AND THE SHARK,
HE HAS TEETH

Studies in German Literature, Linguistics, and Culture

ERNST JOSEF AUFRICT

AND THE SHARK, HE HAS TEETH

A THEATER PRODUCER'S NOTES

TRANSLATED FROM THE GERMAN
BY BENJAMIN BLOCH

WITH AN INTRODUCTION
BY MARC SILBERMAN

CAMDEN HOUSE
Rochester, New York

First published 2018 by Camden House

The original from which this translation is made was first published
in Germany in 1966 under the title *Erzähle, damit du dein Recht
erweist.* It was republished in 1998 by Alexander Verlag Berlin under
the title *Und der Haifisch, der hat Zähne. Aufzeichnungen eines
Theaterdirektors,* ISBN 9783895810121, © 1998 by Alexander Verlag
Berlin, Fredericiastrasse 8, D-14050 Berlin, Germany.

Camden House is an imprint of Boydell & Brewer Inc.
668 Mt. Hope Avenue, Rochester, NY 14620, USA
www.camden-house.com
and of Boydell & Brewer Limited
PO Box 9, Woodbridge, Suffolk IP12 3DF, UK
www.boydellandbrewer.com

ISBN-13: 978-1-64014-017-2
ISBN-10: 1-64014-017-4

Library of Congress Cataloging-in-Publication Data

Names: Aufricht, Ernst Josef, author. | Bloch, Benjamin. | Silberman, Marc,
    1948– author of introduction.
Title: And the shark, he has teeth : a theater producer's notes / Ernst Josef
    Aufright ; translated from the German by Benjamin Bloch ; with an
    introduction by Marc Silberman. Other titles: Erzahle, damit du dein Recht
    erweist. English
Description: Rochester, N.Y. : Camden House, 2018. | Includes bibliographical
    references and index.
Identifiers: LCCN 2018015237| ISBN 9781640140172 (hardcover : alk. paper) |
    ISBN 1640140174 (hardcover : alk. paper)
Subjects: LCSH: Aufricht, Ernst Josef. | Theatrical producers and directors—
    Germany. | Theater—Germany.
Classification: LCC PN2658.A9 A3 2018 | DDC 792.02/32092—dc23
    LC record available at https://lccn.loc.gov/2018015237

Printed and bound in Great Britain by
TJ International Ltd, Padstow, Cornwall

CONTENTS

Illustrations follow page 90

INTRODUCTION

Marc Silberman

T hink of theater during the Weimar Republic, during the interwar period in Germany, and probably the first thing that comes to mind is the eminently hummable "Mack the Knife," the lead song of the Brecht/Weill musical *The Threepenny Opera*. Why is that? First of all, the ballad has become an international hit, sung by luminaries from Lotte Lenya, Ella Fitzgerald, Louis Armstrong, Frank Sinatra, and Bobby Darin to Sting. Second, the musical itself, adapted by Bertolt Brecht and Elisabeth Hauptmann from John Gay's 1728 *Beggar's Opera*, quickly proved to be the most popular play of the Weimar Republic. Within a year of its opening in Berlin on August 31, 1928, there were dozens of additional productions in Germany alone, and translations and productions soon followed as well in Austria, Italy, the Netherlands, Switzerland, Poland, Hungary, Finland, and the Soviet Union. Kurt Weill's jazzy musical settings for Brecht's lyrics hit a nerve like no other music of the time, generating what has come to be called "Threepenny fever." Although the first American staging was a failure, opening at the Empire Theatre in New York City in 1933 before either Brecht or Weill had arrived as exiles from Nazi Germany, when it was resurrected in 1954 in a new translation by Marc Blitzstein, it became the longest running Broadway musical of the day, with six and a half years of consecutive performances. Indeed, *The Threepenny Opera* laid the foundation for both Brecht's and Weill's subsequent reputations as they went their own ways.

Who was behind this success story? None other than Ernst Josef Aufricht, whose memoir presents a blow-by-blow suspense story of how the musical came about, with all its improbable coincidences and last-minute catastrophes. He was the visionary who had leased the Theater am Schiffbauerdamm in Berlin's theater district, an otherwise artistically unremarkable stage that today still functions as the storied Berliner Ensemble, the theater that Brecht established when he returned to East Germany from exile in 1948. Twenty years before that, Aufricht needed to commission someone who could provide a play to open his "new baby" on the occasion of his thirtieth birthday. Brecht, who had been collaborating with Weill on other projects, turned out to be a risky but right choice, bringing together the composer Weill as well as several other talented young bohemians from his circle of actors, stage designers, and musicians.

There was nothing inevitable about Aufricht's success story, but it is clear that he had a good nose for artistic talent and a strong commitment to new, unconventional theatrical fare. Born in 1898 in Upper Silesia (today the southwestern part of Poland), he was the eldest of three sons raised in a well-to-do, secular Jewish family. After the First World War broke out, the eager but underage German patriot volunteered for military service in 1915, which turned him into a pacifist; and his insight into the misery of poverty in the inflationary postwar years turned him into a socialist. Against the wishes of his father, who wanted him to study medicine, he went off to Berlin to become an actor and in 1919 already made his acting debut on stage at the State Theater in Dresden and in the silent cinema. In 1923 Aufricht returned to Berlin—the undisputed theater capital of the Republic—and became the assistant manager and member of the acting ensemble called "Die Truppe" or The Troupe. The hyperinflation that peaked in 1924 led to its collapse after only eight months, but it had opened with a notable production of Shakespeare's *Merchant of Venice* and quickly became the address for non-commercial theater devoted to new texts by young writers. Some of the ensemble's young actors would become famous over the next years, and in a very short time the theater staged a string of noteworthy avant-garde plays, including the first production in German of a play by Eugene O'Neill (*Emperor Jones*). During the next four years Aufricht gradually shifted his energy from acting to theater management, but he was considered an outsider, not especially well-known in theater circles and lacking administrative experience, when in December 1927 he signed the lease for the Theater am Schiffbauerdamm. Yet this fateful move transformed him into one of the most important promoters of experimental theater during the last years of the Weimar Republic.

The collapse of the German Empire in 1918 brought with it a transformation of the country's theater landscape. Court theaters and communal stages became state and municipally subsidized stages, freed to a large extent from both political censorship and commercial pressure. Moreover, a network of privately funded theaters financed by investors and stockholders augmented the stage offerings with both conventional and more risky, modern plays. There were about 150 such theaters in existence during the Weimar years, and the capital city Berlin became the center of the theater renewal that marked the cultural blossoming of the Weimar Republic.

The Theater am Schiffbauerdamm was one of Berlin's privately owned theaters. The only way Aufricht was able to lease it was by convincing his wealthy father to advance him some of his inheritance to cover the security deposit, a technique of wooing well-to-do patrons that he would have to use again and again to bankroll his experimental stagings. Because his prior experience had been with so-called free actors' ensembles not bound to a specific theater or organization, he seemed to be out of his depth managing such a large, unsubsidized theater, but both major Berlin critics and artists saw it as a courageous endeavor, one that Aufricht had the artistic competence to realize. And indeed the initial success of *The Threepenny Opera* was only the beginning of a string of controversial and original productions with first-rate casts. In February 1929, for example, he produced a play about a military putsch called *Poison Gas over Berlin*, which the chief of police closed down after the opening night, leading to one of the first explosive cases of theater censorship in the Weimar Republic. Thereupon followed a second play critical of the military, Marieluise Fleißer's *Pioneers in Ingolstadt* (suggested by Brecht), new threats of censorship that Aufricht was able to deflect, and a reputation within the first season as the most exciting stage in Berlin! He continued during the second season to feature contemporary and challenging plays, avoiding the classical repertoire, but not ignoring the need to provide entertainment, for example with a comedy by Noel Coward.

In some respects Aufricht was trying to implement Brecht's unconventional approach to the theater as a space for political discourse, a place to learn and be entertained by some of the most brilliant and provocative theater people around. He commissioned Brecht and Hauptmann to write a new musical with songs set by Weill—*Happy End*—on the first anniversary of the *Threepenny* triumph, but it closed after only a week, and later he was behind the Berlin production of the Brecht/Weill opera *Rise and Fall of the City of Mahagonny* as well as Brecht's learning play *The Mother*. He took substantial risks, but after the market crash in late 1929, he was increasingly under serious financial pressure. The audience could no longer afford tickets, and banks were in no position to extend credit. Even a reprise of *The Threepenny Opera* in November 1930 couldn't solve the problem; Aufricht had to halve ticket prices to get an audience into the theater. A passionate theater producer, he provides in his memoir a somewhat different perspective on what is often referred to as the "golden twenties" of interwar Germany, not hesitating to include the seamier sides of cultural life. That his success story lasted only three seasons marks his as a representative memoir of a talented German Jew of the period.

The Theater am Schiffbauerdamm was a thorn in the side of the Nazis. As soon as they took over power in March 1933, they homed in on Aufricht, who was at the top of the list as a target to be "cleansed from German culture." He was physically threatened and blackmailed, resulting in his escape first to Switzerland and then to Paris, where his wife and two sons joined him. The second half of the memoir documents the author's shock at losing his home, his language, and his culture. The painful adjustments, the dependency on friends, acquaintances, and strangers, the anxieties but also the unexpected episodes of good luck and generosity will be familiar to anyone who knows something about refugees and exile. At the same time Aufricht never descends into sentimentality but maintains a distance to the events without losing his enthusiasm or colorful sense of humor.

Theater is a language-based undertaking, and Aufricht just didn't have the skill in French to pursue a career in the Paris theater scene. Instead he turned his energy (and what money he had left) into acquiring and managing an experimental farm in northern France, near Calvados in Normandy. The goal was to train young German émigrés in practical skills of farming and animal husbandry that would guarantee their survival in the new homeland. The plan failed within two years, and Aufricht found himself back in Paris, searching for opportunities. In 1937 he was able to lease a large theater and produced a French version of *The Threepenny Opera* that ran for fifty performances during the Paris International Exhibition. And just before the war commenced in September 1939 he helped stage, in German, Brecht's episodic anti-Nazi play *Fear and Misery of the Third Reich* for the German exiles in the city. Other ambitious plans, for example, to make a film of *Happy End* with director René Clair, never found the needed patrons to fund them.

When the German army marched into Paris and installed the Vichy regime in occupied France in summer 1940, a year of anxious waiting, hiding, lying, and searching for forged passports began for the Aufricht family. Finally, in June 1941 they reached New York City with the help, among others, of the legendary Varian Fry in the Mediterranean port city of Marseille, who was able to provide money, visas, transfer papers through Spain, and tickets on a ship from Portugal. Another continent, another country, another language. Aufricht never really felt at home in New York City. He attempted a Broadway career, sought to bring Brecht and Weill together once again for a musical version of *The Good Person of Sezuan* and then for an opera version of Brecht's play *Schweyk in the Second World War.* Neither project came to fruition, but Aufricht did make a series of radio plays aimed at German-Americans, and he was the moving force behind an evening event to raise funds for the German-American and Austrian-American War Bonds committees. "We Fight Back" took place on April 3, 1943 at the Hunter College concert hall to commemorate the recently deceased Stephen Vincent Benet, who had written a radio play about the Nazi book burnings (for this occasion translated into German). Varian Fry opened the event, which included musical interludes (e.g., classical selections but also Weill and Lotte Lenya with songs from *The Threepenny Opera*) and an auction of original manuscripts and drawings by famous writers, painters, and composers.

In 1953 Aufricht and his wife returned to (West) Berlin, harboring hopes of restarting a career in the theater in his native language. As with other artists returning from exile, the welcome was not exceptionally warm. He negotiated with the Berlin Senate to manage a theater, but never overcame the suspicions of city functionaries who saw in him a competitor with Parisian and New York experience and a reputation defined by the fabled quality of pre-Hitler, Weimar theater. Aufricht did succeed in staging one production for the Berlin Festival in fall 1954, a two-week guest performance of three "ballet ballads" by the American writer John Latouche with music by Jerome Moross and sets by his old friend George Grosz, directed by a young master student of Brecht, Egon Monk. It was a kind of epic musical theater, a mix of pantomime, words, music, and lyric-expressive movement, but the critics didn't take to it. Thereafter Aufricht retreated into early retirement, but he and his wife were among the invited guests at the premiere of *The Threepenny Opera* reprise in the Berliner Ensemble in East Berlin in 1960, four years after Brecht's death and one year before the Berlin Wall was built. In July 1971 Aufricht passed away at the age of 73, surrounded by his children and grandchildren in Cannes, in southern France.

Aufricht wrote his memoir between 1964 and 1966. It is rumored that his wife Margot typed it for him, and she was also probably his authority on dates. It was published first in 1966 under the title *Erzähl, damit du dein Recht erweist* (Speak to Establish Your Right), and in August of that year a long excerpt appeared serially in ten installments in the newspaper *Die Welt*, focusing on the centerpiece story about the Theater am Schiffbauerdamm. The memoir was then republished in 1998 under the new title selected by Aufricht's son, *Und der Haifisch, der hat Zähne*, quoting the famous "Mack the Knife" ballad from *The Threepenny Opera*. It remains one of the standard sources for information about theater in the Weimar Republic, often quoted because the author—who was one of the movers and shakers—was also a credible witness. Aufricht's account is not free of bitterness, but he also manages to create an adventure out of his survival story, one filled with challenges, surprises, disappointments, and suspense, but spiced up with wisdom, wit, and a keen eye for the multitude of people he encountered along the way.

TRANSLATOR'S ACKNOWLEDGMENTS

With gratitude to Temy and Nachi Goldwasser, theater lovers and inveterate Weillophiles, who first showed me their copy of this book and told me the story of their meeting with Margot Aufricht. And with gratitude to my father Ariel Bloch, for reading the draft.

AND THE SHARK,
HE HAS TEETH

narra si quid habes ut justificeris
Isaiah 43:26

For Margot

CHAPTER

O N E

I was born at the end of last century in Beuthen, Upper Silesia, in the Bahnhofstrasse, where the first grenades of the Second World War fell, according to military reports. From my early childhood I remember this single incident: I was jumping on my parents' bed, and I came down on one of the edges with my nose. I buried my face in a pillow. When I lifted my head, I saw a bloodstain. I tried it again, touched my head lightly here and there on the white pillowcase, saw several bloodstains, was struck with revulsion, and began to cry. Since then, blood has always terrified me.

Probably with the idea of overcoming this fear, I once went to the slaughterhouse and watched as a cow was hit with a hammer and stabbed to death. Horrified, I dropped my Gaius Julius Caesar (I was carrying my schoolbooks under my arm) in a puddle of blood. I fished it out quickly; the fear that I'd ruined a schoolbook was greater than the disgust. I washed it off at a fountain, and, as all schoolbooks at that time were wrapped in blue wax paper, I replaced the cover at home.

When I was four years old, we moved to the neighboring town of Gleiwitz. Two more brothers were born there. Each birth was connected with the appearance of another wet nurse. The wet nurses came from the country and were dressed in peasant clothing. They wore several skirts one on top of the other, with long jackets over them, buttoned in front, three-quarters length in bright calico. On Sundays their jackets were silk, trimmed with a hand's breadth of lace at the bottom. The wet nurses were young and buxom. One often saw them drinking large quantities of milk and malt beer, a practice required for the increase of their milk. Their smell was sweet and womanly. They stayed and nursed the infants from three to six months, and came to each of the children's birthdays afterwards, where they received a gift of a gold piece. My wet nurse's name was Valeska Kroker. With her earnings she bought herself gold eyeteeth.

Our apartment was on Kaiser-Wilhelm Street. An entrance hall led into the dining room, the smoking room, and the salon. We children were forbidden to enter these rooms unless called for.

The furniture was of precious hardwood hand-crafted by the firm of Pfaff in Breslau. Each piece was in keeping with current tastes, and each therefore looked no different from the factory sets. A huge, richly engraved buffet of brown walnut reached almost up to the ceiling on a massive three-door base where the Meissen porcelain and silver cutlery were kept. Above the base were three drawers for all the items of the family's daily meals: silverware, knife-rests, napkins and napkin-rings, and table cloth. The doors of the upper half were decorated with glass roundels. Displayed on a ledge were a hammered silver tray with coffee and tea service. The table had a draw-leaf and could seat eighteen guests. Eight stiff, tall leather-covered chairs stood around it, with other chairs placed here and there against the wall. Two silver candelabras and several crystal bowls adorned the sideboard, over which hung a grinning monk with a wineglass in his hand, painted by Eduard Grützner. The dining room floor was covered with a multicolored Persian rug.

We had our main meal every afternoon at exactly a quarter to two, every evening at exactly a quarter to eight. The meals were served without a moment's pause between courses, and eaten hurriedly. My father ate without interest and hardly noticed what was put in front of him. If we asked for half a slice of bread at dinner, he answered: "There's no such thing as a half! Anyone who asks for half is eating for pleasure, and isn't really hungry!"

As soon as the maid had cleaned up after dinner, my mother sat at the cleared table with her blotter and papers and put the household accounts in order. My father retired to his armchair in the bay window and read the Upper Silesia, Breslau, and Berlin daily newspapers. The papers had to be folded and in pristine condition, and no one was to have read them before he did. The pages he'd read he let fall to the floor. When they were alone, my parents went to bed at nine.

The smoking room was decorated in dark tones, unlike the dining room and the salon. Facing the entrance of this room hung a copy of Böcklin's *Island of the Dead*. A dark red carpet covered the parquet floor. The furniture was oak, stained almost black. A bookcase with glass doors held all the German classics: the *Great Brockhaus* encyclopedia, Brehms's *Life of the Animals*, and many complete editions of works by popular authors whose names have been forgotten. Once, as a first grader, I was caught looking up "embryo" in Brockhaus. The bookcase was locked and the key hidden from that day on.

On Sundays there were cards at the round gaming table. The only game my father took part in was poker. Director-General Schalcha of the Upper Silesian steel industry arrived every Sunday for poker, a stately figure with his monocle on a black cord. His beautiful black riding horse was recognized throughout the city; later he drove the first electric automobile in Upper Silesia. He was well-groomed and elegant, and gave off sweet fragrances. Another player at the table was Mr. Schindler the corn merchant, whom we children loved. He was a slight man, but with a belly and face protruding sharply forward, and a high, raspy voice. He was married but had no children. We loved the visits to his house because of the pets he kept: several dogs, a monkey and a talking parrot. We were allowed to play with the animals, and were spoiled by the older couple.

My uncle, Dr. Paul Königsfeld, our house doctor and a cousin of my mother, was a regular guest at the poker circle. Tall and wide-shouldered, his masculine face full of dueling scars, he kept his mustache waxed and twisted upwards in the style of Kaiser Wilhelm II. On the Kaiser's birthday he would dress in the dark blue uniform of the Chief of Medical Staff, and I admired him greatly, even though, when asked for his medical advice about my nighttime fears, he prescribed: "A good thrashing, and then lights out!" I was saved from this frightening prospect by a pediatrician my mother consulted in Breslau, Professor Czernin, who recommended a night light.

When the card game was finished, I was called into the room and allowed to take up a collection for the orphans, in a sealed metal box. In those days my father often withheld my allowance as punishment, and for this reason I usually pried the box open later, with a knife and a heavy conscience, solemnly resolving to pay the orphans back as soon as I could.

Only on the more festive occasions did my parents open the salon. The linen slips that protected the furniture were then removed, revealing, underneath, sofas and armchairs upholstered in heavy, striped silk of two colors. These matched the chairs on their gilt, imitation rococo legs, and the bench in front of the mahogany piano, on which two could sit to play four-handed pieces. A Venetian chandelier, brought back by my parents from their honeymoon in Venice, jingled lightly whenever the tenants above us walked with purpose. On a Majolica pedestal, a turbaned Moor held the golden rudder-pole of a green and red painted gondola. Next to a dazzling Venetian mirror was a portrait of my mother in *décolleté* with a wide ostrich-feather hat painted by Eugen Spiro, who had stopped in

Upper Silesia for several months and completed portraits of wealthy ladies at a prodigious speed. The floor was covered with an Aubusson rug.

The splendor of the salon intrigued me. This was life at its largest. There was a certain aunt, a young woman with ambitions to be an actress in the comic opera, who had been married off hastily to a brother of my father's. Her name was Elsa. She was big-bosomed, with black hair, large, dark, glistening eyes and a sensuous mouth. The society men of that time, speaking to one another, would have called her "she-devil," or "sexy." When one of them accompanied her on the piano, she sang songs that made them laugh in a strange way. The servants were forbidden to bring refreshments while she sang. I had to creep to the keyhole to hear the "Song of the Poltergeist," who appears whenever a séance is held in the dark:

Such a charming, devilish little ghost,
his up-and-down will give us such a fright
again tomorrow night!

Or the chanson of the daughter who doesn't like practicing the piano, but is finally prevailed upon by her piano teacher to learn her sonatas. Her governess brings her home after the lesson, and when her mother asks what she played today—here Aunt Elsa sang with feeling and passion:

Oh mother I played a sonata today!
I'm sure you remember it yet!
Like this: la-la, la-la-la-la-la,
Once you've heard it, it's hard to forget!

—and again the men laughed so strangely and the women giggled, and I made a point of remembering the words so I could find out later what they meant.

Unlike the three front rooms, the back rooms of our apartment were drab. The windows in the hall looked out onto a gravel court. My parents had their bedrooms in this part of the house, where we three children lived with our nanny. At the other end of the hall, in a high, narrow and dark chamber that looked like a ship's cabin, the cook, the chambermaid and the winter apples lay in bunks one on top of another. If the door was ever left open, which wasn't supposed to happen, there came from inside this room a peculiar odor, a mixture of humans and apples.

The cook's name was Anna. She gave her earnings to the church and wore a ring on Sundays. She said the ring had been blessed, and that she was a bride of Christ. If she had nothing to do she went to bed early. She got out of bed before five o'clock every morning and went to matins. She was calm and cheerful and a good cook. The chambermaid's name was Martha. She was tall and skinny. She was engaged to the barber who came to shave my father every morning. The barber also came over whenever our parents went out at night, and when Anna was asleep, and stood holding his fiancée Martha in the kitchen, about three heads shorter than she was. I slithered to the half-open door on my stomach, the way I had read in Karl May, and heard the barber pleading with her: "But Marthel, why don't you want to? Kaisers and kings do it, don't they?"

I saw her in a bridal gown at her wedding. The barber sweated in his black suit with a high collar. Both of them had big red hands. When he started his own business, Martha helped with lathering and shaving the men's faces. The barbershop didn't bring in enough money to live by, and Martha often came to cry to my parents and ask for their help.

As the eldest child, I had a bedroom to myself with the obligatory aquarium and terrarium and, most importantly, a worn-out horn phonograph that my parents no longer had use for, on which I played the same operetta hits again and again. The stylus clattered over the cylinder of the machine, and the voices were always too high and compressed at first when it had just been cranked, and too deep towards the end when the spring relaxed.

Hold your cheek against my cheek,
Let only flute and violin speak—

They've come, the Dollar-princesses,
Those princesses of pure gold—

For the first time, I heard the work of professionals, of people who had learned how to put on a performance. The first time I listened to this music, I felt myself spontaneously part of it.

In the evenings, during the last minutes of light, the rats came out in the courtyard, hurrying everywhere and emitting a hellish racket of squeaks and whistles. These twilight-crazed animals seemed to me to lack all playfulness, and even to be goading each other with their fear and malevolence. Rats, with their naked tails, are the only animals I find revolting. With all the others, with spiders, toads, mice and snakes, I can be friendly. I can't pass by a cat without admiring it, and telling it so, if it lets me.

Antonienhütte, in Upper Silesia, was bigger than a village and smaller than a city. It was a market town, its streets lined with ugly tenement flats for workers, several well-tended houses for officials and mining administrators, and one or two villas surrounded by gardens, owned by the managers. The various shops and hotels were clustered around the market place, or the Ring, as it was called in Silesia. One immense and stately house on the Ring was the home of the shipping agent Moritz Koplowitz. He was a distributor of everything that could be moved over the earth's surface, and an employer of many horse teams underneath it. In the mine shafts, hundreds of meters down, Koplowitz's horses pulled the coal trolleys to an access cage, the very cage that had lowered them into the mine as young horses. The old or otherwise unfit horses were brought back to the surface. Startled by the sudden light, they screamed and sometimes went blind. Moritz Koplowitz was a horse enthusiast. He had an excellent team of Hungarian carriage horses, bought in Hungary and transported home.

Koplowitz was short and stocky with a thick mustache and cunning eyes. Married to a tall, powerfully built woman, he was pleased with his income and with the world. His wife's name was Ida. Her sister Flora, a good-looking young woman, lived as their foster child in the Koplowitz house. She was considered poor—besides her trousseau she had received only 20,000 marks for a dowry, provided by her brother-in-law. When she was married to my uncle Hugo I was ten years old, and I went with my parents to Antonienhütte while my two younger brothers stayed with the nanny at home. We left from Gleiwitz by train in the early morning and were picked up at the station by a coach.

All the rooms of the Koplowitz house were crowded with guests. When it came time for the adults to go to the registry office, I and the son of the Koplowitzes, Erich—we were the same age—were sent out for a walk. His father gave him a five-mark piece: "Buy yourselves chocolate, boys!" I myself at that time had an allowance of 20 pfennig a week. We three brothers were held rather close with money, and never spoiled. Every once in a while I spent 10 pfennig on a praline—five marks for chocolate was unthinkable for me. Would we buy several bars of Lindt, or one of those sampler boxes that the adults bring to the table when there are guests for dinner? Maybe something new, unknown to me. The young Koplowitz took a roundabout way to shops, and seemed to be in no hurry. On the Ring it was market day. He bought two bunches of radishes for 5 pfennig at a grocer's stand and gave me one bunch. We ate them, and walked back home. I was too timid to ask about the chocolate. To this day I can feel the disappointment.

In the huge somber hall of a clubhouse in town, tables arranged in a horseshoe were set for the hundred wedding guests. For place cards there were centimeter-thick spruce wood disks, each the diameter of an average dinner plate, polished on both sides, with the bark still attached. On the one side was a photo of the bridal pair under a layer of varnish, with their names burned in; the guest's name was burned in on the other side. These wooden ornaments suggested the trade of the bridegroom, who, like my father, was a wholesale wood dealer. When Uncle Hugo got married he already had a belly, he was no longer young. My grandfather, who considered bachelorhood a disgrace to the family and who didn't tolerate any contrary opinions from his children, had arranged this marriage.

All of us were gathered. In the middle of the hall stood a canopy; four men, honored guests, held the posts upright. A violin and piano duo played the wedding march from *Lohengrin*, "Faithfully Led," and my uncle in coattails, his bride in her gown and wearing the myrtle wreath, crossed the hall. They took their places under the canopy. She was very agitated, and when the Rabbi, with great pathos, gave his closing sermon on gratitude, she began to cry. The whole thing looked so sad to me, I sobbed out loud. My mother led me out of the room and threatened to bring me home to bed if I didn't stop crying at once. Maybe my tears were for the untasted chocolate.

I waited every day for the summer vacation. For me it was like a journey from darkness into light. My family spent its vacations near the sea, or in the mountains, and when my parents took trips abroad I was sent to a summer lodge.

Her name was Eva. She was twelve years old, I was eleven. She had a long, brown braid and a feline face with a flat nose and narrow green eyes. She moved like a boy. The two of us, together with three other children, were watched over by three elderly spinsters during the long vacation in Schmiedeberg. I loved her more every day. When the weeks had passed and the last day had come, I knew something had to happen. I hadn't yet even found a chance to hold hands with her. I brooded all morning over how I could get near her, watching for every opportunity. In the afternoon I finally screwed up my courage. She was in the garden, sitting on a bench under the colonnade. I asked her: would she like me to get rid of her wart? She had one on her right middle finger. She said "Please." I went inside and found the brown cardboard box that had First Aid written on it. When you lifted the lid, it smelled like valerian. There were two rows of tiny bottles inside, a gauze dressing, cotton compresses and English adhesive plasters. I chose a bottle marked "Hoffman's Drops," went back to her and said "Give me your hand." I let a few drops fall on the wart, and held her finger. The scene was so beautiful that I asked her if she would marry me. "Alright," she said. "Then we have to write to each other," I said. She thought it was a good idea. She thought that in order that no one else would be able to read our messages, we should use a secret code. Only the first letter of every word would count. Then she ran off. I shouted after her: "Your wart will dry up in a few days!" I was proud and happy.

I wrote her many letters from home. In the mornings, before school, I would ask the mailman if anything had arrived. At midday it was Anna the cook, my confidante, who would ask him for me. I waited a long time. At last a yellow envelope arrived with a yellow letter inside, something from a child's stationary set, a letter I carried with me for weeks afterwards and read over many times. She had written:

"Dear Ernst, how are you? I'm fine. So is my brother, whom you do not know. Your *Wax Igloo Frank Egret*, Eva."

I wrote her back right away, but there was no answer. I wrote again and got a card from her brother explaining that she had scarlet fever and wasn't allowed to write.

I pined away for her and thought about her all the time, but I didn't write again. A year passed. The long vacation came again, and this time my parents wanted to send me to a summer lodge in the town of Jannowitz. I didn't want to go to a lodge again under any circumstances. So it was decided that I would go instead to Aunt Elsa and my cousins, most of them younger than me. Suddenly a letter came from Breslau. She wanted to know if I was coming to Jannowitz for the vacation. When I grasped the extent of my misfortune, everything went black. A wind came through the open window of my room. I lay on the floor and held the letter in my hand.

The evening before my trip, I heard my parents agreeing in whispers that no matter what happened, I had to be kept away from my cousin Richard. The next day I was brought to the train. On arriving, I immediately looked for Richard and waited for a chance to talk to him, but with no luck. Finally I ran into him on the street. I challenged him to his face that he had kissed a girl. He smiled coolly, the way only a sixth grader can smile at a fourth grader, and said, "I've done a few other things with girls." My amazement was so obvious that he went into detail. "How could I do something like that?" I asked him. "You've got it easy," he said. "The nanny at your aunt's will help you. And give her my regards." I gave the nanny his regards and asked for her help. She acted as if she didn't understand what I was saying, and I thought Richard had tricked me. Later that day, when I was leaving the house, I heard a whistle, and turned around; she was standing at the dormer window, showing her breasts. I hurried back inside and, since there were no adults in the house, straight to the attic. "I guess you're old enough," she said.

Every time I came home from the long vacation it occurred to me how hard it was to breathe. The air was gray and dirty. The white removable collars had to be changed twice a day. Concentrated industry, ironworks and coal mines filled the air with soot. Other than a minority of middle-class citizens, the great majority of people living in the provincial towns of Upper Silesia were badly paid workers, dressed almost in rags. On Friday evenings the streets rang with shouts and challenges from drunken men who had gone to the bar with their week's earnings. The bar typically had no seats, was just a room with a long counter, where for 10 pfennig one could buy a glass of hard liquor flavored with a few drops of raspberry juice, known as a "Gestreifter." We were strictly warned about these drunken men, and we kept our distance from their children, who had no soap or way of washing themselves. I remember stories of heroism from before the First World War about shining young officers on horseback who rode into a crowd of striking workers, and sometimes, struck on the forehead with a rock, fell from their horses.

Outside the towns, where industry wasn't yet developed, forests of spruce, potato fields and grain stretched out far and wide. The flat landscape, the thick forests, the looming obscurity of castles built in no particular style, the pitiful villages of potato farmers who couldn't eke out a living from their small fields and so had to earn their livelihoods as lumberjacks, all of these gave my birthplace a melancholy character.

It was land owned, for the most part, by Upper Silesian magnates. The Princes von Pless, the Counts Schaffgotsch, the Thiele-Winklers and others of distinction sat on estates of 100,000 acres and more. The sons of the lower aristocracy, Barons and Lords, were the trustees for these estates, their chief foresters and district councilors, unless they themselves were landowners.

To see that their wealth was turned to profit and their appetite for objects of luxury and comfort satisfied, they needed businessmen. At that time, Upper Silesia's early industrial boom was, for the newly emancipated Jews, an opportunity similar to what the overseas colonies offered Europeans. Once coal and iron were discovered and smelting plants were built, business grew quickly, and many of the Jewish businessmen became rich. Some of those who achieved wealth and distinction moved to Upper Silesia's capitol, Breslau. They bought villas and large estates, and imitated the lifestyles of the aristocracy. Their sons were sent away to school and prepared for academic careers.

My father was always making plans and always in motion. His day began at seven in the morning and ended at nine at night. He had no hobbies whatsoever, he didn't smoke, hardly ever drank alcohol, and was a moderate eater. All he wanted to do was to work. By 61 he was used up, and died. He had an unremarkable face, at one time with a goatee, later with a small mustache, at that time called a "brush." Though he was small in stature, he didn't appear that way, and the tremendous energy with which he played his part impressed everybody. He'd left the house at fourteen after his father had given him a beating. On his own initiative he had made a fortune and become one of the most eminent wood merchants in the East. He'd set up businesses for his brothers and married off his sisters, gave money generously here and there, and never asked for a thing in return. And yet he was not well liked. His gifts always came with an admonition to thrift, and people who rely on others' generosity are usually not eager to hear about that.

He idolized my mother, a very beautiful woman. I, too, loved and respected her as if she were an unearthly being. Her kindness and even temper were a counterbalance to my father's nervous vigor and severity. She had always remained attached to her home city, Breslau, where her mother and many siblings lived. In the First World War, when I was serving as a soldier, my parents left Gleiwitz with my younger brothers for Breslau. For my mother, who in her modesty would never have asked for such a thing, my father acquired a mansion in the grand style, an automobile, a horse-drawn carriage, and whatever else went with luxurious living, and he bought an estate and manor in the country an hour outside of Breslau by car.

It is said that the eldest son should take after his father, and that is why my father and I avoided one another. I was a daydreamer, more lazy than enterprising, and completely uninterested in school. In Gleiwitz I had attended the Royal Catholic Academy of Classical Studies, which was housed in a monastery. There was a boarding school attached to it, where boys with no financial means were lodged, clothed, fed, and instructed in the priesthood. They also attended classes with us. Quiet, timid, pale-faced and pimpled, they dressed winter and summer in the same black suit. There were also several farmers' sons among the students who often had started school late, at eleven years old, and therefore stayed till they were older than usual. They sat at the ends of the rows, where there was room for their long legs.

The lesson began at eight. Catholic students had to be present at seven-thirty in the school chapel every day for Mass. The Lord's Prayer was recited at the start of the lesson by teachers and by Catholic students, who crossed themselves before and after it; Protestants and Jews stood by silently. Other than this, no distinction was made between religions, neither by teachers nor by students.

Before the beginning of the first hour, the Director could be seen on the steps to the main entrance. Every tardy student had to pass by him, be stopped by him and receive his referral for punishment. The Director was a large, plodding man with stooped shoulders and a fleshy face framed by a reddish-blond beard, and, over a bulbous nose, two intelligent, penetrating eyes. I made sure to miss the entire lesson any time I was going to be late, in order to avoid the chastisements of this much-feared man. He forbade his high school students, prior to graduation, to smoke, drink, set foot in a tavern without an accompanying adult, or play soccer, a game he disparaged as brutal. We were not allowed to carry a walking stick, or to wear any kind of conspicuous tie or dress shoes. We were forbidden to cross the Kaiser-Wilhelm Street without a very good reason, because the other side of the street was where boys and girls sauntered and threw each other looks. The penalty for breaking any of these rules was merciless.

The cattle grounds were an open plot on the outskirts of the city surrounded by an iron railing to which the cattle were tied on market days; the grounds also served as a soccer field, where the less cautious students had an opportunity to mingle with the players. A classmate of mine named Pogszeba got caught by one of the teachers patrolling the cattle grounds, and received the *consilium abeundi*. But he didn't give up. Under a bobbed black wig, convinced that he bore no resemblance to the old blond Pogszeba, he went back to the cattle grounds, was caught again by the same teacher-spy, and expelled. He married a widow with a hat shop and five children and moved to Kattowitz.

When the war broke out in 1914, the Director summoned us to the assembly hall. He climbed the rostrum and we all rose to recite: "Our most gracious sovereign, our beloved Kaiser and king." We shouted three hurrahs, sang "Hail to Thee in the Victor's Wreath," and many eyes were moist with genuine enthusiasm for Kaiser and the fatherland. "At a time when thousands are dying on the battlefield," the Director told us, "it is frivolous to laugh." He forbade laughter for the duration of the war. He stood in the yard during recess and watched our faces.

While we had crowded into the assembly hall, the son of the gymnastics teacher Pshibulla had stayed behind and stolen red water-snails out of the art room aquarium. He sold them to us for 10 pfennig apiece.

When Easter arrived it was time for the Director to deal with the miserable worms who had been condemned to repeat the year. He came to the classes and the teachers went pale; they feared him as much as we did. He sat down in the last row and asked to review the work of the student in question. Usually he changed a grade from an F to a D, and the student was saved.

None of my teachers were pedagogues at heart; not one of them made any effort to establish personal contact with their students. They were either old men or they were young, assertive teacher-trainees who rested on their authority, carried out their lesson plans without interest, and spread a paralysis of boredom. I was a bad student and an insolent one. School was a constant annoyance to me, and I revolted tirelessly against it. It was incomprehensible to my father that a person could ever fail to do his duty; my bad grades, in assignments as well as in conduct, enraged him, and we lived with an unending feud between us. I tried my best to avoid him, and he bore down on me with ever harder punishments. Finally my kind mother intervened. It was decided that a private teacher would be hired for my improvement, with the result that my free time was further diminished, and my aversion to teachers and school greatly increased.

But I had no aversion to books. As was the custom in those days, I was given the collected German classics for my Bar Mitzvah, and my mother and I read dramas and poems together. I recited them in my room aloud and with much emotion.

A performance artist with a one-man-show as part of his repertoire was called a "reciter." In my childhood there was Ludwig Wüllner, a lofty, noble presence with a Roman head and silver-white hair. He didn't sit, like most of the reciters, at a lectern or a table, but stood in his flawless dress-coat behind the podium or on stage, and recited the classics with pathos. There was the more avant-garde Ludwig Hardt, who appeared in trousers and a shirt, and disdained pathos entirely. He sometimes sat on the corner of his desk and was the reciter of the intellectuals. There was the affectionate and cheerful Joseph Plaut, and the most popular, the most vulgar, Marcel Salzer. An unspoken laughter at the expense of those he portrayed existed between Salzer and his audience. At the beginning of the war he made a tour of the military bases and the home front, and his performances were invariably patriotic—for this reason the school didn't prohibit students from attending, and my parents allowed me to go. Salzer, a short, athletic man with sparse hair, leapt onto the stage and was greeted with long applause and anticipatory laughter. When the noise died down he became serious and gave a report from the front, saying that our brave young men in the field-gray uniform were fighting tirelessly, but that they shouldn't forget to laugh when there was a pause in the action.

And not just in the field, our sons,
Come back and laugh with us for once!

With that he ended his introduction and went into the first item on the program: a patrol has taken ten Russian prisoners. The lieutenant can spare only one man to transport them to the prison camp, so he chooses one and instructs him: "You let the prisoners march single-file in front of you, see, and have your weapon ready to fire. If any one of them tries to be clever . . ." here Salzer winked into the audience, "you understand what I mean. Now march!"

The soldier and his prisoners move off. After a long march, the soldier reports to the captain of the prison camp:

"Captain, sir! Private so-and-so reporting with ten prisoners!"

"What do you mean, ten? I only see one, where are the other nine?"

"The others tried to be clever, sir!"

We roared with laughter. The little man came forward, walked to the back, laughed with us, and bowed profusely. The evening impressed me so much that I made up my mind to find an audience for my own recitations. But who would my audience be? My friends would have laughed at me. I came up with the idea of suggesting roles for them from the classics, and putting on readings as a group. They liked my idea because I'd said that we would get girls to read the female roles. It was wartime, and dancing lessons were considered unpatriotic; there was no credible excuse for going out in the evenings to meet girls.

A distinction was made between society girls, who were respected and marriageable and who didn't have reproductive organs until after the wedding—and the other kind, who belonged to the lower class, and who were viable candidates for pre- or extramarital sex. If the first kind lost their virginity before marriage, finding a husband became difficult and could only be achieved, for instance, with the help of a large dowry.

As one of my friends was the son of a foundry director, and one of the potential actresses also had an important father who had been in our house, there were no objections on my father's part to our meetings. He saw the value in social contact, and had respect for art and culture.

We met in the evenings, two girls and three boys, alternately at each of our homes. Our parents greeted us with sandwiches and raspberry juice, and promptly withdrew. We ate first, then distributed the roles, usually more than one to each person. Each of us had a copy of the script, and we started reading.

I usually chose for myself the roles of the scoundrels and schemers. I paid no attention to how the others were reading; it was intoxicating to hear my own voice, and I believed that my performance had the same effect on the others as it did on me. In this way, every one of our evenings was a success.

We felt a special affinity for the plays of Goethe and Schiller. During the vacation we took a walking tour of Thüringen, with Weimar as our final destination. The girls, of course, couldn't come with us, so we recruited a fourth boy for the group. This was Gottfried Bermann, who later became the renowned publisher Gottfried Bermann Fischer.

The thrill we experienced at seeing the streets where the poets had lived and walked is hard to understand today. In our enthusiasm we bought a copy of Schiller's *Robbers,* took it to a park, and there, to the surprise of passers-by, went into loud raptures over the genuine pathos of Schiller's language. In the evening hours we walked through lamp-lit Weimar. We came to a narrow alley flanked by tiny houses where older, mostly fat women were advertising their *décolletés* in the windows, waving to men in the street. I told my friends I was going to accept one of these women's invitations. They took me to a side street and tried to warn me about theft, murder, and disease, but I had made up my mind. I went into the alley and asked one of the women there, who in the dimness didn't seem all that old or spongy-looking, what her prices were. She asked for two marks. Everything else—my watch, the rest of my money, my identification papers—had been taken from me by the others for temporary holding. They were going to give me fifteen minutes and then storm the building, by which time it could be assumed I had fallen victim to some violent act. I went in, put my two marks on the table, saw her turn on a light, and was struck with horror. I managed to blurt out "I'm sorry!" and ran back to my friends. "Wash your hands right away or we'll all be infected!" they shouted to me when they saw me approaching.

One year later I was a soldier. I stood next to an older man at the five o'clock roll-call every morning, a pharmacist in his civilian life, who every morning arrived in line at the very last moment, half asleep and with puffy eyes, and said the same thing: "I just threw out a whore."

CHAPTER

T W O

Most of my friends, one or two years older than me, had already gone into the army as wartime volunteers. They came home in their uniforms to bask in the city's admiration, and waited impatiently for their assignments to the front. I had enlisted for the light cavalry at the outbreak of the war, and had concealed that I was only fifteen (the minimum age was sixteen), but my father found out and prevented me from going. Twelve months later I said to him: "If the war ends and I wasn't there, I'll shoot myself right in front of you!" This time he gave me permission to volunteer for service. Because infantry had the heaviest losses, men were being turned away from other divisions and referred to this one. I had my heart set on cavalry. A schoolmate of mine who had come home on furlough informed me that the field-artillery regiment Nr. 20 in Posen was still enlisting. I reported, passed my physical exam in Gleiwitz and got my mobilization order.

My mother sobbed when I left. My father accompanied me to Posen. We ate a silent dinner at the hotel where we had stopped. The next morning he invited me in an uncharacteristic way to take a walk with him. I saw that something was weighing heavily on him. After a few halting starts he managed to explain to me that soldiers sometimes come down with a kind of infection, a sexual disease. If it should happen to me, he said, he didn't want me to be ashamed and keep it secret, but to tell him. We walked back to the hotel, called for our bags and took a coach to the recruitment depot at Fort Grolman. Formerly this had been a part of a network of fortified outposts; it was surrounded by a high wall and generally made a hard and bleak impression. The cab stopped in front of a gate with a posted sentry. I got out and took my suitcase, said "Goodbye," nothing more, and walked toward the gate. I heard a strange noise and turned around. My father was sitting in the coach and crying.

Beyond the sentry and the gates was a corridor with signs to the order-lies' room, where a corporal greeted me and took my papers. He brought me to the clothing depot. I was issued a uniform of blue fabric with a black collar and black cuffs, rough cotton underwear, fatigues with many patches, a brimless round cap called a "krätzchen," a sword-belt that had the buckle inscribed "With God, for King and Fatherland," and boots that were hard as rocks. The corporal dropped me off in a barrack and gave the senior soldier directions to show me my locker. Inside the locker was a concentrated smell of herring, a smell that otherwise faintly pervaded the whole tunnel-like room. There was a door at one end and a window far across from it on the other. Beginning at the door and running the length of the room were two rows of plank beds, thirty on each side, with top and bottom bunks. Trestles with boards on them were set up in the middle as tables for the soldiers, each with a stool. Two water jugs and a few basins were the wash facilities.

My comrades didn't pay me any attention. They were infantrymen of the second conscription, about forty years old, no longer capable of march-ing, who had been reassigned to artillery, either to squat next to the cannon or be trained as equestrians. "Go to the canteen and buy yourself some cleaning things; you can wash out your locker and polish your boots," the senior soldier told me. I changed my clothes. I didn't put on the coarse underwear I had been issued, but kept my own. The civilian articles that I wasn't allowed to keep I put in my suitcase to hand in later. I put on the pants first, next the hard and much-worn boots (I slipped around in them, not aware that you had to use foot-wraps to fill them up), and finally, hav-ing fastened the black collar, the uniform tunic. I pulled on my cap, and the big moment had arrived: I was a soldier.

But no one was looking at me, and there was no mirror where I could see myself. I didn't have much time to feel like a soldier, either, because there was a drill, I was told, on the hour, and we had to be ready in our fatigues. Someone told me to padlock my locker or I would find it empty when I returned. With the krätzchen and the huge boots on, we looked like prisoners. A drill whistle transformed us all at once into running maniacs. Lockers were piled full and slammed shut, and we bolted through the door into single file along the corridor. A non-commissioned officer bellowed at us: were we cripples? Could he help us get off our stumps? After that we stood and waited half an hour, at the end of which the sergeant-major came, called roll and dismissed us to dinner. There was a fatty noodle soup with potatoes which I didn't have the stomach for; instead I ate slices of the good army bread.

After dinner came the washing and mending hour. I learned how to shine the uniform's belt buckle and many brass buttons by mounting them on a prong used for that purpose. Before nine o'clock, the senior soldier came around with a list and showed me my bed. It was an upper bunk in the middle of the barrack, near an iron oven whose chimney pipe went into the wall directly over my pillow. Wired to this pipe and running to the ends of several of the beds were clotheslines which the soldiers were using for the foot-wraps that had come back drenched with sweat from field maneuvers. The blue-striped sheets hadn't been changed, and fresh ones would be available only in a few days. I lay on top of the blanket in my underwear and held my nose as inconspicuously as possible with my handkerchief. My bunkmate pointed out to me that sleeping in underwear and socks was forbidden, and that I would be punished if one of the under-officers on duty caught me. I crawled under the blanket and waited sleeplessly for daylight.

Can an individual in an antiheroic setting be a hero? The middle-aged men who were with me in training were not my comrades. Their only ambition was to lighten their duties. They cursed the separation from their families and livelihoods. Their conversations all revolved around prognostications for a quick end to the war, and they had only one fear: to be sent to the front. "You want to be shot blind like my brother?" one of them asked me, almost in a rage. To them I was the upstart adolescent with a head full of wool.

I had been losing weight steadily, and was sent to the infirmary for a check-up. The doctor discovered a gastric disorder. I was pronounced fit for garrison duty and transferred from Fort Grolman to another barracks, where I supervised new recruits. November 1918 came. I waited in an anxious crowd in front of the Commandant's office, a blaze of floodlights on the façade of the building. This was the feared center of power where fates were decided, where final decisions about life and death brooked no opposition. But on this evening there was no General's procession with his adjutants; in the approaching car sat four sailors wearing red armbands. They got out and began climbing the steps to the platform, and the crowd was suddenly quiet. The guards didn't stand in their way. The sailors leaned their guns against the wall and embraced their comrades. A thunderous exultation broke out: the war was over.

It was the first political event I had ever witnessed consciously. The impossible had happened, the omnipotent military machine had been broken. People in the street shouted and laughed, many hugged each other, men unclasped their sword-belts and let them fall where they were standing. There was no more singing of "Hail to Thee in the Victor's Wreath."

I oversaw my own demobilization. I stayed in Posen during the Polish annexation of the province and its capitol. At every important site of traffic in the city there were machine guns posted and manned by Polish civilians, many of them still in the German field-gray uniform. None of them ever fired. The endless war and its economic repercussions had brought both Poles and Germans to a state of profound apathy. No one wanted to fight anymore.

The transformation from German Posen to Polish Posen took place quietly, with the exception of a few scattered incidents of plundering. Wealthy Germans left the province. Before it was time for me to leave, I wanted to say goodbye to a girl I had been seeing. I got into a coach and gave the street name and directions in German. The two Polish men opened the door: "Get out, you German pig! We were here first!" One month earlier we had asked the Polish recruits in the drill square: "What's the Kaiser's name?" No answer. "You don't know, you Polish pig? On the double, march! march!"

Then suddenly Warsaw closed the borders to Germany. For the first time in my life I had to escape and leave behind everything I owned. Some Polish friends got me through the barriers at the main station and onto a train designated for German authorities, one of the last of its kind to be allowed through.

I went back to my parents' home in Breslau.

CHAPTER

THREE

I saw the political and social changes as if through a mist. A single thought excited me: my school years and my military service were over, and I had an entire life to spend however I wanted.

During the war I had been in charge of bringing two troop transports to General-von-Pape-Straße in Berlin, and during the trip I had been able to fulfill my greatest wish: I'd attended a [Max] Reinhardt production at the German Theater. I saw *Othello* with Paul Wegener in the title role. It was a brilliant performance in many respects, but it failed to attain the full scope and substance of Shakespearean drama, and I was disappointed. The second time, I went to a production of Wedekind's *Earth Spirit* on the Königgrätzerstraße stage, with Ludwig Hartau in the role of Dr. Schön. Wegener's Othello had been the product of meticulous intellectual craftsmanship; Hartau was the first great actor I ever saw on stage. He was the decisive encounter for the direction my career was to take, a direction I'd first perceived in the clattering phonograph, in Marcel Salzer, and in the readings with my friends of the literary group. I wanted to be an actor. The only thing standing in my way was my father.

I signed a contract with a traveling theater for the roles of the youthful *bon vivant*. The director may have believed what I said about having performed small parts with the Posen City Theater, but he hired me for the good clothes I owned. Elegant civilian dress was very expensive and hard to come by after the war. I kept putting off mentioning the enterprise to my father, and the family discussions of where I would start my medical studies—wartime volunteers who had finished their high school education were exempted from admissions exams—continued harmoniously. When

I finally told my father that I had decided to pursue a career on stage, and that I had already signed a contract, he laughed and walked out of the room. I got my suitcase and began to pack. My mother brought my father back in. For the first time he gave me suggestions instead of orders. I didn't have to study medicine, as previously agreed, but could, if I wanted, take courses in Art History or Literature. I could while away the first two semesters at Heidelberg if I wanted—he also wanted to give me a larger allowance. He spoke slowly, in measured tones, the whole time leaning with his arms on the table, and I saw that he was trying to keep his knees from shaking, so great was his disappointment that I, the first of three sons, was going to give up my studies, and on top of that become an actor. I didn't answer him. I finished packing my suitcase, closed it, and left the room. Immediately my mother was convulsed with tears, and my father was running after me. He caught me at the front gate and took me back inside. We reached a compromise: the contract with the traveling theater would be annulled, and I would be trained the right way, by a professional actor in Berlin. I would also matriculate at the university, as a precaution, in case it turned out that my talent for the stage fell short.

I traveled to Berlin with my father. I was going to live in the city where every night the great actors walked the stage. I was sure that I would become one of them.

An uncle who lived in the city knew I. B. Neumann, the leading art dealer for expressionist paintings, and gave us the address of his gallery on the Kurfürstendamm. We found the place and introduced ourselves to Neumann. He put a small painting before us, a self-portrait by Beckmann, which my father hardly looked at. He was collecting Leibl, Spitzweg, and the German impressionists, Liebermann, Slevogt, Trübner, Corinth. I was impressed by how much my father knew. Later I owned this small painting.

I. B. Neumann knew Hartau well, and called him up. I wanted this actor to be my teacher. Ludwig Hartau belonged to the physically imposing character actors who took up the whole stage with his vehemence and tenderness. His type, which had its last example in Heinrich George, has since disappeared from the German stage. Hartau was squarely built, with a massive upper body and legs somewhat too short. The elegance and agility with which he moved were astonishing. He had a wide neck and a finely modeled head with a forest of black and gray-streaked hair. His face was flat, wide-planed, with burning eyes. This gaze affected one of our serving maids so acutely that she lost control of the venison roast and almost let it slip off the serving plate.

Hartau made a few inquiries about my father's financial position and accepted me warmly as a student. The price for one hour was very high, 100 marks. He asked to have a preview of my talent. I went to him in his apartment and recited a poem by [Max] Bierbaum. He didn't listen, concluded that I was very talented, and made an appointment with me for the following morning punctually at nine. I was to have memorized Valentine's monologue from *Faust*. The next day at nine I arrived in Tempelhof at his apartment, which was furnished in the middle-class style. The maid led me into the study and asked me to wait. I waited patiently. I noticed that his wife and both of his children, a girl and a boy, were walking on tiptoe. At 12 o'clock noon I heard his booming voice through the walls, and the laughter of his daughter, and, soon after, sounds of breakfast from the adjacent dining room. The meal took a long time, as Hartau was a gargantuan eater. In a restaurant he would eat three consecutive meat dishes, then ask the head waiter, "What can you suggest? I'd like to put something substantial in my stomach." He died at 47 of a degenerative heart disease.

Now he opened the obligatory sliding door between dining room and study, and entered in his nightgown. I bowed; I revered him. "I'll be right back," he said, and went out again. He bathed and shaved himself, then dressed. At two o'clock he slid the door open again: "Follow me, I've got a lot to take care of!" He introduced me to his family, said a loving goodbye to his children, and we left. He told me about the theater, it was all he talked about. Nothing interested him but his roles. "If I had it my way, I would be on stage every minute of the day," he told me. He signaled a cab, and we drove first to his manager's office, Meinhard and Bernauer, in the Charlottenstraße Theater. I waited a long time in the cab. He came out very agitated, explaining as he approached my window: "It didn't go well with the advance this time"—he was always in financial straits—"I had to give them the unfortunate father and all that hard luck story, or they wouldn't have coughed up a penny!" He got back into the cab and we continued on our errands, till we finally stopped in front of a house in Motzstraße. "Wait here," he said to the driver. A pleasant-looking, middle-aged woman opened the front door. She was medium height and "full-figured" as the phrase went, about 30 years old, pale-skinned with black hair and dark eyes. "The actress Monika Gerhardt!" he called out to me from the top of the steps.

We sat in the spacious drawing room of the house. "Here, in this room," said Hartau, "you and a few other students of mine will be offered group lessons twice a week. The cost with Ms. Gerhardt isn't as much as with me—thirty marks an hour."

I talked a little with Ms. Gerhardt, then suddenly Hartau turned to me and said: "Go downstairs and pay the cab. Here are the keys for when you come back up." I came back and waited alone for another hour in the drawing room; the two had vanished. When they appeared again, we said goodbye to Ms. Gerhardt, caught a taxi, ate hurriedly at Huster in Hedemannstraße, and drove to Hartau's dressing room at the Königgrätzerstraße Theater, where he was playing the officer in Strindberg's *A Dream Play*. Never again will an actor, the bouquet in his hand in front of his bride's house, say those words with such tenderness, shimmering with expectation: "Victoria, Victoria! She'll come out now, I hear her already . . ." never again with such hopelessness.

His dressing room was crowded with people: shop owners delivering delicacies he'd ordered, creditors with invoices, actors in costume and make-up. There was a recess in the back wall with a built-in wash basin under a cupboard with a mirror, and next to it a low stool. "Sit down," he said to me, and began putting on his makeup. I sat in a rather awkward position, with my shoulders hunched low and my neck craning up from under the cupboard. "You are sitting on a stone in front of Gretchen's house with your eyes to the street. Out with it, Valentine! 'When I was at some drinking bout, where big talk tends to blossom out . . .'" I cleared my throat, and found I couldn't say a word. "Come on, out with it! You can't be embarrassed in front of a few people if you want to be an actor!" In a thin voice I began my monologue. That stool was a martyring stake. He corrected me, let me start over again once or twice—the whole time fluidly following the directions of his wardrobe assistant, turning this way and that and lifting his arms—until a signal bell called him to the stage. The others in the room seemed to be used to this kind of exhibition; they hadn't once turned their heads. During the intermission we continued with Valentine's monologue until the bell rang a second time. "Enough," he said abruptly," tomorrow morning at ten o'clock, here in the dressing room. I have a rehearsal. I've written you down for one hour today." This sum was drawn from the advance he had received.

I was in the dressing room at ten, and so was another boy, my age, apparently another of his students. The boy's name was Fritz Scharf, and he was the son of a slaughterhouse owner. He was skinny with a pointed, street-wise face, and the customary Berlin "lip." He didn't have the slightest bit of awe for Hartau. Whether or not he could act I don't know; we never had the opportunity to try our talents. Hartau came in from the stage during a break in the rehearsal. "You've both heard of *Romeo and Juliet* by Shakespeare?" We nodded. He laid a folded chair on the floor and said:

"This chair is the grave of the seemingly dead Juliet. On this side is the grating that separates the family crypt from the rest of the tombs. I'm going to be Romeo for you. It's night, and I'm standing outside the grating with my servant Balthasar:

Give me that mattock and wrenching iron!

—he takes both—

Hold, take this letter

—he gives Balthasar the letter for his father—

But if thou, jealous, dost return to pry
In what I further shall intend to do,
By heaven, I will tear thee joint by joint,
And strew this hungry churchyard with thy limbs . . .

—the wildness of these lines comes out in a hoarse whisper, he's holding the tools with both hands, stiffly, his whole body is shaking with determination—

Thou detestable maw, thou womb of death,
Gorg'd with the dearest morsel of the earth,
Thus I enforce thy rotten jaws to open . . .

—he shoves the iron between the bars of the grating and leans into it with his shoulder, you hear the splitting of the bars as they crack. He stands motionless for a second. Then he sees Juliet, and sinks slowly to his knee—

Oh my love, my wife!

—a sob throws him forward, the ground is drenched with his tears . . . I can hardly stand the grief—
    "So," he said, and got up from the floor. "Now you're going to do the scene. If you want to do nothing but weep for a whole hour, I won't interrupt you." Scharf nodded and made the gesture for payment behind his back.
    The lessons with Hartau were not acting lessons, they were demonstrations of a peak achievement in art, and of the standard that governs the life of the artist: the complete transformation of private life into a single, uninterrupted performance that must be a matter of principle for every actor, but that is found so seldom, and only in the great talents.

CHAPTER

F O U R

I t was a glorious time. More naive than today's twenty year-olds, not at all disappointed or embittered, our optimism was boundless. The long, bloody war had passed and become a ghost. Its victims had not died in vain, its suffering had not been endured in vain, it had taught us to love peace. There would never be another war, we had lived through the last one!

Poverty presented itself to our conscience, and we knew its remedy: socialism. We knew it was our responsibility to denounce tradition, which stood in the way of the new life. No less in the arts. Painters painted with their left hand in order to free themselves of what they'd learned, and create works of immediacy. The Dadaists arrived with their objective of mocking every concept and teasing the artistic world. So, at least, the intelligent ones like George Grosz; the idiots among them thought they had found a new direction.

The theater was liberated from censorship. Wedekind's *Pandora's Box* could have its first performance. A lesbian couple, an old man who deflowers his twelve-year-old stepdaughter, Jack the Ripper—these were the characters involved. Nothing like it had ever before been seen on stage, and the public stormed the box office. Movie theaters showed "educational films" depicting prostitution, drunkenness, gambling and drug addiction realistically. The films had a moral to them, they warned about vice, and the public came in droves to enjoy the spectacle.

In one feature film, *Baccarat*, Ludwig Hartau played the role of the big industrialist ruined by his gambling habit. At the center of the action is a young violin virtuoso, famous and spoiled by women, who also veers from his course into moral and artistic bankruptcy at the Baccarat table, and finally takes his life. Hartau held the silent film in contempt, as most stage actors did at the time, and took his part only because of the money—but he thought that for me, an actor with no experience, this would be a good assignment, and guaranteed that I could handle the role of the young violinist. By the time the film first played at the Marmorhaus, I had an acting contract with the Dresden State Theater and couldn't come to Berlin. I never saw the film.

During the film shoot I had gotten into contractual problems with the producers. Hartau gave me the name of a lawyer whose oldest daughter was a colleague of his at the Königgrätzerstraße Theater. I found attorney-at-law Schoeps in his private apartment in the elegant Meinekestraße, a street with no restaurants, hotels or shops. I saw his nineteen-year-old daughter, Margot, and made up my mind to marry her at once. I myself was twenty.

A few months later, in Dresden, I took a day off and came to Berlin for the wedding. I was still a minor, and needed my father's consent. "Who's the bobbed beauty you've been spending your time with?" the director [Berthold] Viertel asked me. "My wife. Please don't tell anyone." In Dresden and the surrounding areas there were more boarding schools for girls than anywhere else in the country. The young women would go on outings to the State Theaters and go wild over actors and singers. A married or family man was no object for this kind of excitement. Since I was again appearing in the roles of the youthful *bon vivant* and shy lover, it would have hurt my career to disappoint my female audience.

The management of the Dresden State Theater lay in the hands of an ensemble-elected manager and board of stage directors. Despite this democratic innovation, its backstage etiquette had preserved an air of the royal court theater. We younger actors addressed the seniors with "Sir" and "Madam," and no one dared make an indecorous joke in the lounge. The roles for each new play were hand-delivered to the actors by a theater employee. Another picked up the briefcase with the script from the director's apartment every morning at nine-thirty and delivered it before the rehearsal. Both of the hairdressers kept their combs stuck in their long beards and were addressed as "Herr Barber." They dealt exclusively with coiffure, wigs, and beards. Every actor did his own makeup; the conception of a character's face and dress belonged to the study of the part. A stage guard in uniform patrolled backstage on tiptoe during the performance, and gave a discreet "Psst" when anyone was talking before their entrance. The new theater—the old one had burned down—was built in a modern style and had a compartment with a chamber-pot in every dressing room. The emptying of the chamber-pots was the business of the dressing room attendant.

There was an unusually wide revolving and retracting stage designed by Linnebach, the great theater technician of that time, and an auditorium that seated 1,600. These dimensions forced the actor to adopt a volume and a degree of accentuated speech far beyond what the sense of the modern text permitted. The exaggerated attitude of the characters brought back the pathos of earlier court theater. There was no smaller second house for small comedies or conversation pieces. We were reduced to a vulgarity that stifled my joy at being an actor. Later, in my own Theater am Schiffbauerdamm in Berlin, I heard how the outstanding speaker Erich Ponto, whom I had brought from Dresden to a Berlin stage for the first time, had a "thick" sound. "A provincial actor like him," warned the director Karl Heinz Martin at a rehearsal, "will never make it in Berlin." It wasn't until opening night of the *Threepenny Opera* that Ponto felt at home in the small theater, when he gave his incomparable performance in the role of Peachum.

During my engagement at the Dresden Schauspielhaus, which lasted three years, I got to know Berthold Viertel. He was a director specializing in modern authors: Hasenclever, Kaiser, Stramm. His intelligence and ability earned him every actor's esteem, though his open-mindedness often got him into trouble. On one occasion a quarrel with the popular comedian Mayer drove both men into a rage: Viertel had nothing against using the word "shit" on stage, but Mayer hadn't given two children a good upbringing so they could learn that kind of expression in the theater. We talked to Viertel, and agreed, as we had already agreed more than once, that it would be better for him to take his ideas to Berlin. As a consolation, we went for a look at the gallery that was showing work by the young painter [Otto] Dix.

There I saw a collage for the first time. It was an immense oil painting with bloody pillows and other objects attached to the canvas. Dix called it "The Barricade." It made a big impression on us. For me, it was the impetus to begin collecting modern art. For very little money I bought Klee, Nolde, Archipenko, George Grosz, Beckmann, Jawlenski, Felixmüller and many others. The walls of my Dresden apartment were covered with these paintings, a collection which I completed in Berlin, and which I eventually lost.

The most notable appearance at the Dresden State Theater was the actor Lothar Mehnert: tall, stately, a Caesar's head, one predestined for the part of Mephisto, or the president in *Love and Intrigue,* or King Phillip in *Don Carlos.* He possessed a natural elegance, a coldness and brutality that were sometimes offset by great affection and humor. The originality of his private life was well known throughout the city. He made the impression of a sovereign, lofty homosexuality. He'd once pursued a high school boy on the main boulevard. The boy, either perceiving his intention or simply intimidated, stopped in front of a store window. Mehnert came up alongside him and fixed him with his gold-rimmed monocle. The boy walked further and was pursued further. In his distress he jumped onto the back of a passing streetcar. Mehnert stood in the middle of the boulevard, and, pointing his impeccably rolled umbrella, howled after the student in his well-known nasal voice: "Coward! Coward!" Night after night, he stayed awake in his walk-up flat in Dresden-Neustadt. He snorted cocaine and drank many bottles of red wine. In order to sleep a few hours in the early morning, he would take a large dose of veronal. He looked like an old man before he was fifty, and died of a heart attack.

I had just signed my contract, during the first weeks, and Mehnert invited me to his home for a glass of wine. When I arrived at nine in the evening he was already filling two crystal decanters. He offered me a deep leather armchair and, because the place wasn't well-heated, brought out two wool blankets, wrapped me in one of them and himself in the other. He poured red wine into two old tumblers, and handed me an antique engraved tobacco box filled with white powder. It was cocaine. I thanked him and declined. We discussed the theater avidly. I was thrilled that the great actor was talking to me as his equal. "Shall we change the scene to my smoking room?" he asked, and opened a door to a small room where there were two sofas with a smoking table between them. He lay down on one and invited me to lie down on the other. We lit our cigarettes. Mehnert touched a switch, the light on the smoking table went out, and a second one came on, across the room, on a small copy in bronze of Androcles removing the Lion's thorn. I jumped up from my sofa. "Mr. Mehnert, I've wasted your evening. I'm engaged to be married and completely normal. I shouldn't have accepted your invitation . . ."

"Go," he interrupted me, and held a hand in front of his eyes. "Go at once! Let me never see you again. You have torn a veil clumsily. Go!" I went out, though not really dejected, because his pathos struck me as comical.

The next day in the theater, he gave me his hand, beaming, thanked me for the delightful evening and hoped he would be invited to the wedding.

A single unparalleled sensation I had in Dresden was at the birth of my first son, Heinz. I immediately had a great tenderness for the child. I bathed him, took him on my arm, brushed his satin-soft hair. But the designation "papa" or "father" was strange to me, almost embarrassing. I said to him: "Come to uncle!"

I broke off my five-year contract after three. In the last year I played character roles, and felt well-adjusted in my profession. I was the First

Student in *Faust*, the Worm in *Love and Intrigue*, the Hunchback Arnold Kramer in Hauptmann's *Michael Kramer*, and, as my last role, Jean in Strindberg's *Miss Julie*.

But I never felt at home in Dresden. The majestic city was spoiled by the provincialism of its inhabitants. The people I had spent time with, the journalist Hugo Zehder or the publisher Rudolf Kämmerer, the painters [Peter August] Böckstiegel and [Walter] Jacob, were not natives.

When I boarded the train with my wife and the baby boy, leaving Dresden behind to settle in Berlin, I set out on a trip for the city that would feel like home to me. In the Landauer Straße, Rudesheimer Platz, we found a suitable apartment where we would live until our expulsion in 1933.

CHAPTER

FIVE

I n 1923, the director Berthold Viertel and I founded The Troupe in Berlin, with Viertel as Managing Director and myself as Assistant Director. The dramaturg was Heinrich Fischer, recommended to us by Siegfried Jacobsohn, Editor of *The Stage* (later called *The World Stage*).

The inflation gathered speed. Actors went over to film for some degree of security against the daily devaluation. Members of The Troupe agreed to a contract of one year, during which time they were not allowed to shoot a single day of film. They worked, one and all, for equal pay and a dividend of the theater's net profit per season. Why they did this is hard to understand today. They were seasoned professionals who didn't take on only one engagement at a time, but signed contracts with several first-rate theaters: Rudolf Forster, Sybille Binder, Fritz Kortner, his wife Johanna Hofer, Lothar Müthel, Heinz Hilpert, Aribert Wäscher, Leonhard Steckel, Erna Schöller, Paul Bildt, and Walter Franck, among others. The revolutionary goal of The Troupe was to build an ensemble that made no commercial concessions, that didn't call itself a "star theater," and that didn't tolerate filming during the season. Our business manager was a State Theater civil servant who had cancelled his contract, with pension rights, in order to come to us. He was married, had children, and owned a house with a garden in a Berlin suburb. He was small and unprepossessing. When he smiled, he revealed a blue front tooth that gave his expression a certain morbidity.

After a few months of balancing our empty accounts and struggling in vain with the financial chaos, created in part by our director's artistic fanaticism with night rehearsals and the delays these caused, the business manager finally left us. He sold his house and garden and leased the Theater am Nollendorfplatz in order to launch his girlfriend, a lousy soprano. He let his correctly trimmed hair grow long, took to carrying a monocle on a black band, went broke in two months, and hanged himself.

The landlord of the Comedy House at the lower end of Friedrichstraße, who had agreed to take a percent of our proceeds as rent, was named Heinz Saltenburg. He was the manager of several theaters, and the prototype of an uncultured businessman. He had no face. The front side of his head could be identified by a rimless monocle and two dimples. His round scalp shined like a billiard ball; he had it shaved daily. His voice was loud and deliberately pert. But despite his lack of refinement, he put up successful cosmopolitan productions.

Our office-rooms consisted of a dark storage space for props and a small room with a white, ink-flecked writing table. Four tattered chairs stood in the corner. The spacious and well-furnished Manager's room was reserved by Saltenburg, though he never used it. He heated the house only during the evening performances, which interested him because of his share of the proceeds. We rehearsed every day of the week, even Sunday, frozen blue for ten hours at a time. Saltenburg wore a sable-fur, drove the most expensive car, a Maybach, and had nothing but contempt for us idealists. Whenever we talked to him he had an eight-inch imported cigar in his mouth. He summed up his opinion of how little money we were making: "Literature is just decoration!" Both he and we felt ourselves validated by the other's opinion.

For our premiere we chose *The Merchant of Venice*. At the first rehearsal Viertel called the entire cast into the auditorium to make an announcement. He read out a letter from Rudolf Forster which asked that we please excuse him, he couldn't be present at the rehearsal because he was filming that day. Our outrage was boundless. Forster was turned out of the ensemble. Later we agreed to take him back, as long as he would play in both pieces we'd chosen, with the same pay as the other members and an equal share of the season's profits.

In the meantime the first rehearsals had started. Paul Bildt replaced the absent Forster in the role of Antonio. Kortner played Shylock, and his wife, Johanna Hofer, played Portia. Apparently he had worked with her on the role beforehand, because when Viertel suggested that she change the intonation of a certain line, Kortner flew to her side and attacked the director sharply. The two men, both dangerous cholerics, went at each other shouting. We were afraid it would come to blows. To save the smaller Viertel from injury, we held Kortner back by the arms and hands. The rehearsal was called off and a court of honor convened that afternoon to reestablish Viertel's authority.

We met in our small office. Fischer, myself and a friend of Viertel, a Dr. Münz, demanded that Kortner apologize to the whole ensemble. He refused outright. He said he'd had no intention of punching his adversary. "So was it to stop you from talking that we were holding your arms, Mr. Kortner?" I had to ask. At that he stood up, walked over to me slowly, spat between my shoes, and went back to his seat. No one spoke for a few moments. Then we settled that he and his wife would accept the director's suggestions while we worked on *The Merchant of Venice*, and after that both of them would leave the company.

Despite the merits of a superior cast, the play was no great success. Viertel's uncertainty in the visual area—he was a masterful director of the word in contemporary pieces—left us victims to the work of Dicker and Singer, two stage designers from the Dessau Bauhaus. Dicker was a slight woman who was always poking at some needlework she had with her. She was deaf to any objections on our part, and listened only to her colleague, Singer, a haggard blond man in a Russian tunic. The set consisted of cubes, blocks and Spanish walls. These were painted over with diagonal and horizontal lines.

"If you don't understand that diagonal lines are pessimistic, and represent the gloom of the ghetto, and that horizontal lines are optimistic and signify the cheerful world of the Venetians, then I can't discuss art with you," Singer explained. "I divide the actor's body into planes, which he then brings to life." Viertel, who had wanted this production to be original, rejected all of my protests against Dicker and Singer. These decisions were his prerogative as director, and I had to comply.

In the first dress rehearsal, Kortner came on stage wearing the costume devised for him by Dicker and Singer, a slender black barrel, a sort of straitjacket that allowed him to move only his forearms. After the first few lines he tore off the straitjacket, to my gratification, and from then on appeared in a costume of his own. No one challenged his highhandedness for fear of putting the premiere in danger. None of the directors could subdue this great actor; he played as a star, and it was a good thing he and his wife left the company.

Following *The Merchant of Venice*, our production of *Fetched from the Devil*, by Knut Hamsun, was a justified failure. The lead was played by Viertel's wife, Mea Steuermann, who was out of place on the Berlin stage, who spoke well, but too loudly. This production, which fell below the standard of Viertel's other work, came across as lifeless. The silent part of the ninety-year-old was turned down by one and all as a walk-on role. I took the part myself, and had a singular success, with both the press and the audience, because I alone on this loud evening didn't get on everyone's nerves.

After the full rehearsal we decided to put off the premiere by a few days. We rehearsed without sets, the walls were raised, and suddenly our performance could breathe. It was as though someone had cut the strings of a corset for us. But Viertel, who felt the improvement, was still unable to make a change, and the stark, green stucco walls remained.

It was no surprise that we didn't see any profits this time. I went to see my father and explained to him that it would come to an ugly situation if The Troupe were to liquidate and count its losses now, without first letting the contracts run their course. He gave me enough money to release me from my obligations, and I promised to give up The Troupe. Not only did I not give it up, but we put the money toward new productions.

It was Forster's turn now, with a lead role in the debut of *Next to Each Other* by Georg Kaiser. The set design, in response to my urgent appeal, was given to George Grosz. The plot is set in the present day. Kaiser portrays, side by side, inflation racketeers and black-marketers with their extravagant amusements, the stuffy middle-class family idyll in a lockmaster's house, and a wretched pawnbroker with his hunchback daughter. The pawnbroker finds a letter in a pawned coat, and sets out with his daughter to prevent a threatened suicide. They get in trouble with the racketeers and the police, and in desperation put an end to their own lives.

It was the single big success of the seven plays we put on in eight months, and the single one that brought in profits, despite the deserted neighborhood and the forgotten theater. The play called for a large cast, and as we had lost a few of our number, I took the "classy nighthawk" role.

After *Next to Each Other*, Forster took the title role in the debut of *Vinzenz, or The Mistress of Important Men*, by Robert Musil, a somewhat unfortunate piece of literary finery. When I came in to see how things were progressing a few nights after the premiere, I couldn't quite grasp why the sense of the play had become unclear in certain stretches. It also struck me that the dialogue was going by much too quickly. During the intermission I went backstage to Forster's dressing room and asked him.

"My good friend," he explained to me very obligingly, and with the irresistible charm he had both in life and on stage, "it will no longer be possible for me to speak these long sentences for an equal dividend." With difficulty, straining to use the same cheerful inflections, I asked: "And how much do we need to pay you to do all of your lines?" "Three equal dividends!" When I brought this to Viertel, he flew into a rage and smashed a picture on the wall, injuring his fist. He regained some of his composure while the wound was being bandaged. I went back to Forster and we agreed on a double salary.

Viertel went to Vienna to find an attraction and brought with him Friedrich Kiessler, the inventor of the "Raumbühne" (Space-Stage). Kiessler designed costumes and sets for our next production, *The Emperor Jones* by Eugene O'Neill. His concept called for a raked stage, raised in the back and dropping toward the audience at a sharp angle, so that the actors were forced to balance in this unusual position while trying to walk and stand normally. The scenery consisted of beams, boards and rafters with colorful linen draped over them. Dimly lit, they had an eerie effect, but because the actors couldn't play in darkness, the stage lamps had to be kept on, and the dilettantism of the whole thing was exposed.

This powerful drama set in the primeval forest, with a black man as its central character, was not done justice because of the stage designer Viertel had found to punish us and himself. A new man was in the role of the black Emperor Jones, the Munich actor Oskar Homolka, who belonged to that category of heavyweights—Schildkraut, Steinrück, Jannings, Klöpfer—who, like the ichthyosaur, have become completely extinct in the theater. He was so powerful in this role that only the Kiesslerian "Space-Stage" could ruin the evening.

Inflation broke its floodgates. We would count out the wages every day at one p.m., and by two p.m. the money had a new rate. We hurried to the nearest restaurant to eat. The Comedy House stood at the end of a back-court, and on its right side was the side entrance to a gloomy old public house called "Bodegas." There we ate bad meals and drank many glasses of schnapps to warm ourselves. If there was any money left after that, we took it to the first shop and spent it before it became worthless.

Instead of one mark, a million, then a hundred million, then a billion!

Then things took a turn. The president of the Imperial Bank, Dr. Schacht, invented the rye mark. "Who was it who made the rye mark? Dr. Schacht, Dr. Schacht!" The security was no longer gold, but rather the country's total agricultural product. The million- and billion-mark notes went into the trashcans, and pictureless, hastily printed notes were circulated.

One mark was again one mark, but all of the money I had earned was worthless. We didn't give up; we found a patron, [Richard] Weininger, an elegant society man married to the Czech daughter of the house of the coal magnate Petschek, whose brother, [Otto Weininger] author of the pessimistic book *Sex and Character*, had committed suicide very young. Weininger supplied us with Czech crowns, which we were extremely lucky to have while the inflation lasted, but which returned to their normal value once the mark had stabilized. In spite of our trying situation, we managed to stage two more plays during this time, two one-acters by Karl Kraus together on one evening, *Dream Piece* and *Literature, or You Ain't Seen Nothing Yet,* a Magical Operetta, the best directorial work Viertel did with The Troupe. Heinz Hilpert and I sang the psychoanalyst's couplet in *Literature*: "There under the threshold, we make bold . . ."

After a few evenings, our literary audience had run dry and we had to come up with a new play immediately. We had also been losing cast members at a steady rate, and could now only afford to put on a sparsely-casted comedy with makeshift stage decorations. We played one of the weaker Wedekinds, *The Love Potion.* The play and our production of it were lifeless, our parting tune. We had performed for eight months, had rehearsed daily, mornings, afternoons and evenings in an unheated theater, we had a stranglehold contract with the management and hardly any revenue to speak of, we were buffeted by the shock waves of the inflation and trying to hold on to unpaid actors, and yet we would have considered ourselves lucky to be able to go on working under the same conditions. The productions of The Troupe had, despite their shortcomings, the high standards of Berlin's best theaters.

The small group of actors who were left over had year-long contracts, and were still owed four months' wages. A meeting was called in Café Riedel on the Belle-Alliance-Platz. We convened around a large round table in one of the club rooms, all of the members and Karl Kraus. When everyone was present, Viertel stood up and announced that our funds, and every possibility of raising new funds, had come to an end, and that we could no longer perform. Then he started crying. When he had come to himself again, he went on to explain that we had found someone willing to put forward two months' wages, a total of 9,000 marks, if everyone would agree to do without the other two months. This would leave no outstanding debts to the contracts. Everyone who agreed should raise their hand.

Aribert Wäscher's face was red. "Who's the heel who had this idea?"

"I am," said Kraus.

A long silence followed. Then everyone raised their hand. Kraus received the promissory notes from Viertel and me, and we all went our ways. It was a beautiful, sunny day in May, and I had a feeling of total emptiness.

SIX

"**M**r. Herzfeld will see you now." The banker received me in his private office, Unter den Linden 21.

"Your father has credited you for 100,000 marks with us. He has also given me instructions to deposit 50,000 marks security in your name at the Police Headquarters, and to guarantee your lease of the Theater am Schiffbauerdamm from its owners. Please be so kind as to follow me."

He led me into a bathroom and put his hand on the flusher. "I can pay you the sum in cash. If you throw it in here and pull"—he pulled the cord—"then it's gone, and so are your worries. If you open a theater with it, then it's also gone, but you have a big problem on your hands." I thanked him and transferred my money to another bank. I had no nerves, at the time, for that kind of joke. On my way home I bought a small blue notebook as a temporary ledger. I sat down with it at my writing desk and entered: "Blue notebook . . . 5 pfennig."

I now had a theater in Berlin that had to open in nine months. I offered Erich Engel, whom I consider to have been the most important director of the twenties, the production of the first play. He was interested, and we met at the bar of the Hotel Bristol, where he did most of his work, in order to discuss which play it would be. I remember his first suggestion, to hire a star cast for Wedekind's *Spring Awakening*, a work which at that time was seen as revolutionary and aggressive. I decided against the project; it was the kind of thing better suited to Reinhardt's intimate theater. We considered one of the chapters in *The Last Days of Mankind* by Karl Kraus, and rejected it. This long book was written for the reader and not the stage—the characters have no theatrical life. Later, I acted in a studio performance of

"The Last Night," from the same work. Despite much admiration from the press and the ambitious literary public, it never became part of the regular repertoire.

I needed a staff of assistants. "Are you looking for a Dramaturg?" Mrs. Eugenie Schwarzwald asked me. She was known for the soup kitchens she had set up during the postwar period in working class neighborhoods of Berlin and Vienna, and was also the director of a girls' high school. "Come with me tomorrow at noon to meet Dorothy Thompson" (a noted American political journalist, later the wife of Sinclair Lewis) "and I'll introduce you to an intelligent and cultivated young man."

On the following day I was introduced to a stooped old man of about twenty with a round face and glasses. Robert Vambery was laconic and awkward. At the door he delicately pulled on a pair of galoshes. This, I thought, is exactly what I don't want. But he seemed friendly enough, and I invited him to visit me in my office. I hired him, and had, as was later proved, found my best colleague.

I drove to Munich. Heinrich Fischer had been signed on by The Troupe as Dramaturg for the Munich Kammerspiele. I offered him a multi-year contract as my assistant. He was happy to accept the better position, and above all to make the change from Munich to Berlin. Fischer, heir and trustee to the literary estate of Karl Kraus, was an intellectual in perfect form: sharp, learned, and prepared to defend his beliefs. Together with Vambery, the two were unimpeachable in their artistic opinions, steadfast in their convictions, and uninterested in money. Because I resembled them in this last point, we made a good team.

We had the accustomed tendency of the political left. We had been witnesses to the ruin of the Kaiser's empire and looked to the Republic for the founding of a new age. We were pacifists and socialists. Any person or movement that contradicted these ideologies was our enemy. The slightest spark of the old tradition sent us into a rage; we trampled over the already cold ashes of the past and overlooked, all the while, the glimmers of a new fire.

Fischer took a short vacation from his work in Munich for preliminary arrangements, came to Berlin, and we went looking for plays together. Although the entire financial and artistic risk was in my hands, I often speak of "we" when referring to the management of my theater. I never claimed the dignity of a first-in-command. Anyone could speak to me at any time, and I welcomed every good suggestion.

We knocked on all the sales agencies' doors. The president of Bloch and Sons, an intelligent and witty man named Wrede who later shot himself in Paris at the beginning of the emigration, went out of his way to offer me something unusual. The opening of a notable theater in Berlin under new management was an important event, and of great interest to him. After long reflection he took down a copy of Hermann Sudermann's still unproduced *The Rabbit Skin Trader* and handed it to me, suggesting that I make it my first production. Sudermann was the sentimental and untruthful vogue-author of our parents' time. I took the book with me when I left, went down the steps and threw it in a garbage can next to a bench on the Nikolsburger Platz, where, in its time, the publishing house had its offices. When I later undertook the premiere of *The Threepenny Opera*, Bloch and Sons took over the promotion of the work. And it was at this same bench on the Nikolsburger Platz that Brecht would ask Weill, on their way to signing the contract, to sit down to discuss their ten percent royalty, and would bargain Weill's agreed upon two and a half percent to one and a half.

I advanced Die Schmiede publishing house 2,000 marks for an unfinished comedy by Georg Kaiser, *Mississippi*, and the Dreimasken Press 1,000 marks for an unfinished play by Paul Raynal. These visits to the publishers led to nothing in the way of an opening show. We decided to find all the authors who lived in Berlin at the time. We went to Toller, Feuchtwanger and others, but none of them had a play ready. "I'll kill myself if I don't find anything!" I told Fischer. He answered me, "At this point all we have left is to ask around at the artists' pubs—either at Schwannecke or Schlichter."

So we went to Schlichter on Lutherstraße.

On the walls hung paintings for sale by the owner, the artist Rudolph Schlichter. There was a man sitting in the back room. It was Brecht. I didn't know him personally, but was familiar with his literary experiments for the stage, and thought highly of his poetry. His long face often had the ascetic expression of a monk and sometimes the cunning of a gallows-bird. He had dark, avid eyes that absorbed everything in front of them. He was lean, with sloping shoulders. His unkempt proletarian outfit with cap, jacket, and bare neck I always took to be a Brechtian "Verfremdung." Despite his somewhat off-putting appearance, he was attractive.

We took two seats at his table and asked the crucial question. He began to tell us the plot of something he was working on. He must have noticed that we weren't interested, because we asked for the bill.

"Then there's another thing I've been working on," he said. "I could show you six or seven scenes tomorrow. It's an adaptation of John Gay's *Beggar's Opera*. I call it *Gesindel* [Rabble]. It was first performed in 1728—not in London, but in a barn in one of the suburbs. It's about a corruption scandal, about a gangster who's friends with the Chief of Police and does business with him. The gangster kidnaps the daughter of a powerful man and marries her. This man is the King of the Beggars; he puts them in costumes, trains them, and assigns them to work according to their abilities. The end comes in the seventh scene, which I've only sketched so far."

This story smelled like theater. We made an appointment to pick up the manuscript the next morning in Spichernstraße, where Brecht had a furnished apartment.

Fischer went to Spichernstraße, and because the place wasn't far from my parents-in-law in Meinekestraße, I waited for him there. It began to rain, and he came back with the typewritten, damp and lightly stained manuscript. We read it. I was immediately struck by the nerve and the dry humor of the work (both ring a bit duller today), and by its intimation of a new style. I decided to open my theater with *Gesindel*. Fischer was of the same opinion. We telephoned Brecht, who informed us that there was also a musician with him, Kurt Weill, whose two one-act operas, *The Tsar Has His Photograph Taken* and *The Protagonist*, with texts by Georg Kaiser, could be heard in the Charlottenburg Opera. I went to the next show and found Weill's music too atonal for a theater piece. In order to have an alternative ready, I asked Theo Mackeben, whom I had hired as Musical Director, to find the original score by Pepusch.

Together with Engel, who also showed a great liking for the text, we now began to think of a cast. We saw the play as it is written, as a humorous literary operetta with occasional flashes of social criticism. The single aggressive song, "First comes the food, then the morals," we took seriously. The political reality had not yet proved, drastically, that when morals disappear, so does the food. Brecht and Weill weren't offering edifying messages. The profound scholarly interpretation of *The Threepenny Opera*'s socio-political message, in which Brecht himself later participated, has attached a false meaning to the play.

We put Harold Paulsen in the role of Mackie Messer. He was supple and alert. He could sing and dance. His actions never seemed entirely in his control, and the effect was unsettling. For Polly we found Carola Neher. She was ideal for the role, a marsh blossom under the moon of Soho. Her flat, regular features and her cat-nose could be as funny as they could be sad. She was, next to Lotte Lenya, the best interpreter of Brechtian texts and songs by Weill. She had a great haughtiness in which one could hear, also, the jangling of a shattered heart. "Do you love me?" she asked me once later. "Yes," I said, "on the stage."

For the role of Peachum I hired my old colleague from the Dresden State Theater, whom no one, till then, had ever been able to convince to work in Berlin. A short, spindly figure with a wrinkled face and a big nose and two foxy eyes, Erich Ponto had astonishing versatility as an actor. He played the quiet and touching Jau in Gerhart Hauptmann's *Schluck and Jau*, and possessed the rigor and wit for the role of Mephisto.

Mrs. Peachum was Rosa Valetti, the great mistress of Berlin cabaret with the furrowed face, the caustic voice and the sharp Berlin tongue. Tiger Brown was the shapelessly immense cabaret comic Kurt Gerron. His daughter Lucy was the ballad singer Kate Kühl, with her deep and arresting voice. The small role of Constable Smith was taken by Ernst Busch. When Brecht and Weill came back from the south of France, where they had been working further on the text and the music, both were impressed with the cast.

Rehearsals began on the 1st of August; the premiere and opening of the show were scheduled for the 31st.

Our offices were on the second floor, and could be reached by a flight of stairs from the courtyard. Fischer and I sat in a medium-sized room, facing one another at a two-person desk. In a smaller room next to us sat Ms. Schwarz, our secretary and bookkeeper in one person. She was our entire office staff. Finally, Vambery's small room: the script department. On the ground floor next to the stars' two dressing rooms, opposite one door that led to the stage and lighting bridge and another that led to the auditorium and my private box, was Room 4—so called because its door had a number 4 nailed to it. There was a corner closet where the directors hung their jackets, a sofa, two armchairs, a number of wooden chairs, and a writing table for furniture. On all of these, as well as along the walls and in the middle of the floor, stood empty coffee cups and full ashtrays. The pulse of the theater went through this Room 4. At all times, at night too, when there was work to do, the room was always packed with members and non-members, with actors and theater students, directors, playwrights and journalists, agents and publishers, ticket salesmen, chatterers and parasites, who together made up the working milieu of the theater. From Room 4, this mass of people spread itself into the offices, into the corridors and the auditorium, and from there coursed back again. We had no office hours. We kept open doors every hour of the day and often much of the night. We discussed and argued *ad hoc* in the theater, not in meetings or assemblies, where those in attendance think more about showing off as speakers, and the issues become of secondary importance. Our discussions weren't only theoretical, either, but rather dealt with perfecting the production at hand.

During the first days of rehearsals, Kurt Weill and his wife were announced in my office.

"I would like to play my music for you tomorrow. And I have another request—I would like my wife to play Jenny, one of the whores."

I was unpleasantly surprised. I'd never heard of Lotte Lenya as an actress or otherwise. "Fine," I said anyway, because she looked talented, had graceful movements, and appealed to me. "Weill is going to compose a song for me," she said at the door. She's rather shameless, I thought. And: what's such an attractive woman doing with the stumpy Weill?

There was a piano in the props room. We rolled it out to the stage, Mackeben, Fischer, Vambery, and I, and stood waiting. The small, mild, bespectacled man, with a soft metallic voice that expressed precisely what he wanted, began to play and to sing. I believe we were all at a loss, hearing this music for the first time, until Vambery crept over to me and whispered in my ear: "This music has as much of a chance of success as the play does." The longer Weill played, however, the more my prejudice abated. For all its strangeness, the music had a naive quality, at once sophisticated and exciting, that touched me.

Mackeben began work on arrangements for the songs, putting together a jazz band and simultaneously holding down the piano part and the function of Musical Director. Because there were no performances during the day, the musicians began their rehearsals in the morning.

By the 4th or 5th of August all members were back from their vacations, except for Carola Neher. She was married to the dying lyric poet Klabund, who had an incurable tuberculosis. The two were staying together in a sanitarium at St. Moritz. We wrote, we telegraphed, and no answer came. When I finally reached her by telephone, she told me in a soft voice that Klabund was in his last agonies, but that I shouldn't give away the role. We telephoned twice a day. In less than a week he died, and she got on a train and appeared at the next rehearsal. In her black, high-buttoned and long-sleeved dress she spoke the first lines, and I saw and heard how perfect she was in the role.

A few rehearsals later we were ready for a first run-through. It was in the evening. We wanted to try it without interruption and without discussion. It was normal, of course, that we soon came to an impasse and chaos broke out. Quite naturally there were interruptions, there was discussion between the actors, between the author and the director, the text was rewritten in places, changes were made in the blocking, there was screaming, reassuring—and suddenly Neher declared that she refused to continue, her role was too small. Brecht stepped in instantly:

"I'll take care of this. Please—curtain down!"

He had a small table brought on stage. He asked Neher to sit next to him, and began writing. The overworked actors waited in the auditorium, and I tried to find words to lift their spirits. By five in the morning their patience had worn thin. They wanted either to rehearse the last scene or go to sleep. I went up on stage; Brecht was busily scrawling lines, and Neher eagerly snatching them up. When I suggested to the two that they might continue their work in my office, she stood up, hurled her script at my feet, screamed "Play the thing yourself!" and ran out of the theater. It was a week before the premiere, and we had no one in the lead female role.

"Take a bunch of roses, Polly's bridal gown and Erich Engel with you, and try to change her mind," Brecht suggested, "you know what you've lost if she doesn't come back." Because he was right, I asked Engel, who was loath to interrupt his rehearsals with time so short, to accompany me. Carrying the roses and a box with her costume in it, we drove to Neher's apartment. We rang the bell. I gave the roses to the housemaid, and we were asked to wait in the small dining room of a modestly furnished residence. It was a very hot August day, and we waited. We waited half an hour, then opened the door to the corridor and shouted "Miss! Miss!" many times, and "Hello?" No one answered, and we sat down again. After another half-hour the housemaid came in and announced:

"Madam isn't receiving visitors today."

"Tell Madam that I was too well brought up to say what she herself would say in this situation."

We drove back to the theater with the costume box. Now we had to recast the role. Time was very short. We mobilized all of our forces, spoke to agents and made friends with directors. Horrible actresses came forward. Most of the talented ones were rehearsing, like us, for a season premiere. Finally we had the luck of finding Roma Bahn. This graceful, blond, blue-eyed woman was austere and unsentimental. In four days she had learned the unusual music and the difficult text, and was flawless on opening night.

Like a cat hunting mice, Mackeben lay in wait for actors who were done rehearsing; he caught them as they were coming off stage and dragged them to the piano. Although the action of the play was continuous, such that the singers had to perform with their backs to the orchestra and the conductor—the orchestra was placed in a huge organ shell at the back of the stage—they were well-prepared for their task through the intensive work with Mackeben. In the Paris production, the French actors refused to sing without support; there the orchestra was, as is customary, in front of the stage, and the conductor gave them their cues.

The clear landscape of Brechtian lines, the thin air of Brechtian diction, were unfamiliar to the actors. The unusual writing style and music seemed strange to them, they groped and couldn't find the solid ground of conventional theater. A general uneasiness spread among the ensemble. On top of that, the play didn't seem like it would ever be ready. I made an announcement that I had invited my parents to opening night on August 31st, my birthday, and that they were coming that night even if we only had half a play. My boldness saved me; without it the production would have been put off forever.

The first falling-out between Engel and Brecht was over the songs. Brecht wanted them to be sung as though they weren't part of the plot. The stage lights went down, and four old-fashioned petroleum lamps were lowered from the fly space. One singer stood alone in the spotlight. The organ shell became visible in the background with Mackeben on the bottom level at the keys, flanked on either side by a musician, and over these another pair of musicians. Each of them played a number of instruments. When the song was over, the organ disappeared back into darkness, the lamps were pulled up, and the lighting returned to the way it had been before. Engel would not accept this arrangement under any circumstances. And as Brecht wasn't prepared to compromise, Engel suggested that they strike the music entirely. Obviously this course was not taken.

Harold Paulsen, who had played mostly in operettas, dressed for the role of Macheath in a black tailored suit by Hermann Hoffmann, at that time a first class men's tailor. The lounge jacket was double-breasted to the waist in the style of the turn of the century, and the pant legs narrow-fitting, with stirrups. In lacquered shoes, white leggings, a thin stiletto cane in hand and a bowler hat, he sailed over the stage. The jacket was buttoned high, and a white, stand-up collar with upturned corners gave him a superior air. He completed this costume with an embellishment after his own taste, a streaming, bright blue silk scarf. The blue scarf to match his eyes—that was the only reliable security, the thing he wouldn't do without, which he put between himself and the incomprehensible madness around him. He clung to the blue scarf with both hands and wouldn't give it up—sooner the role. Paulsen became heated when a remark was made. All hell broke loose. The situation quickly escalated, and the play was in jeopardy. Brecht stepped in with an idea. "Let him be as pretty and charming as he wants," he told us in the office, "Weill and I are going to introduce him with a ballad that goes into the details of his horrible crimes, and the effect will be even more chilling with the bright blue scarf." In this way the most popular song of *The Threepenny Opera* came into being: "And the shark, he has teeth . . ."

The fifth scene, the brothel scene, wasn't getting off the ground. Helene Weigel, Brecht's wife, was supposed to portray the crippled Madame of the house. She rolled across the stage on a frame with wheels, was lifted to a table, and from this height directed the operation. Upon the discovery of an inflamed appendix, however, her doctor advised against this squatting position, and so the role which couldn't be choreographed had to be removed. We rewrote the fifth scene in the Hotel Bristol during lunch hour.

Drawn by the sensation of a "Mission Impossible"—that's what our project was being called in theater circles—many curious people came to the rehearsals. The opinion was widely held that the play would not run an entire season, would probably not even outlast its premiere performance. The theater director Karl Heinz Martin and others, among them Rosa Valetti's husband, Mr. Singer, walked out of the theater during the dress rehearsal because they felt so sorry for me, as Martin explained to me in the city. Singer signed a contract for his wife with the Comedians' Cabaret, which was to open a day after *The Threepenny Opera*.

Karl Kraus, who had been present at most of the rehearsals, hidden in one of the private boxes, wrote the second stanza to the *Jealousy Duet* between Polly and Lucy, because he was certain the audience wouldn't be satisfied with only one. Brecht was happy to accept this gift.

The dress rehearsal lasted till six in the morning, and then the actors, the musicians, and the technical personnel left the theater. We who remained sat down together. The play was three quarters of an hour too long. Various songs, among them the *Solomon Song*, with its outstanding interpretation by Lotte Lenya, had to be cut. The seventh scene, Peachum's main scene, had to be cut in half. Then we all went home exhausted. I slept one hour and was back in the theater at ten o'clock. Today, I said to myself, I don't want to see a single member of this high-strung cast before the show begins. Someone was already waiting for me there. A young man, Naphtali Lehrmann, approached me with a request. He played the part of Filch. Brecht had recommended him for the role, although he wasn't an actor, but an unemployed apprentice interested in getting into the book business. Addressing me with all the arrogance and contempt of a member of the Young Communists facing his employer, he began:

"You've hired me for the minimum wage of ten marks a day. I'm not an actor, nor do I wish to become one. You can't put me on the blacklist, or find any way to threaten me, I don't own anything. I demand thirty marks an evening or I'll disappear this instant, and you have no premiere." I said, "Agreed!" and hoped to replace him the next day.

"I demand a two-month contract immediately, and a larger advance," Lehrmann announced. I called Brecht and asked him to come to the theater to speak with his protégé. I showed the young man to a chair. Brecht arrived and spoke to him for a long time, and finally appealed to the young man's conscience. The result was twenty marks a day plus the advance.

Next came Erich Ponto, carrying two suitcases, into my office. He was packed and needed to leave quickly to catch the midday train back to Dresden. He'd heard about the extensive cuts in the seventh scene, which affected mostly his lines, and he refused to play only a part of the role for which he had been hired. Now I was at a loss. I could only plead.

"For your wife and children's sake," Ponto answered me—he'd been a frequent guest in our house—"I'll unpack my bags!"

I went out of my office and onto the stage. A mid-height stage curtain, a little over man-high, was hanging across it, drawn up at the sides and running on a wire that had been painted black to make it invisible. It replaced the bigger curtain that came down only during intermission and at the end. It was a heavy, red, silken material, hemmed with green and embroidered with colorful parrots. Behind this middle-curtain the stage technicians worked silently in felt slippers and very little light. "This curtain will be the shroud of the premiere," I said to Caspar Neher, the stage designer. After a heated discussion, he gave in. There happened to be a supply of plain white sackcloth in the house. Rollers were fastened the length of the material and it was pulled across the wire. Neher took a can of black paint and a thick brush, and painted the final title of the play across this curtain: *The Threepenny Opera*.

And then came the horse, or rather, the steed. It was a life-size, galloping dapple-gray stallion with fiery nostrils, which was supposed to burst from the upper level of the organ shell on two rails and slide onto stage bearing the messenger of the queen. Unfortunately, the angle of the rails had been miscalculated such that both messenger and steed would have continued along their path and landed in the audience. To start making adjustments in the machinery with only four hours till curtain was not possible. "The horse stays, or there's no play!" declared Brecht categorically. In the meantime he had given directions that four wheels be attached to the horse, and, beaming, he pulled the animal on stage. "This is how it'll be done tonight: an extra pulls it out by the reins with Gerron in the saddle." I objected: "We're not running a children's theater here!" "Then," suggested Brecht, "we'll have it on stage before the curtain goes up." Someone remarked accurately: "But then the *deus ex machina*, the mounted messenger of the Queen who comes just in time to prevent the hanging, loses its whole point." "In that case," Brecht answered, "we'll just cover it, and uncover it for the mounted messenger." He had a tarpaulin brought out, and covered the horse.

"I don't want this ugly block on stage for the final scene," I said. In the audience Weigel was wringing her hands and moaning: "The horse, the horse!" Brecht now had everything staked on the horse, and he'd come up with a new idea—but it was never heard. The head technician Sachs came up to me:

"There are a few projection screens I haven't tested. If you want to start at seven-thirty"—it was already six, the cleaning women with their brooms were coming into the auditorium—"then I'll need the stage now."

"Please clear the stage and let down the iron curtain, the rehearsal is over!" I had to announce.

"This is the last time I ever set foot in this theater!" Brecht screamed. "Me too," said Weill and Neher. Fischer challenged them: "Would you gentlemen like to give us that in writing?" And as they were all proper theater people, they arrived punctually at seven-thirty for the premiere, and the queen's mounted messenger made his entrance on foot, and stood on a little grass plot spread out for him by an extra.

The onstage construction was still underway as the audience filled the auditorium. I got dressed in my office and went to my private box.

We didn't have the usual program booklet with pictures and advertisements, but instead a newspaper called *The Cue*, edited by Heinrich Fischer, featuring essays on theater and literature. Alfred Kerr, the Pope of critics, eagerly opened his newspaper and found two poems by his enemy Karl Kraus on page one. He stuffed it angrily in his coat pocket. As he had also been seated, by an oversight, next to his hated rival Herbert Ihering, both men froze up.

I rang the bell to begin, and the overture started up in the form of a fugue. The audience was disconcerted. The curtain went up, revealing some of the cast standing around a barrel-organ. Gerron, dressed as an organ grinder, began to turn the crank and sing "And the shark, he has teeth . . ." but no sound came from the organ, it hadn't been switched on. Finally, in the second verse—and what a deliverance that moment was—the orchestra set in. The Peachum couple crossed the stage with their daughter Polly behind them. Macheath, a dark shadow with the light blue scarf, the stiletto cane under his arm and his cocked hat, appeared and crossed after them with a light panther-step, himself followed by the lurid gaze of the whores. Lenya, in her sharp voice, ended the scene with the sentence: "That was Mack the Knife!" The scene caused amazement, but not applause. In the second scene, Erich Ponto taught the audience in his precise and suggestive manner about his difficult profession: how to put a human being into the unnatural state of mind in which he's willing to part with money. The rejection of the scene was easily felt. Not a single hand moved. I noticed Fischer's knee—he was sitting next to me—bouncing rapidly. The wedding scene was next. There was no laughter at any of the funny parts, the audience froze. Suddenly—the men on stage had just sung the *Cannon Song*—came the breakthrough. The audience didn't gradually thaw—it went straight to boiling. Clapping, shouting, stamping, they demanded a repeat. I had forbidden all repetition of songs as unserious, but since the audience wouldn't let the actors continue, and they looked helplessly into my box, I gave the consent for the *da capo*. From that moment on, every line and every note was a success.

Intermission came. I went backstage and couldn't believe my ears. The tranquil Weill was raging and bellowing: "This pigsty! This hog sty! My wife won't play another minute! I won't allow it!" He held the program out to me, and indeed, Lenya's name did not appear in the dramatis personae, the same Lenya who had just had a huge applause for her *Tango Ballad*. She helped me calm Weill. After the performance we called all the newspaper offices and corrected the oversight.

I didn't know that this evening would go down in theater history as the biggest success of the twenties. The theater expert and manager of the Volksbühne, Heinrich Neft, congratulated me on this great artistic success and gave me friendly advice to try another play immediately. He estimated *The Threepenny Opera*'s run at a month. Carola Neher congratulated me: "How long does this other one have a contract for? I must play Polly!"

After the premiere, I ate dinner with my parents-in-law, and later in the night, at a pub, met the married actor couple Straub-Reuß. With these two and my wife I drove, unaccustomed to sleep, to Werder, on the river island, for breakfast.

I bought the *Twelve O'Clock Midday Edition* when we came back, which appeared at nine o'clock to give it a head-start on the *Berlin Times at Noon*. "A Great Victory!" ran the headlines. The reviewer prophesied a run of 500 performances.

In the theater, ticket orders came in on two telephones. The show was already sold out for three weeks. That was good, because I had only 12,000 marks left in the bank. Many unforeseen expenses, for example a new heating boiler, a fire extinguisher system and other necessary repairs in the theater, had all but drained my savings.

The Threepenny Opera ran for full houses, as Walter Steinthal had predicted in the *Twelve O'Clock Midday Edition*. There was no end in sight. I was in the theater before noon to turn people away, and in the evening to oversee the performances. I began to get bored; I missed the rehearsals. We decided to realize a project, finally, that we had discussed before the opening: the founding of an experimental theater whose direction I would give over to Heinrich Fischer.

For our first production we chose *Orphée* by Jean Cocteau, an author who had not yet been performed in Germany.

There were two kinds of matinees. There were the 3:00 p.m. performances, at half price, of the same plays that appeared in the evening program. And there were the literary matinees, Sunday mornings at eleven, presenting works for discussion whose artistic merit was undeniable but whose popular effect was unpromising. Because I have an aversion for attending theater during the day, especially during the bright hours before noon—rehearsals are different, they don't require an illusion—we decided to start the studio performances at midnight on Saturdays, after the regular evening show.

The arrangement was not paid for by the usual ticket sales. Rather, the board of directors provided the house fully equipped: props, costumes, and technical personnel, and the actors got a share of the profits. Since there was usually no more than one show, and its audience was comprised largely of complimentary guests and members of the press, it was clear to everyone involved that little money would come of the enterprise. It nevertheless attracted our best talents, who knew that the literary matinees would be attended by the most respected members of the press and by a select and avid audience; these were the critics to whom one wanted to prove oneself. All of the Berlin theaters, with the exception of the State Theater and the three opera houses, played *en suite*, so the actors had time to rehearse for studio performances with another company.

I had seen a staging of Offenbach in Hamburg by Gustaf Gründgens. When Erich Engel withdrew from the project on account of lack of time, I brought Gründgens to Berlin to produce the Cocteau. We got along splendidly with the intelligent and witty Gründgens. In the middle of the interview came a call from Engel, telling us he'd found a way to rearrange his appointments around the production of *Orphée*. I asked Gründgens, with whom I hadn't yet made any binding agreements, if he would step down. He must certainly understand that, for the opening of the studio, such a well-known producer as Engel was preferable to a name hardly known in Berlin. Gründgens didn't understand. But he put a good face on the matter and gave back the script, thanked me for my good intentions and left the theater.

Engel came the next evening, apologized, and again retracted. Now we sat between two empty chairs and were without a director. Vambery, Fischer and I went to Roberts on the Kurfürstendamm after the performance. It was the first American cafeteria in Berlin. Its specialties were the various salads one could choose from, and it was a pleasure serving oneself. While we were eating, Gründgens came in, walked past us with a muted greeting and sat down at another table. Vambery took a copy of *Orphée* out of his portfolio and put it on the table. I picked it up it: "Who has the nerve to offer it to him again?" Since neither of them answered, I went over to Gründgens's table and asked him if I could sit down. I laid the book in front of him.

"Tomorrow before noon I expect you to come and sign our contract!" He smiled, took the book in his hands and accepted immediately. He was neither surprised nor insulted. I myself was astonished; I didn't yet know that a person predestined for a certain career goes after it directly, and doesn't allow himself a single delayed reaction. Once Gründgens was a success, he had time to make up for it.

I became acquainted with him as an actor on the day of the dress rehearsal. The woman in the part of the Goddess of Death, Maria Koppenhöfer, got sick. The doctor allowed her to participate on opening night, but not at the rehearsals. I asked Gründgens to read the part. We were all surprised when, instead of the dark-haired Koppenhöfer, a blond, short-haired creature stepped onto the stage in a long black evening dress and long leather gloves. Gründgens played brilliantly in the part. When the curtain fell, he came to me in the audience, knelt affectedly, himself overcome by his achievement: "Let me play Madame la Mort tomorrow night!" It was hard to make him understand that my theater would be compared to the transvestite club "Eldorado," and my license as theater director put in jeopardy.

The production was a success. We repeated it the following Saturday night. After the premiere, at Karl Kraus's table in a restaurant, we discussed whether putting on a surrealistic play was part of a theater's obligations.

The conductor Otto Klemperer, who had seen *The Threepenny Opera* about ten times, also came to both performances of *Orphée*. As head of the Kroll Opera, he hired Gründgens as an opera director. He met Karl Kraus in my theater and offered to put on his adaptation of Offenbach's *Perichole*. The operetta was performed in the Kroll Opera house—only a few times. It lasted, despite an early starting time, until after midnight.

Public transportation didn't run after midnight during the week, and very few of the Kroll Opera subscribers could afford to own a car or to hire a taxi. The production could have been saved had Kraus allowed cuts to the script, but since he had stipulated in the contract that none were to be made, and because he was inflexible about this, the work had to be taken off the program.

Karl Kraus was not a large man; he had an unremarkable face, and, behind a pair of rimless glasses, a watchful and unsparing gaze. The ordinary face of an office drudge became animated and inspired when he spoke. His left shoulder was crooked, a fault which he corrected when he sat, stood, or walked. He wore a dark blue, single-breasted, high-buttoned suit and a stand-up collar with the corners turned in at the front.

Karl Kraus's readings of his own texts and his adaptations of Shakespeare, Nestroy, or Offenbach—he called these presentations "The Theater of Poetry"—were big events in Berlin's artistic life. Kraus sang and read sitting at a table. He was accompanied by a pianist placed on one side of the platform. Herbert Ihering wrote of Karl Kraus as a dramatic reader: "We are witnesses to a miracle: ethical will and spiritual passion as the creative force of a dramatic art . . ." The prominent theater figures attended these evenings with enthusiasm, until one by one they were targeted and shot down by Kraus in his journal, *Die Fackel* [The Torch].

Kempinski, our regular restaurant, had two entrances: one on Leipziger Straße and another on Behrenstraße. It was frequented by the city's businessmen and visitors from the provinces. In the neutral atmosphere of this spacious restaurant, in which he could remain unnoticed, Karl Kraus ate his eternally unchanging supper of boiled beef with potatoes and gravy with a dill pickle and a custard, a beer, and finally a mocha. He was joined at his table by more or less the same people every evening, a retinue of male admirers who knew almost every issue of *Die Fackel* by heart, and who, ecstatic in their good fortune, never took their eyes off the master. The severe Kraus was indulgent with them. The normal guests at the table had to be sure never to criticize anything by him, written or spoken, or they were exiled from the table forever, as I myself would be later.

Women were seldom found at his table. I remember only the actress Maria Bard, whom Kraus respected, and the poet Else Lasker-Schüler, whose poem "An Old Tibetan Rug" he considered one of the most beautiful in German poetry.

At midnight the proprietor, a small man in a frock-coat with a round face, a thick white mustache and a bald head, would appear, bow with a smile and announce: "As wonderful as life may be, sooner or later we all need some sleep!" The party paid, stood up, and betook itself to any other pub where Kraus wouldn't be recognized and where he knew no one. We often went to a certain gloomy place at the Weidendammer Bridge, next to the Theater am Schiffbauerdamm; it had a back room where all the waiters getting off the night shift went, and it stayed open till early morning.

The nights spent with Kraus were occasionally tedious, when he was tired or uninterested, and let the others at the table talk. But when he spoke, his guests were unable to leave, he detained them with his great charm; the fascination surrounding this unique personality was so strong that no one wanted to go home.

The actor Fritz Genschow brought me a new play by Peter Martin Lampel. The Young Actors' Group had made a name for itself with the recent success of Lampel's *Revolt in the Reformatory*. The new piece was called *Poison Gas over Berlin*. The Group wanted to rehearse it in my theater and put it up for discussion as a matinee. Lampel dramatizes an incident that had taken place in Hamburg: the German Army, against the agreements of the Treaty of Versailles, had produced poison gas. Through a technical error gas had escaped from the canisters and killed several civilians. Persons depicted in the play were Commanding General Seeckt, head of the Reichswehr, and the forever politically embroiled Colonel Schleicher. Both appeared in persona, portrayed by actors in costumes and makeup. In the final tableau, marching to a cry of "Victorious we shall overthrow France," the troop crosses the stage before a saluting General Seeckt.

Despite the play's many dramaturgical shortcomings, as pacifists we were fascinated by the theme. I suggested to Genschow that we include *Poison Gas* in the evening program, and for two months play *The Threepenny Opera* in another theater. We moved it to the nearby Comedy House. I augmented the group with several crucial actors and took all the financial risk, and thereby all the artistic responsibility, upon myself. I had no idea of the trouble I was getting into.

It started with a telephone call from Administrative Adviser Adriani of the Theater Unit at Police Headquarters. He needed to see me in his office at once. I assumed it was the building ordinance police, whose yearly inspection hung like an eternal Sword of Damocles over all of the old theaters, and who now would demand a costly and long overdue structural renovation. I asked Adriani to tell me over the phone what it was they wanted, but he insisted that he had to speak to me privately. With an uneasy feeling I got into my car and sought him out. The kind man assured me adamantly that it had nothing to do with censorship. I didn't understand what he meant. In a roundabout way he asked if he could have a look at a copy of

Poison Gas. He had heard scandalous things about the play. He wanted to read the manuscript not in order to create difficulties but to spare me a few.

"You just submitted the 'non-profit forms'"—this meant tax exemption—"for your theater. It would be undiplomatic to provoke a scandal at this point!"

"So it *is* censorship!"

He asked that I refrain from using that word again. I understood his sensitivity; the Social Democrat Severing was Interior Secretary, and his party had voted with great aplomb for the abolition of censorship. I took my leave without making any promises and called my legal representative, Attorney Joseph, who advised that I send the book to Adriani, and that for the sake of the non-profit exemption I should stay on the man's good side.

"I'll find out from him whether they can approve your petition any sooner."

A few days later the telephone woke me up before nine in the morning. A senior privy councilor from police headquarters requested my presence that morning at ten in Police Commissioner Zörrgiebel's office. They would send a chauffeur. I thanked him and declined: I had my own car, and I wanted to eat breakfast, shave, and take a shower first. I would be there at noon. He asked if I couldn't come unshaven and unshowered today; the Commissioner had to deliver his report to the Department of the Interior by eleven.

"I am not going to change my habits for you this morning, especially since I never requested this conference." We hung up. A few minutes later the phone rang again: I was expected at noon.

I had Attorney Joseph come with me. In the waiting room, an official asked me to follow him alone.

"I'm driving home this minute if my lawyer isn't allowed to come in with me." We were asked to come in together. Commissioner Zörrgiebel informed me very obligingly that he had not read Lampel's play, but that a copy of it was in the hands of the Reichswehr, who had given directions to the Department of the Interior to intervene. He advised strongly that I discontinue the play and spare myself all kinds of unpleasantness.

What kinds of unpleasantness, I wanted to know.

Legal proceedings on the dissemination of falsehoods and the defamation of an official. Possibly the closing of the theater.

"If you think you can threaten me, Mr. Zörrgiebel, if you think you can intimidate me . . ." Here I was interrupted by Mr. Joseph, who asked that we adjourn until he had taken counsel with his client. We left.

"I believe you want a theater, not a battle with the authorities. I think there's a way you could use this situation to your own advantage." Joseph tried to persuade me to find a pretext for dropping the play, but it was too late for his advice. The headlines of that day's twelve o'clock newspaper read: "*Poison Gas* Scandal." The press demanded a production and attacked the authorities sharply. I had been given a new role: resisting censorship.

We drove to Joseph's office and founded a "Coalition Against the Reinstatement of the Censor." A majority of the theater critics and leading figures in literature, as well as many other personalities in the public eye, among them Einstein, Thomas Mann, Heinrich Mann, Feuchtwanger, Toller, and of course Brecht and Weill, joined as members.

At the first meeting, the principal reviewer for the *Vossische Zeitung*, Monty Jacobs, talked about the importance of examining the literary value of work we would stand up for. Brecht snapped at him: "You'd like that, wouldn't you? You want to organize a literary coffee klatch. We fight unconditionally against all censorship, even if it's *Puss in Boots*."

About twenty years later, returned from his emigration in communist East Berlin, where censorship was absolute, Brecht was prepared to change the pacifist conclusion of his opera *Lukullus* into a glorification of defensive war, when the successful premiere was followed by a ban.

The well-known defense attorney, Social Democratic Member of Parliament and former communist Paul Levi, an aristocrat in appearance and a collector of ancient Chinese porcelain, offered me his services in the battle over *Poison Gas*. His violent end in the early 1930s was never explained; the public prosecutor was satisfied with the report that he'd opened a window during an attack of high fever and fallen out.

Levi phoned the Interior Minister from my apartment: "Severing! You're not going to fool us with some rotten compromise. We want to know—are you shutting down the play or not?" This only aggravated the situation. I was forbidden a public performance, and granted only a single, private showing for an invited audience, after which I would be informed whether or not I could continue playing the piece.

The guest list would be drawn up at Police Headquarters. A set of blank invitation cards for this one-time performance would be given to the police, who would send out a limited number of tickets in my name; beyond this, the authorities would not be involved. For Lampel's sake and that of the Young Actors' Group I had to agree to these conditions.

Two police officers came to pick up the invitations and to discuss the order of arrival of cars in front of the theater. They sat down in my waiting room. By chance, the actor Riewe was with me in my office, made-up for the part of Schleicher, wearing the Colonel's uniform. We crossed the room and the two officers stared in disbelief. "Well, then!" Riewe barked at them. They sprang to attention and saluted, then, bewildered, turned to my secretary for clarification. But she did not come to their assistance, as she was "not authorized to give out information."

The chief of police had distributed our tickets to all of the government departments, to members of parliament, the army, and the chancellor's office at the university, to the theater critics and the political editors of the newspapers. I had laid aside about thirty tickets in the second balcony, and instructed my secretary to send them to the youth organization of the Social Democrats, in order to have a few sympathizers as a claque. Through an error on the part of my office, the second balcony tickets went to the Young Communists. This error resulted in a catastrophe.

The next day was the premiere. As I crossed the stage to make sure all the actors were in costume, I saw Brecht, who had been drawn magically to the rehearsals during the last few days, speaking insistently to one of the actors. When he saw me, he handed the actor a note and vanished. Embarrassed, the actor gave me the note. I read it.

"You're supposed to read this to the audience?"

Brecht had instructed him to step in front of the curtain after the first signal bell and inform the officers in the audience that the actors refused to perform in front of armed soldiers, could they please check their sabers in the cloak-room. I tore up the note, refusing to let this kind of provocation put an early end to all of our work. I went into my private box to watch the audience just as Commissioner Zörrgiebel was coming in. He was greeted with shouts from the second balcony: "Bloodhound, criminal, slave driver! Let's hang him!"

In less than a minute the offenders (it was the group with my free tickets) were removed from their seats by some of the many plainclothes officers placed throughout the auditorium. The curtain rose. The actors, mortified by the icy, hostile atmosphere that hung over the audience, played without conviction. The critics had promised themselves an unprecedented sensation after all that had surrounded the play before its premiere, a sensation the play could not deliver. They were disappointed and wrote coolly. The production of *Poison Gas over Berlin* was banned the next morning on account of its threat to public safety. The Department of the Interior took the verbal assault against Zörrgiebel as grounds for its discontinuation, and, in doing so, hoped to avoid the accusation that it had yielded to the pressure of the Army in its censoring of the play.

No one took this explanation seriously. Demonstrations against the censorship were held on an almost daily basis. The president of the Academy of Arts, Professor Liebermann, himself a painter, published a general invitation to the debate: "To Censor or Not to Censor." Assemblyman Bohnen from the State Legislature and Professor Heller, an expert on state law, took the part of the censor, while Liebermann, Alfred Kerr, and Walter von Molo spoke against it. The manager of the Staatstheater, Leopold Jessner, said he felt sorry for me. "You open your theater with an international success" (a great many theaters in Germany and abroad had acquired the performance rights to *The Threepenny Opera*), "and your second piece is a huge political scandal with headlines on the front page of every newspaper . . . how are you going to go on from here without disappointing everyone?" The premiere of *Pioneers* gave him the answer.

While my negotiations with the authorities were coming to a crisis, we began the rehearsals for *Pioneers in Ingolstadt* by Marieluise Fleißer. *Poison Gas over Berlin* had been banned with about three weeks left in the run. The ever-prosperous *Threepenny Opera* was bound by contract to another playhouse. Since I could not simply close our doors for three weeks, I borrowed a piece with a small cast from the Renaissance Theater, *The Illness of Youth* by Ferdinand Bruckner. It played to half-empty houses and helped reduce our loss to 50,000 marks—a huge amount for a private theater in the twenties, today in the 1960s more or less the subsidy of Berlin's German Opera for a single day.

The premiere of *Pioneers in Ingolstadt* provoked a new scandal. In her 1963 novella *Avantgarde*, Fleißer writes: "The struggle against the theater"—that is, my Theater am Schiffbauerdamm—"had long been on the political program of certain parties. Its success was too great and too long-lasting, it was run by a Jew,"—that is, myself—"the house poet was a left-wing extremist,"—that is, Brecht—"and this was an opening for the right wing to close it down. That period had its own peculiar thorns, and the air was already charged with what lay ahead."

The play does not tell a story. As the curtain goes up, a military company marches to the booming of a brass band into Ingolstadt. The maid-servants stand at the roadside and wave. The soldiers flirt with them, and start building a bridge. The construction makes progress from scene to scene, as does the acquaintance of the soldiers with the maidservants. In the final scene, the soldiers march away over their bridge to the booming of the brass band. The maidservants stand and wave at the roadside. One of them was a timid blond played by Hilde Körber, another a cheeky brunette played by Lotte Lenya. Fleißer writes that it was Lenya's best role.

Outside my office a strange little man was sitting and following me with his eyes. He stood up and bowed shyly every time I went by. Finally I addressed him:

"Do you want something from me?"

He nodded, and I asked him in.

"I'm an actor. I'd like to join your company."

I had to laugh, and I asked him to excuse me. "You look like a tadpole," I told him. He had large, bulging thyroid eyes. "They're rehearsing on stage. Ask for Brecht. Tell him I sent you for the role of the village idiot."

Brecht had anonymously taken over as stage director. On his suggestion we'd hired someone from the provinces who wasn't qualified for the Berlin theater, and so Brecht had taken over. Suddenly I became very ill. A strep throat, and no antibiotic had yet been developed. Brecht sent word to me by my wife that I shouldn't worry about the rehearsals, he promised not to make any stinks, and advised me to sign a three-year contract with the actor who had tried out for village idiot. I signed the contract for Peter Lorre, who later went to Hollywood.

I consider *Pioneers in Ingolstadt* my most successful production. Caspar Neher, the greatest stage designer of my time, had conjured up a transparent atmosphere upon which the bridge took form, assembled realistically, piece by piece, by the soldiers. The stage direction was so understated, one didn't notice it at all.

Fleißer does not write in Bavarian dialect, she writes in Bavarian diction, authentic in her poetry and her real-life depictions. The public was capable of appreciating this peculiarity, but wasn't yet accustomed to the overt treatment of sexual matters. When the cheeky brunette takes a sergeant into the cemetery, a disturbance rose in the audience. When, in a later scene, the timid blond crawls into a tarp-covered equipment crate with one of the soldiers and the crate begins to shake, some spectators protested with shouts of "Shame on you!" though they were quickly silenced by others with "Quiet!" and "Shh!" In the final scene, the scouts set a trap for the unpopular sergeant. He falls into the river, and comes back on stage dripping wet. He blasts on his whistle, the soldiers form a line for their punishment drill and stoop together to shoulder a beam. "Knees bent! Knees straight! Knees bent!" He chooses one, kicks him in the behind and roars: "Lower! Lower! I see you were draining the family stocking last night!" The audience made a row for minutes on end. I thought we wouldn't be able to continue.

When the curtain fell, applause and rejection were felt in equal measure. I went on stage. The actors were uneasy. A gentleman with an attendant approached me and introduced himself:

"Deputy Chief of Police Weiß! Do you think we'll stand for this sort of thing? I forbid you to perform it again!"

"I forbid you, Mr. Weiß, to upset my actors!" I shouted back. "If you want to talk to me, find out where my office is!"

In my office, Deputy Chief Weiß declared:

"I was a Lieutenant in Ingolstadt. I never witnessed any such incidents."

"Sir Lieutenant Weiß—" Fischer addressed him.

Weiß's attendant, a senior privy councilor, interrupted: "You as foreigner will be asked not to interfere!"

Fischer slammed his fist on the table. Born in Karlsbad, he had a slight accent. A senseless quarrel ensued, and when it had died down, we announced that we were ready to appear at headquarters the next day. I went home depressed—not because I feared a ban, but because I feared an artistic failure.

Brecht woke me the next morning.

"You're in a deep hole, ten fathoms underground. Pull yourself out and come to the theater. We're meeting with Fleißer."

It was Sunday, there were no newspapers, and we didn't know how the press had reacted.

"Fleißer," said Brecht, "is a woman, and speaks softly. She'll apologize, she'll say there were things that went wrong with the production, and she's worried something may have gotten Herr Dr. Kerr's attention."

Fleißer, who did everything Brecht told her to do, lifted the receiver and made a stammering inquiry to Kerr, who assured that he was at that moment writing how marvelously he had been entertained. This news put us back in good spirits. We sat down together and considered cuts in the script. There was nothing in it, in terms of worldview, that we needed to defend, and we knew that a ban would help no one. I telephoned Weiß and informed him: the embrace in the cemetery would take place behind a burial mound, the defloration in the equipment crate would only appear as a reference in the script, and the kick in the behind, along with the line that followed it, would be removed altogether. Weiß was content. After this, the production ran its course without incident. Kerr's review made it possible for me to close *Pioneers* with a profit. A number of his colleagues threw dirt on Fleißer; Kerr was the only one who understood the work, both text and performance.

As soon as the agreed-upon two months were up, I brought *The Threepenny Opera* from the Comedy House back to my theater. Carola Neher played Polly. Anyone who saw her in this role will never forget her. At the beginning of 1933 she married an engineer, a Romanian communist. The two fled to Moscow for political reasons when Hitler seized power. There her husband was shot. She was interned at Kazan Prison and lost without a trace in Russia.

The sky that spring was blue every day, a disaster for the theater box offices. One Sunday morning my wife and I drove with the Mackeben couple to the Grunewald for a walk. It began to rain. The rain came down just in time for the theater, before one o'clock in the afternoon. I invited them to the best restaurant, to Horcher. The Sunday rain increased my theater's profits that evening by a few thousand marks.

When I had first acquired the Theater am Schiffbauerdamm from its owners, the Volksbühne, I had signed a contract whose terms required me to hold 600 of my 800 seats, at a ticket price of 1.75 marks, for members of the Volksbühne Association. At that time there was no subsidy, yet, from the City of Berlin. *The Threepenny Opera*'s high budget brought the necessary seat price to an average of 2.90 marks; even a full house couldn't bring in much of a profit with this quota of 600 reduced-price seats. I applied to annul the contract with the Volksbühne. It cost me 25,000 marks. The theater was closed July and August. The summer cost 70,000 marks—a composite of salaries for the actors with permanent contracts (Neher, Gerron, Hörrmann, Lorre, later Theo Lingen, and many beginning actors), for the office and technical staff, my own staff and the monthly rent of 9,000. I needed money. My wife's dowry provided fresh working capital.

After the success of *The Threepenny Opera*, Brecht, Weill and I agreed that we should open the next season as a team. Brecht and his assistant Elisabeth Hauptmann had put together a story about a Salvation Army girl and a gang leader, using characters out of American popular fiction. Two acts were ready in rough form; the title was *Happy End*.

Brecht, who had begun to adhere more closely to Communist Party dogma, didn't want to claim responsibility for this frivolous story, and adopted the pseudonym Dorothy Lane. Weill, however, made it a condition that Brecht use his own name for the song editions.

The part of the Salvation Army girl was written for Carola Neher, and I got Heinrich George for the part of the gangster. Before everyone left for the summer vacation, we set a date at the end of July for the start of rehearsals, by which time the finished play and the music would be turned over to stage director Erich Engel and Musical Director Theo Mackeben. My staff returned in the last week of July: Fischer; Vambery; the director's assistant, Dr. Halewicz; a newly recruited second director's assistant, Emil Hesse Burri; Engel; Caspar Neher; and Mackeben. Brecht was missing, and with him the last act, which he had not sent as promised. I telegraphed his holiday quarters at Ammersee and received no answer. Caspar Neher, who didn't like being mixed-up in "theater affairs," reluctantly explained to me that I'd insulted Brecht, that he wouldn't send the third act, and was waiting for my apology in Augsburg.

No doubt the third act wasn't yet finished, and Brecht simply wanted to blame someone else. I consulted with Weill. At Mackeben's house in Brückenallee, he played his music for *Happy End*. Mackeben snatched the notes away from him:

"Give me this! This music is too good to be played by you!"

Mackeben was a first-rate concert pianist. I heard Weill's most beautiful song, "Surabaya Johnny," and could barely wait for the rehearsals. It was, however, pointless to begin with the work. The third act determines the success or failure of a theater piece. Weill suggested that I telegraph Brecht: "Play withdrawn—am returning to vacation."

"Leave tomorrow and take Lenya with you. Brecht will assume the message is a trick and phone me from Augsburg. I'll tell him that you've gone to the lake with Lenya."

My wife and Lenya and I were in Warnemünde two days before the theater called with news that Brecht was in Berlin and wanted to speak to me at once. We drove at high speed, Lenya and I alternating at the wheel every hour.

At the theater there were no messages of apology and no third act, only a few notes and an assurance that the play would be completed in a few days. We decided to go ahead with the rehearsals. We needed to recast the male lead. During the vacation Brecht had cut out sections of the gang-leader role and created a new character, written for Weigel: a secret female leader of the gang, called The Fly. She marries the Salvation Army officer at the end, played by Sigismund von Radecki (today known as an author), who made a bizarre impression on account of his extraordinary height, his bald head, and his deep bass voice, with which he delivered the Salvation Army song about the "Whiskey Dealer."

Heinrich George refused to play the remains of a gutted role, as he called it. Oskar Homolka, who had fallen out with Piscator during rehearsals for Walther Mehring's *The Merchant of Berlin* at the Theater am Nollendorfplatz, took over the part of the gang leader in its revised form, and made it possible for us to go on rehearsing without delay.

Engel had worked on two acts and now asked for the third. Brecht couldn't give it to him. The two separated after a hostile conversation, and I had to speak to them in different rooms. Engel requested that I dissolve his contract, or find another play. Brecht would never write the third act; anyway the content of the story was already told in two. Brecht said Engel was a used-up, tired old man, and kept reminding me of *The Threepenny*

Opera, which had also been unfinished when I first took it on. Inspired by the actors, he explained to me, he had written the conclusion during the rehearsals.

I wanted to believe him and had to believe him. The ensemble I'd hired was an expensive one. Engel stepped down and Brecht took over the production, and rehearsals ran smoothly. Only in the fragmentary last act did it come to a conflict: the actors felt that their characters were unresolved at the end, and they demanded more text. I had a meeting with Brecht in my office. I accused him of having deceived me. We shouted ourselves hoarse. Then I resigned myself. I gave up criticizing him because I saw that it was pointless. Engel had been right: in the end, there was only a fragment of a third act. My only hope now was that the outstanding cast, the music by Weill, and the interpretation by Mackeben would save us.

In the last days before the dress rehearsal, Brecht was surrounded by an odd group of characters. One of them was named Slatan Dudow, later well-known in East Berlin. Some of them were from Moscow. Brecht introduced a certain Dr. Reich to me as being a master of cutting text. The man wanted to suggest a few in *Happy End* for a fee of 2,000 marks: "In Moscow I played Lear in an hour and a half," he explained. "They call me Dr. Strikes." I turned and walked out.

The dress rehearsal started late and ran without a hitch until shortly before the finale, when it was interrupted by the hulking Kurt Gerron. The actor advanced to the footlights and looked out at Brecht: he had no desire to be an extra all through the third act, and he demanded new lines. Several actors, whose roles had been similarly whittled away, started to murmur along with him. Brecht, over-excited, turned on Gerron in full fury:

"You fat clown! You miscarriage! If you ever lose any weight it'll be because you're out of a job!"

Gerron screamed back: "You should have written a play, instead of dumping your shit all over the stage!"

Then Brecht: "I demand that this man be disciplined at once! Or I'll leave the house!"

I couldn't speak; I found this dialogue too funny. I leaned forward with my face in my hands to hide an attack of laughter while Fischer intervened:

"No one's going to be disciplined at four-thirty in the morning. Please keep your verbal attacks to yourselves and let's finish the rehearsal."

The premiere's public reception, until the second intermission, was as enthusiastic as it had been for *The Threepenny Opera*. Then came the third act. The audience, audibly disappointed, rustled and coughed. I stood backstage and counted the minutes. When the act was over, and the ensemble gathering to sing the finale, I saw, hardly believing my eyes, Helene Weigel suddenly step onto the stage. With a shrill voice, reading from a piece of paper, she yelled into the audience:

"What's a pick-lock compared to a stock market share! What is breaking into a bank compared to founding one!" and other vulgar Marxist provocations. The bored audience, torn abruptly from their lethargy, demanded the curtain with a cry. Two gaudily colored stained-glass windows were lowered from the rigging-loft, depictions of Henry Ford and John D. Rockefeller. From the wing, Theo Mackeben played and sang the last finale of *Happy End* as loud as he could, "Hosanna Rockefeller, Hosanna Henry Ford." Tears ran down his cheeks; he sang alone while everyone else lost the tune in the muddle.

It was Brecht's group of hangers-on we had to thank for this harangue from Weigel. They had felt that *Happy End* was inadequate in its ideological underpinnings. I didn't bear a grudge against Brecht. We had each played by our own rules and lost. The loss on my side stood at 130,000 marks. A short Brecht-break set in at my theater.

The long faces of the cloakroom women guarding the two jackets and five hats on their racks while rows of hangers remained empty, the ushers with their piles of unsold programs, the stale cookies left lying on the counters of the theater café, the cashier who brought me the anemic sales report, the depressed actors who had to play in front of tiny audiences, these were the nightmarish images of failure.

If this sort of situation was repeated too often, a manager went bankrupt and disappeared without a trace in the wreck. He couldn't expect any help if he didn't help himself. He had to sell tickets. If he failed to do this, he was no theater manager, though he might still make a good superintendent in the provinces, as was shown by the example of Gustav Hartung. In spite of his failure in Berlin, Hartung was received with open arms in the subsidized Staatstheater in Darmstadt.

We opened the following season with a debut performance of Ernst Toller's *Fire from the Cauldrons*, the story of the two marines Reichspietsch and Köbis, forerunners of the 1918 revolution, who had led a seamen's revolt in Kiel. Toller portrays the failed mutiny, the court-martialing of the two plotters, and their execution by firing squad. The apotheosis of the final scene—red flags and a tirade of Communist propaganda—was cut after difficult negotiations in which Fischer and I entreated Toller to give us the authority. It was during an evening rehearsal. Toller asked to be left alone while he made his decision, and he asked to see a copy of the script. He gave it back to me an hour later. On the first page he had written: Such and such a date, twelve o'clock midnight. In memory of the hour in which a man gave up. Signed, Ernst Toller.

He was a loving and lovely man, in love with his own pathos, his beautiful eyes, his ample temperament. He hanged himself in a New York hotel room during his emigration.

The production boasted an exemplary cast: the two main roles were played by [Hermann] Speelmanns and [Albert] Hörrmann, the petrified military attorney very quietly by Erich Ponto, an ill-natured Navy officer by the slender and elegant Theo Lingen, and the first mate by the sympathetic Heinrich Gretler, with his benevolent seal's face. For most of the sailor parts we chose actors who wouldn't come across as comic under the realistic direction of Hanns Hinrich. Caspar Neher built a practically functioning ship on stage. We were able to show the engine room receiving a direct hit from artillery.

Both the play and the production were a sensation with the press for opening night and the night after. Felix Holländer wrote in the *Eight O'Clock Evening Edition* that I deserved thanks for such an evening.

Ticket sales were next to nothing. We sent out thousands of free tickets to trade unions and workers' organizations to fill the theater for at least a month. The tickets were not taken. The topical realism of the twenties theater was dead.

"You want to know what the workers and the unemployed" (whose numbers were increasing rapidly) "are interested in seeing?" someone asked me. "Go to The Plaza!"

A former train station converted into a theater with 5,000 seats, The Plaza was sold out at noon. There were three performances showing daily. The price of a cheap seat was 30 pfennig. The Rotter Brothers brought their played-out operettas there, having arranged contractually with the house manager to hire only third-rate singers in order not to spoil the audiences and to keep their tastes undemanding. When the Count of Luxemburg lit his cigarette with a hundred mark note, the audience forgot their dull misery and applauded with spirit.

Those days, with their stock market crashes and locked bank counters, crept into peoples' homes and into their beds with them as nightmares. The circling vulture of Black Friday, November 1929, could no longer be driven out of the sky. The small upper class of the mega-city, the perhaps 50,000 who were interested in the literary theater, wanted only to be entertained, and the income of the serious artistic stages dissolved. The former dancer Eric Charell filled the 3,000 seats of Reinhardt's big auditorium every evening. He put on grand spectacle operettas, though with better taste than

the entrepreneurs Rotter, who would play as many as twelve theaters at a
time. In *White Horse Inn* the revered buffo Max Hansen sang the part of a
waiter, and the beloved Paul Hörbiger moved the audience with his nobil-
ity of mind and good nature in the role of Kaiser Franz Joseph.

I went back in history and took a costume piece set in the eigh-
teenth century for my next production. The author Paul Kornfeld was
a small, bespectacled, lively, intelligent, and funny man. The play was
called *Jew Suess*. Our innocence—or confidence—could not have been
greater. We portrayed a Jew in a black caftan and sidelocks. He arrives at
the court at Württemberg, through his cunning and intelligence makes
himself indispensable to the Duke, ascends to the all-powerful office of
Finance Minister, drains the people of every penny through taxes of his
own invention, and loads himself and his carefree master with riches.
He gives a magnificent banquet, himself appearing in a white dress coat
trimmed with precious stones. The Duke, in a radiant mood, attends the
feast, and Jew Suess's career is at its high point. The Duke feels suddenly
unwell, falls over, and dies. The enemies and those envious of the Jew take
immediate action. The townspeople, who have always been rebellious,
are immediately up in arms. The Jew is arrested, tried, and strung up
in a cage. We cut the scene with the townspeople; a crowd of care-worn
women in shawls and furious men stamping in their stupid excitement
was a motif as old as last year's snow.

The play's large cast and wide range of settings called for a well-versed
director. Engel had left the theater and taken a one-year contract with the
AFA movie company.

Later, during the emigration in Paris, I met the AFA producers. They
had brought with them thousands of humorous excerpts from their movies, and were filming the first humorous French military sketches. The
French didn't laugh, however, and the film went into the waste basket.

I offered the production of *Jew Suess* to Superintendent Leopold Jessner.
With his modern stage productions after the revolution, Jessner had done
away with the heavy pomposity of the old courtly theater. He was a large,
well-groomed man with an aura of authority. He had an exclusive contract
with the State Theater, but he was able to push through this one outside
production as an exception. I paid him the high salary of 8,000 marks.

We hired Ernst Deutsch for the main role, for which he was perfectly
suited. For the part of the Duke I brought the large, sunny, and masculine
Otto Wernicke to Berlin from Munich. At the head of the clique of Suess's
antagonists is a minister to the Duke, who was played by Erich Ponto. Theo
Lingen was the scheming ambassador of an enemy state. Gina Falckenberg,

Eleonore von Mendelssohn, Lotte Lenya, and Hilde Körber gave the banquet scene its radiance. Caspar Neher conjured up costumes of starched cloth which were then sprayed with color. When you threw light on them, they appeared luxurious and costly.

The play was amusing as long as it showed the rise of the Jew, until the intermission. After the intermission, it became singularly tragic. Jew Suess is laid in chains, put in prison, sentenced to death, and hanged in a cage. A play that starts out amusing and later becomes serious or in any way sad will invariably be rejected by a Berlin audience. The production lost money. It had been too costly to sustain itself with narrow profits.

I leased the cloakroom proceeds for one year to a Professor Epstein, who specialized in this line of work. He paid me 60,000 marks in advance.

The Berlin theaters' revenues were in constant decline. We could no longer cover our expenses. The Association of Stage Managers held one meeting after another concerning the measures we could take as a group, but an agreement between so many staunch individualists was not reachable.

As it would not have served the glamor of the theater to make its financial difficulties public, these meetings were kept strictly secret. Therefore we were surprised, one morning, to see the words "Theater in Danger" appearing in the headlines. The Secretary of the Association, whose duties included seeing to it that the doors remained locked during our meetings, had sold the details of our secret protocol to the press for 20 marks.

As always, when things were difficult, I asked my wife for help. She had already assisted once with stage direction; now she became my colleague.

"Go to the theater and see what you've been missing," wrote Alfred Kerr in his review of our premiere of *The Garden Pavilion*. The author Hermann Ungar, press attaché for the Czech Embassy in Berlin, had written a number of successful novels. He never saw his premiere on stage, however; he died at 35 of appendicitis. The play was a mixture of literature and plain obscenity, a mixture that succeeds just as well today.

In a small provincial town in Czechoslovakia, the daughter of a well-to-do middle-class home decides to lose her virginity. She asks the servant Modlitzki for his assistance. Modlitzki places himself at her disposal on one condition: his proletarian dignity must remain intact. He'll do her bidding as a woman, it must be understood, and not as a bourgeois seductress. He warns her, drawing the curtains of the garden pavilion, "And don't even dare to offer me refreshments."

The father sets his heart on a trip to Paris. The plans and preparations go on for several months. Modlitzki notices that something is weighing heavy on his master during this time. All men travel alone to Paris for a particular purpose—but he has never done this sort of thing outside of the house. How can he embark on such an adventure in a land where he doesn't speak the language? Modlitzki has the answer: master might just as well take care of this business at home. He arranges a rendezvous with someone in his chamber, and the master then has his head free for the sights of Paris.

In a free-standing villa built by Caspar Neher on the revolving stage—a villa in the style of the 1880s with all its quaint atrocities of red bricks and turrets—Uncle Kudernak putters about. The fat uncle, a devoted glutton, appears in every novel by Ungar. The doctor forbids him his gormandizing, which is threatening the old man's eyesight. The uncle answers: "I've seen enough, but I haven't eaten anywhere near enough."

The servant was played by the not yet shapeless and not yet splotchy-faced Oskar Sima, the father by Erich Ponto, his wife by Hedwig Wangel, a famous portrayer of mothers, who would soon leave the theater and found a home for "fallen women." The precocious daughter was Hilde Körber; Uncle Kudernak the comedian Szöke Szakall. Szakall tended to mumble, which allowed him to make a career in Hollywood despite his limited English. The play made money, and I recovered from my losses.

When the shortage of new plays came to a crisis, Peter Martin Lampel was the man to turn to. If one couldn't find a single piece ready for performance, Lampel took an unready piece and had it ready in five days. He always found an original milieu and presented it honestly and capably. Only the staging didn't proceed in an orderly fashion. Awed by his gift of observation, one believed that any such problem could be brought to his attention and resolved, which was not always the case. The premieres were never failures, nor were they ever great successes. We put *Schoolboys* and *We are Comrades* on the experimental stage, and both for a short time on the evening program.

On his birthday, my older son Heinz received the newly published book by Erich Kästner, *Emil and the Detectives*, four times as a gift.

"Why don't you make this story into a play for the children's theater?" my mother asked me.

She was right. I met with Kästner and asked what he thought of staging *Emil and the Detectives* as an afternoon show during the Christmas season. A month later he handed me the finished play; the idea had worked.

Since for children the best often isn't good enough, I hired Karl Heinz Martin as director, Theo Lingen for the part of the thief, Lotte Stein as the mother, and for the part of Pony Hütchen, the eleven-year-old, beautiful

Christiane Grautoff, who, five years later during the emigration, married the much older Ernst Toller.

Like two kindergarten teachers Martin and Lingen took charge of the many children at the rehearsals. The production delighted parents, children, and critics alike, but the profits were weak. I inquired at the various ticket offices and asked parents for the reason.

"It teaches the children impertinence," they answered me. "We'd rather send them to the Nollendorf Theater to see *Little Peter's Journey to the Moon.*"

The performances moved from the center of the city to the Nürnberger Straße Art Theater, in order to be nearer the children in the Kurfürstendamm area. There, too, the auditorium remained half empty. Many years later, this delightful play would bring in full houses.

Every summer at the end of the theater season, I drove with my wife to Silesia in the car. We had the 350 kilometers to the Adelsbach estate to put behind us, and seven hours of driving on the then two-lane and exceedingly curvy highways. We stopped for a midday rest in Krossen-an-der-Oder, about the halfway point. Here, the cord that pulled me back towards Berlin finally snapped. The city let me go, and we arrived in the country.

The pines of the march gave way to the spruce woods of my Silesian homeland. Its dark, impenetrable green and its fragrance were my familiars. Arrived at the estate, I parked the car in a shed and didn't use it until the drive back. My wife and I took the green lodens out of the wardrobe trunks, I hung a rifle and a field-glass from my shoulder, my wife only a field-glass. We walked on field paths into the hilly woods, single-file up and down the narrow deer paths, without a sound. We avoided all noise; no one wanted to talk after the loud Berlin theater season.

We were the first to arrive at the castle. Our two sons came by train with their nanny and were picked up at the Bad Salzbrunn station by a horse-drawn carriage. My parents and two brothers came from nearby Breslau, often only for the weekend. My wife's parents and sister, all three of them enthusiastic hikers, shared our partiality for this estate in the Waldenburg highland.

I invited only a few guests: the painter George Grosz and his wife Eva, Toni and Theo Mackeben, Robert Vambery. Erich Engel came once with his intelligent and lovely girlfriend Sonja Okun.

Every year, my old friend Heinrich Neft visited us for a month. He was the ideal country guest. You didn't have to entertain him, he appeared only at mealtimes. He fished for carp in the castle pond and trout in the mountain stream. In the evenings he took his hunting vehicle and, accompanied by a game-keeper, drove into the woods. We couldn't eat all the carp that he caught. They were held in a tank and set free after he had gone.

The night watchman finished his shift at six o'clock every morning, came into the immense castle kitchen and lit the stove. Everything needed for the kitchen was provided by the estate managers and gardeners. Freshly picked fruit and vegetables were brought into the house for us, and my wife filled many vases with bright flowers. We had horses and wagons at our disposal for riding and driving. A spring, tended by a pump master, provided refreshing mineral water, the Adelsbach source, which in its composition resembles the curative waters of Salzbrunn. In Salzbrunn our coachman rested his team of horses at the tavern "Zur Krone"—the old guesthouse that Gerhard Hauptmann's parents managed when he was a child.

The Adelsbach castle, situated in an expansive park, is a heavy structure from the late renaissance with walls one and a half meters thick. Today it is a protected historical site under the supervision of the Polish government. A four-kilometer underground passage leads to fortress ruins in the forest. We had this entrance sealed off because of the danger of its collapsing.

My attachment to these summer grounds was what kept me from leaving my country. When we lost the estate, we were forced to set out on a long and complicated journey. I have not forgotten the fragrance of elder and linden that came through the open windows of the tall and cool castle rooms, that of the ripe wheat, and the sap of the pines at noon.

Squaring the Circle, written by the Russian [Valentin] Kataev, was a parody about the housing shortage in Moscow. At one point in the action a trade-union secretary comes on stage waving posters with party-line slogans. We eliminated this scene and played Kataev's piece as a witty, somewhat frivolous comedy that looked like contemporary topical theater. Two young couples live together in an attic. The room is divided into two halves by a line of chalk. [Heinz] Rühmann and Peter Lorre played the husbands, Hilde Körber and Lotte Lenya the wives. In the role of the poet who often comes to visit them was Theo Lingen. The play was a big hit with the public and the press. We estimated it would run for at least six months; attendance dropped off rapidly after a few weeks. The audience, increasingly affected by the economic crisis, could no longer afford the expensive theater tickets. Uproars and clashes among the countless political parties, whose youth organizations, guided by either the Nazis or the Communists, precipitated bloody street slaughters, put a fear in people of leaving their apartments in the dark. A theatrical success in financial terms could no longer be realized. Soon I needed money again, and I asked the business manager of the Broadcasting Society, Ltd. to my office. The society had nothing to do with either radio or broadcasting: that was simply its name. It was an organization that sold reduced theater tickets to its members for a majority of the Berlin stages. One became a member for 50 pfennig.

Theaters are generally empty at six in the evening. I told the business manager of the society to come at this time. He came with his loan shark. A contract was signed which provided the Broadcasting Society with a certain number of heavily reduced seats for a quarter of a year. I received payment in the form of 20,000 marks' worth of endorsed bills of exchange, which could not be redeemed in the usual way. They remained valid for three months. The loan shark unlocked his briefcase, paid me 16,000 marks in currency on the table, and took my bills of exchange. When calculated over a full year, his gain was 80 percent. He was short, vigorous and stout with sparse blond hair, and his suit of expensive fabric crackled when he sat down. He wore bright gaiters. "I've got a girl in bed in the hotel next door," he told us, "I left her two glasses of brandy on the night table." In high spirits due to this fast and profitable transaction, he slipped on his hand-quilted, bright yellow pigskin gloves, and pulled the fingers smooth. "I'm going to give it to her three times." I thought, is this all worth it, just so that the curtain goes up in the evening?

The critic Herbert Ihering paid a visit to my office at the theater, an unusual occurrence. Critics didn't visit producers in their offices. I assumed he was going to recommend an ultra-left-wing piece for my next production. He often championed works containing more ideology than artistic value.

Ihering didn't recommend a play but rather two young people he had brought with him. One of them, a tall, thoughtful man, was the stage designer Wilhelm Reineking, the other, of medium height and an alert face, the director Arthur Maria Rabenalt. Both were working in Darmstadt.

"We're the four horsemen of the German theater. Wherever we show our faces, bankruptcy strikes."

"You're a little late for Berlin. But show me your portfolios."

They laid out a plan to adapt old, dusty operas for new audiences by applying new text and modern staging techniques.

"I see your bad luck spreading its wings," I told them. "Berlin has three city opera houses it can't afford, and one of them, the Kroll Opera house, is being closed just now. The proposal that I, one of Berlin's unsubsidized private theaters, which are all balancing on one leg at this point, take on an opera, is so beautiful that I'll do it. I'll make you an offer: I provide

the house with accommodations for rehearsals and an evening performance along with 5,000 marks. Props, chorus and orchestra will all have
to be hired with that amount. The singers will have to make it a matter
of honor—to rehearse without wages and perform for a dividend of the
net proceeds. The two of you and the choreographer and prima ballerina
Claire Eckstein"—she was Reineking's wife—"as well as Robert Vambery,
my dramatic producer, and Theo Mackeben, in charge of musical arrangements and direction, will receive no salary. If this production succeeds and
becomes part of the regular evening program, each of you will receive 50
marks per performance."

They accepted my offer.

Rabenalt and Reineking had experimented in Darmstadt. At my theater they found, as the two often maintained, the ideal colleagues. For the
first production of the newly founded Opera Studio, we chose *The Daughter
of the Regiment* by Gaetano Donizetti.

We considered it the dustiest opera in the repertoire. Vambery relo-
cated the plot—the changeful fate of the Colonel's daughter Marie—to
present-day Lima in South America, and wrote an ingenious comedy to
complement Theo Mackeben's transparent instrumentation of the original
music. Mackeben enriched the opera with a few selections from Donizetti's
other works, a practice often attributed to the composer himself.

The stage decorations were as entirely new to stagecraft as the half-
height curtain in *The Threepenny Opera*, later so often repeated. It was
assembled out of moving parts which could be arranged and transposed
variously according to the scene. In addition, for every aria, a small,
painted back-cloth came down from the flies: a tree, a green meadow, or a
barricade. The arias, duets, and trios were delivered with musical precision,
while the singers' actions remained realistic throughout. Combined, the
two had a surrealistic effect. Claire Eckstein developed a dance style which
afterwards, in America, was adopted in ballet and musicals with great success. She instructed the dancers in youthful steps and gestures.

Not until the dress rehearsal were the men transformed into honorable
sirs: they were then given mustaches or beards, patriarchal coattails or a
General's uniform. The women wore dresses with long trains and wasp-
thin waists, great feathered hats and high-buttoned ankle boots. When this
ensemble, in its elegant dress, began to dance and execute leaps, the audience applauded from beginning to end.

Heinrich Gretler, Theo Lingen, Trude Hesterberg, and a new discovery,
the young, beautiful Maria Elsner with her glorious soprano voice—today
in the 1960s her name is Lady Fischer and she lives in England—sang and

acted the main roles. Claire Eckstein's partner was the American dancer of the grotesque, Edwin Denby.

The premiere was the most joyful and most applauded of any performance during my career in the Berlin theater. Many eminent names of the opera and theater, conductors such as [Otto] Klemperer, singers like Richard Tauber, and directors like Max Reinhardt attended the evening. The success was such that I knew I had to put *The Daughter of the Regiment* on an evening program. As there was no room on my own stage—*Squaring the Circle* had just begun and I promised myself a long running season—I signed a contract with the Berlin Theater management, and *The Daughter of the Regiment* moved to that stage. Rabenalt and Reineking went separate ways. Rabenalt specialized as a director of fluffy movies and made money. Reineking stayed in his line of work and earned prestige as an artist.

The *Berlin Times at Noon*, Thursday, January 2nd, 1931:

We are Halving the Price!
A practical attempt by Ernst Joseph Aufricht,
Producer of the Theater am Schiffbauerdamm

"During the last few weeks, repeated attempts have been made—in discussions held in the theaters, in meetings of the Stage Workers' Union and Guild, and in numerous proposals and counterproposals from professional and lay circles—to untangle the Gordian knot around our theater. I would now like to attempt (at least for my theater) to cut that knot, and cut it exactly in the middle: starting today, all entrance prices for my theater are reduced by half. The most expensive seat will cost 7 marks, the least expensive, 75 pfennig.

"This is now possible only because, finally, even the actors have begun to understand that our crumbling economy demands a sacrifice. After the last negotiations passed without raising much hope that an equitable wage agreement with the actors could be reached through the Union in the foreseeable future, I began to implement my own solution, in individual cases, wherever possible. I have, to my best ability, and where there has been little willingness to oblige, made replacements among my ensemble for equivalent but less expensive talent, and have found in almost every case the good sense that alone has made possible the existence of my theater and a few other Berlin theaters.

"The new regulation of ticket prices is effective not only for the comedy *Squaring the Circle*, a relatively inexpensive project and therefore ideal for the first step in this experiment, but also for the next piece, *The Daughter*

of the Regiment, which is to return to the Theater am Schiffbauerdamm
shortly following its guest appearance at the Berlin Theater. Here we have
succeeded through negotiations with theater members (and, significantly,
without replacing a single one of them) to bring before the public this
opera with its 30-piece orchestra, its chorus of nearly 20 and its cast of
first-rate actors for a ticket price from 75 pfennig to 7 marks. The wage
reductions have been set not only for almost every solo part, but also for
members of the chorus and orchestra. Only the extras, who from a purely
social point of view have always received less than adequate compensation,
have remained at their original wages.

"The significance of this radical price reduction must surely be clear to
the public: the almost complete elimination of season's tickets and problems with ticket inflation, the return to normal booking, and the stable
balancing of budget with entrance fees. If it is possible to run a theater,
one ranked Category A by both the Theatrical Guild and the Association,
at its hitherto existing level of excellence, with ticket prices that are hardly
any higher than those of the big cinemas—almost half the price of any
other Category A and B theater—then perhaps there will be sufficient evidence to reconcile the disunited body of directorships in its approach to
this question of box-office failure, and to replace it with an actionable and
unified readiness."

People came with chocolates for the ticket woman. They no longer
needed to purchase their tickets through organizations offering reduced
prices; they could now buy them at affordable prices at the theater box
office. But profits did not rise to the extent we had speculated. The half-
price tickets did not bring us full houses.

Whenever I tried to make it easy for myself, I made it more difficult. In July
1930, in order to mitigate the cost of the summer-long closing of our doors,
I had put on a Noel Coward piece with the German title *Tratsch* [Scandal].
I had my name taken down from the façade and out of the program. I used
the term "summer season" wherever possible.

The comedy was arrayed with irresistible actors: Maria Paudler, Rudolf
Platte, and Hans Schweikart, who also directed the production. The critics annihilated the harmless and well-accomplished endeavor; they didn't
accept entertainment theater from my company. Monty Jacobs of the
Vossische Zeitung walked out in the intermission, not without first loudly
remarking: "I'm getting out of this theater of profound thought!" Alfred

Kerr praised the performance, but found it out of place in the Theater am Schiffbauerdamm; his review began and ended with "yawning." The sales were nonexistent. I closed the theater and went on vacation.

The results were similar in 1931 with a play by [Alfred] Savoir that had had a series of successes in Paris. It took place in the circus milieu, was of no literary value, but had five show-stopping roles that I could cast with favorites. The part of the lion tamer went to the Bavarian Goliath, Fritz Kampers. Whip in hand, he rocked back on his chair and contemplated his huge thighs in skin-tight white leather. The decadent Lord was played by Gustaf Gründgens, reduced to a wisp for the part through a severe regimen of diuretics. The Lord haggles with the lion tamer over a certain equestrienne, played by Carola Neher. Gründgens, taking a look at Kampers: "When I look at your thighs, I feel like throwing up."

The two clowns were played by Lingen and Lorre.

We were having full set rehearsal the morning of the premiere. Suddenly Gründgens appeared on stage, looked around for a moment, and took a reeling step through one of the set walls. I screamed something onto the stage. Gründgens crumpled like a sack. We were frightened, and tore off his shirt and tie. Someone put a wash basin with cold water next to his head and began to prepare a compress.

Gründgens awoke out of his faint, bent his head over the basin and sobbed for a while over the water. Then he lay back, closed his eyes and was insensible again. We carried him to the couch in his dressing room. In the meantime the doctor had arrived, summoned by telephone, and Fischer and I retreated to our office. We were anxious, we feared a postponement of the premiere. The doctor came out after a few minutes:

"The man is perfectly healthy. Pay him no attention, eventually he'll get bored and go back to his normal behavior."

Fifteen minutes later I heard someone whistling in the courtyard; it was Gründgens leaving the theater. He arrived punctually that evening in his dressing room.

The curtain goes up. We see the back of a big tent and hear the sounds of a circus performance. In the foreground, in a small, open tent, stands a bar. Gründgens, inimitably elegant in a dress coat and top-hat, enters and climbs onto a barstool with evident disgust. The bartender waits humbly.

"A Manhattan!"

The bartender begins to mix the drink. Gründgens stares motionlessly ahead of him. In the middle of this taut silence the entire circus tent, for unexplained reasons, collapses in the background. Loud laughter in the audience. I thought: the performance is done with! Gründgens doesn't bat an eyelash. He doesn't make the slightest change in his position. For him, not a thing has happened. The audience understands him: he wants to keep going. The laughter ceases, the performance continues.

When Gründgens came offstage after his scene, I left my private box to look for him. I heard a terrific noise through his dressing room door; Gründgens was demolishing the room. He smashed mirrors, windows, and lamps with a stool. He needed to let off steam, it seemed, for the sake of his nerves. I assigned him a new room.

Despite the resounding applause that evening, the critics were merciless the next day, and I was forced to abandon the production.

One week later, Ödön Horvath's *Italian Night*, a play we had intended for the studio, had a surprising success and I was compensated for my loss.

At a table in the long and narrow nightclub Schwannecke sat a large, chubby, boyish man with beautiful brown eyes who fixed me with a stare every time I went by. He had a roll of typewritten pages in his hand. I finally stopped in front of him and asked whether he wanted anything from me.

"Yes! I've written a play: *Italian Night*. A topical political comedy. Maybe you'd like to read it."

I took the pages and made a note of his name, Ödön Horvath, and his telephone number. I began reading that night, and read the play to the end. I asked him to come to the theater the next morning and sign a contract to begin work on it immediately.

"My wife doesn't give a damn who eats my sausage," Horvath has the innkeeper say, who rents rooms to Communists, Nazis, and Democrats alike. Horvath was fascinated by these obtuse human monsters. They had become dear to him, and he put them up against the whipping post. The boorish Merkel Franz, played by Fritz Kampers, who puts his hand in the beer glass of his delicate fiancée, Blandine Ebinger, to cool himself off, embodied for Horvath the brutality and meanness of the subhumans who abound in human society; they were what gave him his melancholy, and inspired his talent for writing novels and plays.

We began rehearsals for *Italian Night* right away.

A few months earlier I had made a trip with my cousin Günther, an intelligent and lively student, by car from Berlin to Thüringen. We started in the evening hours and drove all night. Hundreds of transport vehicles passed us, loaded with armed SA troops. We were shocked, but drew no conclusions as to the significance of this frightening experience immediately touching our lives.

In Horvath's brilliant comedy, an SA man in uniform comes on stage and is made a laughing-stock. Elsa Wagner, as the wife of a Democratic city-council member, makes an imbecile of the storm trooper. I had invited district leader Hinkel and author Arnolt Bronnen, who early on had become a National Socialist, to the premiere. The two Nazis wouldn't let themselves be provoked; they applauded the successful evening as the others did. Horvath's plays appealed to premiere audiences in Berlin and to the critics, but they never reached the broader public. *Italian Night* was, of all Horvath's Berlin productions, the longest running. It comforted the audience with its ironic treatment of political reality. It was my last production in the Theater am Schiffbauerdamm.

SEVEN

B etween 1931 and 1932, the death of the theater began in Berlin. What no one would have thought possible: Max Reinhardt gave up his five theaters and went to Vienna. The Rotter Brothers, leaseholders of many playhouses, fled from their debts to Liechtenstein. Long established theater managers vanished. Piscator at the Nollendorfplatz had given up early on, as had Charell at the Große Schauspielhaus. Heinrich Neft of the Volksbühne, proud never to have received a subsidy, was forced to ask the City of Berlin to support his Theater am Bülowplatz with 300,000 marks a year. Temporary engagements, some of which lasted no more than a single month, played to empty houses.

I ended my lease with the owners of the Theater am Schiffbauerdamm at the end of the 1931 season. The summer with its huge expenses, the theater's location in the dead central city, and the scarcity of appealing plays helped me in my resolve to leave. Our profits were a third of what they had been, and the wages for a stage actor boosted sky-high by the advent of sound film. There were only isolated, sensational hits, and only three stars, [Elisabeth] Bergner, Richard Tauber and Hans Albers, could fill an auditorium.

The economic crisis intensified; unemployment was at four million. The Deutsche Bank closed its counters. In order to prevent a rush of panic, the banks and the savings and loan institutions limited withdrawals to 200 marks for a time.

I founded the Ernst Joseph Aufricht Production Company following the American, or the English, model. No longer obligated to enforce the daily rise of the curtain, I could take time to find a suitable play, one that could be cast as its roles demanded. I could try out a play in the provinces, then choose any one of the distressed theaters in Berlin. Size and character of an auditorium are important elements in the success of a production.

I rented a ground floor space at Kantstraße 162, on the corner of Joachimstaler Straße, and arranged my office there. Returning in 1954 I would find as my successors to these rooms the "Remde's St. Pauli" nightclub and striptease.

Heinrich Fischer went back to Munich. Vambery became my assistant manager. My financers were the banker Dr. Fritz Schönherr and Richard Bluth, head of an insurance company.

[Trude] Hesterberg was always on the lookout for an artistic undertaking. She had sung in our adaptation of *The Daughter of the Regiment*, and wanted to know why I didn't put on *The Rise and Fall of the City of Mahagonny*, by Brecht and Weill, with herself in one of the roles.

"*Mahagonny* is an opera with a number of singing roles, a men's chorus, a women's chorus, and a thirty-piece jazz orchestra. It would require a long rehearsal period. It's too expensive for me."

"Have you met my friend Fritz?" she asked me. "Pick me up at the Comedians' Cabaret this evening."

Fritz was a wide-shouldered, athletic man with a nose broken from boxing. He had great charm and great thirst. He was in his mid-thirties, head of a private bank in Potsdam and a Social Democratic city-council member in Kreuzberg. He loved Hesterberg, who was older than he, and later married her. When I returned to Germany in the early fifties, I heard an ugly story that Fritz Schönherr had been an informer for the Gestapo. As he was of a more than average intelligence and a natural decency, I take this rumor to be false. He was shot in the battles in Berlin during the first days of May 1945.

Fritz asked me: "How much money do you need to produce *Mahagonny*?" I named a sum of 50,000 marks: 20,000 for preparations and 30,000 as a security for thirty guaranteed performances. "Come to the bank tomorrow and I'll give you the money." And so he became a partner of the Ernst Joseph Aufricht Production Company. He didn't appear in person, he appointed the author Franz Jung as his representative.

I made a contract with Max Reinhardt's managing office to lease the Theater am Kurfürstendamm. I leased it fully outfitted for this piece, with technicians, lights and heating included, for a percent of the profits. The Reinhardt management agreed, in addition, to remove the cover from the sealed orchestra pit and to raise the stage. We needed distance between the action and the audience. We transformed the fashionable character of the auditorium with sheets of raw plywood.

Brecht and Weill made their definitive break from one another during the *Mahagonny* rehearsals. Caspar Neher would be the librettist for Weill's next opera. Brecht and Weill would, however, collaborate once more, in 1933 during the emigration, in the Paris production of *The Seven Deadly Sins*. It played at the Théâtre des Champs-Elysées for a short time and was soon taken off the program.

During our rehearsals of *Mahagonny* Brecht fought vehemently for the primacy of the words, and Weill for that of the music. Lawyers came to the theater and threatened each other with interim injunctions. Brecht knocked the camera out of a press photographer's hand because he had taken a picture of him together with Weill.

"I'll throw the false Richard Strauss down the stairs in full war paint!" Brecht screamed at Weill.

"We can understand every word, Paulsen!" I shouted encouragingly onto the stage.

"Don't pay us any attention, Paulsen!" put in Alexander von Zemlinsky, who belonged to the Weill camp. The coveted conductor had offered, out of interest in Weill's opera, to be its musical director. For this reason I had not been able to reserve the post for my friend Mackeben, who had little experience with this type of large orchestral work.

We made no progress because of the differences of opinion. Caspar Neher, who had designed the set, had also taken over production. He was a quiet and careful man, a friend to both antagonists, and nevertheless could bring about no agreement.

In an attempt to keep Brecht away from the rehearsals, I offered to take on his play *The Mother* (after Gorky); the Theater am Kurfürstendamm had a large, empty room in the cellar, and Brecht could begin rehearsing there right away. I was aware that this production would entail a loss, and would limit my funds to three thousand marks.

After the launch of *Mahagonny*, we began our production of *The Mother* in the Comedy House, which I had similarly leased for a share of the income. The play had few parts. Helene Weigel played the title role. We made use of whatever props and costumes I had in my storeroom. I wouldn't have taken on this Brecht project, but a work so full of ideology, and with Weigel in the central role, was sure to fascinate him. My calculation paid off. Brecht preferred the cellar and left us upstairs in peace.

Rehearsals for *Mahagonny* lasted a month; preparations for the rehearsals had taken twice as long. During this time Zemlinsky had put together a 35-piece jazz orchestra. Eight singers were chosen for the men's chorus and five for the women's chorus, among them Lale Anderson, still unknown at that time. They rehearsed for weeks on end. Harald Paulsen, the original Mack the Knife, played and sang the main role. The girl who charged by the hour was played by Lotte Lenya, with her natural grace and languor, and the authoritarian and avaricious manager of the City of Mahagonny was Trude Hesterberg—both women ideal for their roles. The supporting roles were sung by opera singers who could also speak lines. Both choruses were musically superb, in diction and gesture as exact as the famous Rockettes at Radio City in New York. The projected texts between scenes were a thorn in my side; they were removed from the screen, and spoken instead by the actor Albert Hörrmann, elegant in a dinner jacket.

Mahagonny had debuted one year earlier in the Leipziger Opernhaus, with singers and a stunning musical interpretation under General Musical Director [Gustav] Brecher. The text by Brecht, however, had been garbled and inaudible. In my Berlin production, both composer and author came into their own, every note by Weill and every word by Brecht was heard. At the Leipzig premiere there had been some disruption in the audience and even, at the second performance, which I attended, threats of violence. A team of police had been posted along the perimeter and the aisles, and the house lights kept on throughout the show. I waited tensely; nothing moved. In the light, no one dared set up the smallest protest. There had been no third performance after these two.

The Berlin premiere went off beautifully, and found its place among the great theater evenings of the early 1930s. Weill, rich as a Croesus with musical ideas, gilded the Brechtian text with the last rays of a setting age, the Brechtian Walpurgisnacht of injustice, cruelty and brutality which foresaw elements of the imminent future. We played *Mahagonny* for over fifty evenings. Never before had a modern opera been performed *en suite*, and so many times.

I stood on the walkway between stage and dressing rooms at the Renaissance Theater, a house I had never visited before. I heard an intermittent splashing sound.

"Is that a broken washing machine?" I asked Vambery.

"No," he answered, "the audience is laughing."

The Four Reporters were performing their play, *Hier irrt Goethe* [Here Goethe Errs]. They were a group of students enrolled in the Munich theater seminar with Professor [Artur] Kutscher. They had written their own play, composed the music, designed and prepared their costumes and set.

They themselves played the roles and the music. Two of them later went on to make careers in the theater, Helmut Käutner as a producer and an actor, Norbert Schultze as a composer, among other things of the world-famous song "Lilli Marleen."

Trude Hesterberg had turned my attention to the Reporters, who were giving indoor performances of their Fasching Carnival spoof every after-noon. I drove to Munich accompanied by Franz Jung. When we had settled in at the Hotel Regina, he knocked on my door and asked for money.

"My wallet is over there. Help yourself."

He left the room, and when I went to put away my wallet, I found that Jung had taken it. Luckily, I had a few coins in my pocket and wasn't entirely helpless. I went out and saw *Hier irrt Goethe*. The Reporters were very funny. I was still uncertain whether the Munich Carnival phenom-enon could be transplanted successfully to Berlin. But before anything else, I went in search of my wallet.

Jung, a former member of a nationalist student fraternity, his face full of dueling scars, his eyes inflamed from drinking and sleep-deprived nights, an anarchist and a Catholic (I saw him kneeling at mass, resolved to go to hell because there was one), author of a defense of the Albigensians as well as of various works for the theater, editor of an economic newsletter in Berlin and during his emigration, was a sympathetic helper when one needed help, and a downright saboteur when one didn't. He was a man without fear, because he despised the material world and had no use for it.

I found Jung at the apartment of the writer Oskar Maria Graf. The two were blind-drunk. In my wallet were the return tickets, but no money. I asked Mrs. Graf if she could bring Jung to the station in time to catch our night train, then returned to the Regina, phoned my wife and arranged a sum of money to be wired. The Reporters were waiting for my answer in the hotel. I had time to kill until the money arrived, so I sat down and wrote up a contract with them for a guest appearance in Berlin. They would receive scant compensation in addition to the shared profits. They were very happy.

At the train station, I had to load the belligerent Jung onto a sleeper car. I opened the door, and he entered and fell on the floor next to the bed. He refused to get up. A box of cigars given to him by Graf had burst open, its contents lay scattered around his body. I found him in that position, among the cigars, the next morning, and had a hard time waking him. We walked out of the station and into the fresh Berlin air, both of us hung over: he from the alcohol, and I from the excitement of the contract we had closed. Of the premiere, Alfred Kerr wrote in the *Berliner Tageblatt*: "An audience hasn't laughed like that for 100 years."

The Reporters were sold out at the Renaissance Theater for many months, and toured with their show for about two years in the provinces. They brought in money for themselves and for us. I had sublet the Renaissance Theater from the head of an insurance company, Major [Richard] Bluth, who had tried, in this theater, to launch the acting career of his red-haired, beautiful wife. He had made Ernst Deutsch his partner. The enterprise had misfired. I asked him if his ticket sales ever came close to those for the theater programs of *Hier irrt Goethe*. "Can I join your company with my money?" was his response. Luckily I accepted his offer; his courage would save me from the worst when March 1933 arrived.

Horvath invited me to visit him in Bavaria. He was working on his new comedy *Casimir and Caroline* in his parents' house in Murnau. I enjoyed reading it, suggested a few changes, and stayed eight days with him. I couldn't resist taking over the production, and decided to begin with it at once. I gave the roles of the two lovers to Luise Ulrich and Hermann Ehrhardt—the latter I snatched away from a rural Bavarian theater. Both enlivened their roles with genuine rustic charm. We rehearsed in Berlin, made a number of guest appearances in Leipzig and then, after making a few necessary corrections, returned to Berlin for the premiere performance in the Komödienhaus. Despite an enthusiastic response, and financial guarantees in both cities, we went into a deficit. Our losses didn't weigh too heavily, however, as the Four Reporters' surpluses, and later those from the Admiralspalast, were enough to allow this kind of literary experiment. Francesco von Mendelssohn, reputed to be unserious because of his extravagant manner of living, began as assistant director at my theater, and then staged both Horvath plays with unusual ability.

Horvath's next work, *Stories from the Viennese Forest*, was too expensive for me with its large cast and prodigious set design. It was performed under the direction of Reinhardt at the Deutsches Theater in Schumannstraße with a superior cast. Once again the premiere was a success, and once again it soon had to be taken off the program.

The departure of the Rotter Brothers had left many theaters in the city center empty. The Theater in the Admiralspalast, with a capacity of 2,200, was owned by a Dutch syndicate that during the inflation had bought the greater part of the houses in Friedrichstraße for next to nothing. The board of directors sent their administrative head to see me and to inquire whether I was interested in being their guest. They would assume all risks and expenses. I promised to help and, in 1932, became Artistic Director of the Admiralspalast.

I knew that only one of the box office magnets like Hans Albers could fill this theater in the central city that had become so empty by night. Albers had often insisted that I let him play Mackie Messer in *The Threepenny Opera*, and that I only needed to name a date. I drove to the UFA studios and talked to him in his dressing room. It didn't take long to see that his film obligations would leave him no time to rehearse the new role before the end of the season. A reprise of Molnar's *Liliom*, the work whose title role he had played with great success one year earlier in Alfred Polgar's Berlin version at the Volksbühne, with music by Theo Mackeben, could be undertaken at once. I visited the original director Heinrich Neft, bought the old stage decorations from the Volksbühne, turned the stage direction over to Karl Heinz Martin, and within three weeks saw *Liliom* performed for full houses in the Admiralspalast.

Albers was a true folk actor. He went at the audience like a bull in the arena. He snorted at his girlfriend, and the audience reveled in his impudence; he sobbed, and they broke out in tears. He was the physical paragon of the approaching age: tall, blond and blue-eyed, with the gait of a hunting beast.

With him as the lead, we could have played *Liliom* hundreds of times for full houses. But the filming by day and acting by night was too much for his voice, he went hoarse, and we had to discontinue the production after two months.

I had provided for this. The tenor Richard Tauber was performing in Amsterdam. I drove to Holland with the librettist and the composer of a new operetta, written precisely with Tauber in mind, a work called *Spring Storm*. The text was as bad as the title. The music was by the Czech opera composer, Jaromir Weinberger, whose *Schwanda* had played in every German opera house. I took comfort, almost refuge, in the music, from the vulgarity and banality of the libretto. Tauber sang his part, full voice, in the Amsterdam hotel room, and was very excited. He signed a contract, and I completed the ensemble in Berlin. The reviews were mixed. Nevertheless, we finished with a profit. The name Richard Tauber was enough to pull people into the theater.

The year 1933 began. The Nazi newspapers now enjoyed wider circulation, and they began their attack on the production. Jarmila Novotna, the female star, was Czech, and had allegedly made hostile remarks against Germany. The comedian Siegfried Arno was a Jew. Tauber, I believe, was half-Jewish, and was to be eliminated like the others. As ignorant of the situation as we all were, he sent Hitler a letter stating that he had a medal of distinction from the Pope, and demanded of the Führer a retraction of the press attacks against him. The attacks were redoubled, and the theater was forced to close. I ran into Tauber a few weeks later in Zürich, as an emigrant.

The Völkische Beobachter named me "The Red Director." My acquaintances pressed me to leave Germany; they said it was high time. I knew it and didn't want to know it.

I am talking with Bluth in my office. The door is flung open and—what I've waited for every hour and still never thought possible—an SS officer with two henchmen behind him asks me sharply:

"Are you Aufricht?"

I nod.

"Get up and come with me."

"Where are we going?"

"To Hedemannstraße for interrogation."

On this street was a Gestapo house with cellars from which the interrogated re-emerged as bloody clumps.

I remain frozen in my seat.

"Don't make any problems!" the Officer barks at me angrily.

In this unforgettable moment, Bluth stands up. With the voice of an active officer, who has learned how to command, he introduces himself:

"Major Bluth!"

The SS men stand at attention. Bluth energetically signals the leader to follow him into the next room. The two henchmen take positions on either side of my chair. A sweat of terror runs in streams down my face and my back.

Vambery, seated in the back of the room, comes forward and reads an article from the morning paper out loud: Göring has prohibited all forms of vigilantism. He wants to help me. The two SS men pay him no attention. The door opens again, and the officer whistles his escorts aside and signals them to follow him. They leave the room. I recover for a moment, and then ask Bluth:

"What did you arrange with the man?"

"I gave him fifty marks."

When my father-in-law arrived to take me to lunch on nearby Meinekestraße, we told him what had happened. A Prussian notary and council member, he couldn't understand the situation. He turned to Bluth enraged:

"How could you give such a hoodlum your money?"

Bluth replied, "I could have showed him this Browning I keep with me now, and told him to get out of the building. I would have called von

Papen, with whom I attended the officer training course. But I don't think it would have helped your son-in-law. I would advise him not to sleep at home for a while, and to move his work over to my apartment, and let me represent him in all his official business."

I spent the night at the house of my parents-in-law and went to my office the next morning. Punctually at the same time, the SS officer arrived, this time alone. "I've asked my superiors: taking money from a Jew is allowed—today a hundred!"

I gave him the money, telephoned my wife, she brought me my suitcase, and I took the next train to Switzerland. My emigration had begun.

The misfortune that had befallen me was no longer reversible. A community had thrown me out. I went through foreign lands. When I came back, it wasn't to my home that I returned.

CHAPTER

E I G H T

M y emigration began in March 1933 in Zürich. The opulence and the security of this beautiful city made me uneasy, as I began to understand what was ahead of me. The marvelously funny and intelligent entertainer from the Comedians' Cabaret in Berlin, Paul Nikolaus, summed up his situation at one of the many exiles' tables:

"As a political comedian in the German language, I can perform in Zürich and in Basel for fourteen days each a year. My money will last me at the most two years. Why should I wait for the time to pass?" He said goodnight, went home and slit his wrists.

I didn't stay long in Zürich but left for Czechoslovakia to meet my wife and our two small boys, accompanied by a nanny (a luxury that wasn't to last much longer). We decided that I should go on to Paris and leave the family behind temporarily, at a boarding house. During my time at the Theater am Schiffbauerdamm I had declined the offer of an exchange guest appearance with the Théâtre Pitœff, as I'd felt that the only theater for me was in Berlin. Now I had to try to persuade myself that the Parisian theater was waiting for me.

The train stopped in the Gare du Nord, and I broke a shoelace as I was getting off. At the hotel, I found that I couldn't express to the house servant that I needed "de lacets noirs"; I could only show him the damaged lace and grin at him. He grinned back at me and disappeared. I threw the torn shoelace, in my confidence that it would be replaced, into a bin from which it couldn't be retrieved. I waited in vain for the man to come back. I began to comprehend that I was reduced to an infant, or an imbecile, in this place where I couldn't make myself understood, and I began to realize the extent of my misfortune. On the streets—it was a radiant spring day—I saw and heard the busily contented people so willing to charm and be charmed by one another with their language, I was blinded by the beauty of the city, I stumbled numbly and mutely among the foreign sounds that had nothing to do with my school French, and felt ill. I telegraphed my wife.

Twice in my life, during the years that count, I've lost my language. The first time it was French, and the second time English that I had to learn anew to think, speak, and write. I am a slow learner and a perfectionist, and it was hard for me.

I retreated from the blinding Paris streets into a darkened hotel room. I didn't want to see or to speak. My wife convinced me to drive to the seashore, which with its unbounded distances, its untouched and untouchable vastness, for a time shut out all associations and thoughts about recent events. Here I slowly recovered from my state of shock; slowly I accustomed myself to the idea that my world, the Berlin theater, had irretrievably gone under. I had to make up my mind to work in France and earn a living.

At the beginning of the thirties, the Paris theater was a purveyor of tasteful and lively entertainment for the good society that still existed in that city. Performances began at nine o'clock in the evening, usually with a one-act "lever du rideau"—a curtain-raiser, as it was called. Most of the audience arrived at nine-fifteen, in time for the play itself. In this way the evening meal, typically an affair of two to three hours, was not cut short by an evening at the theater. Having eaten and drunk heartily, the play-goers were in the mood to be entertained with a light repartee of sex and humor. A funny beginning and a sentimental conclusion were the preferred formula. The famous Comédie Française, which cultivated a classical style, the Grande Opéra, mediocre and outmoded, and the Opéra Comique, where small operas and classical operettas were played with great charm, were the three state-supported theaters. A tiny experimental theater, L'Œuvre, fought and gasped for its existence. The few directors who put on literary pieces, Copeau, for instance, or Dullin, had by this time exhausted themselves artistically.

Surpassing all of these stages in merit was the Théâtre Athénée, under manager, director, and leading actor Louis Jouvet. His repertoire extended from classical Molière to contemporary Giraudoux. Rehearsals went forward without regard for material expense, paid for by Jouvet himself, a well-paid film actor who hated film. Theatrical talent, high intelligence, a dogged, iron will and all the charm of his nation were combined in this man.

My wife tried to persuade me to travel further, to London. But by that time I had begun to fall in love. I began to love Paris, and I never will not love it again, though I was, during the war, twice incarcerated by the French as an enemy alien. I wanted to stay in France and integrate myself there; if not as a Frenchman myself, I wanted at least to be regarded by them as something other than a tourist. I saw how so many of the emigrants annoyed the French with their hard German accents, and that only those willing to change their way of living were able to lose it. I understood that it took years before a French person says, *Il est de nous*: he is one of us.

The first wave of emigrants came mostly from the intellectual professions, which had suddenly been made inaccessible to Jews, "degenerate" artists, and political dissidents of every kind. They were doctors, lawyers, musicians, writers, journalists, painters, architects, theater and film people. All had lost their status overnight; their income and possessions seized, some of them in danger of losing their lives, they had left Germany in a panic. They'd fled with little means and a single suitcase of their best clothes. Dressed to the nines they huddled on the café terraces of the Champs-Elysées or Montparnasse, and annoyed the cafétiers with their consumption of coffee and croissants, driving away native customers who preferred the more expensive aperitifs. Because no one could bear to admit that he had lost his existence, they negotiated business transactions with the empty air, contrived fantasy projects, traded intrigues as in better days, and warned one about the other. Nevertheless, it wasn't boring. It wasn't exactly the dullards who had fled. At a small table at Fouquets sat the great, corpulent comedian Kurt Gerron with a mountain of peanut shells in front of him, the remains of an attempt to fill his stomach. He was the original Tiger Brown of *The Threepenny Opera*, and a sworn enemy of Brecht. "That huge pile of shit," Brecht would say, "even a Hitler won't be able to shovel away." He couldn't know that Gerron, trying to escape to Holland during the war, would fall into the hands of the Gestapo and be gassed.

Brecht lived in a small hotel room near the Luxembourg Gardens. His kidneys rebelled. He lay in bed under his leather jacket in the tiny room. I visited him with Walter Steinthal, editor of the *Berlin Twelve O'Clock Midday Edition*, to look into a possible theater project. Brecht had the idea for a "theater of trials," in which Nazi crimes would be reviewed alongside various other crimes out of the history book. For example, Nero would be indicted and stand trial alongside Göring, the one for his burning of Rome, the other for his burning of the Reichstag. Steinthal, now dispossessed of his newspaper, hoped to be compensated by the German Embassy and to finance the theater with that money. As he was a man who enjoyed talking, Steinthal set off on a lengthy, lovingly worded speech. He was silenced, finally, by the bedridden Brecht, who flew into a rage and shouted that we were no longer in Berlin, we were refugees, we had no time—he couldn't know how much time we still had—and laid his watch on the bedside table to enforce a three-minute speaking limit. Steinthal left the hotel furious, and Brecht remarked accurately: "If the man doesn't call within ten minutes and ask you to meet with him below and talk it over, then he's not fit for the theater and not worth our time." Steinthal didn't call, he received no money, no lines were written, and I didn't lease a theater, but we did begin to get on each other's nerves. At the invitation of the writer Karin Michaelis, Brecht moved to Denmark. Steinthal went on to America. I decided to take a vacation from Paris, and since it had been near the sea that I had recovered from my previous shock, I leased a farm at Cabourg, not far from Deauville on the coast of Normandy.

CHAPTER

N I N E

In the Province of Calvados, where the apple brandy of the same name is produced, where tall hedges separate lush meadows, and the moist, mild sea climate keeps the marshland grasses green almost all year long, I found a dainty Louis XV castle with a farmyard and pigeon-house, a park and a pond. The property had been mostly untouched for 150 years, and had a symmetry and harmony with nature that one often finds in the Romance cultures. I turned the place into an educational farm, primarily for students who wanted to be retrained as farmhands. An impatient son of friends of ours didn't want to wait until we came to Petiville, the small place in Calvados, and I agreed to let him travel ahead of us to the farm, which was still unoccupied by people or animals. He was one of the many young emigrants from Paris whose family had lost the means to keep their children in school, and who, having grown tired of inactivity, were looking eagerly for ways to learn a new set of professional skills. Overjoyed, he telephoned his parents and described the landscape and the sea to them, and in particular two tame, white ducks he had discovered upon his arrival at the farm. These two birds, I later explained to the parents, had lived many years on the lake at Petiville. They were geese, incidentally, and not ducks. "Please don't tell him," the mother said. "It would upset him. He wants so much to be a farmer."

We moved to Petiville and sent for our children, who had gone back to Germany once more to live for a short time with their grandparents and attend school in Hangelsberg. When we met them at the station they carried, under their jackets, belts with swastikas and daggers with blood grooves engraved on the clasp, and a National Socialist songbook. We sunk these objects in the pond.

I began to populate the farm with people and livestock. I hired a German emigrant with a diploma in agronomy, a Russian emigrant French teacher, a French master gardener with assistants, a milkmaid and a cook native to the region. I bought a draft-horse, pigs, and an old, hulking Buick for animal, human and vegetable transport. A poultry yard was fenced-off for various fowl: geese, ducks, chickens, turkeys, guinea-fowl, doves, and peacocks. The rabbits, of course, were not forgotten; their meat is a roast much beloved in France.

The horse was a stocky dapple-gray. Before I paid for it, I met with it once or twice to get a sense of its character. It was a mild, pleasant creature that was willing to do a lot of work. It had the heavy build of a Belgian draft horse, only its head was smaller. These Percherons, as they are called, are bred in Normandy as workhorses. The only colors in their coats are black and white, but with all the shades in between.

I needed a training cow, an old animal patient enough that it could be milked by beginners. I found a ten-year-old named, of all things, Vercingétorix. When you got her going at a trot, her udders began to flow by themselves. For a full pasture of cows, however, I would need six more of her kind. We bought a ticket for the Loterie National with the little money we had left. The day after the drawing, my wife and I drove to Cabourg. We bought a newspaper, went and ordered coffee in a bistro, and compared our number with the winning tickets: our ticket had won. The prize money was enough for six cows.

The cows of Normandy are ruddy brown, sometimes dappled, often with a white head. They are butter cows that give milk in small amounts, but very rich. They are long-legged and never get very heavy. For meat-making, slender bulls are imported from the Charente in early spring and fattened on the succulent meadows.

I bought milk sows for breeding from a Count who raised racehorses for Aga Kahn, and Yorkshire pigs.

"Why do you want to settle in this area?" he asked me. "We foreigners aren't very well liked in Normandy."

"You, Count, are certainly not a foreigner!" I knew that he belonged to one of the oldest aristocratic families in France.

"Yes I am," he said, "I am a Breton. There's a cabinetmaker in Bavent," (a small city in the region) "who's lived and worked there for thirty five years. The people there still call him *le sale Parisien*—the dirty Parisian."

Having grown up on the Silesian estate with an adequate knowledge of farming, I now oversaw the instruction of our young recruits in field, livestock and farmhouse management. My wife taught the girls housekeeping and cooking. It was amazing how quickly the girls adapted to their changed lives. They worked with great dedication and patience. In the hard times that still lay ahead, it was often the women who rescued their families from the worst dangers. Whatever sensitivities they had, they knew that there had to be food on the table. They threw their strength behind whatever was necessary, working in the house and at the oddest jobs they could find to bring in money. The young men had it harder. Time and again they found themselves turned off by the largely monotonous duties of farming. They came up with the strangest ideas, and these were at times reflected by the behavior of the animals put in their care. I had to send away the butcher we brought in to slaughter a pig when I found the animal had been put to work pushing a girl on a swing.

A year went by almost without incident. That was the term of the French Visas stamped in our students' passports. When they went to apply for extensions at the Governor's office in Caen, the capitol of Normandy, they were turned away. Our household began to dwindle in number, and I knew it was time to make the trip to the Governor myself.

"Why did you file with the Department of Agriculture and the Department of Education?" he asked me reproachfully. "Why request permission to start a school for farmhands? Now there are inquiries pending, and we have to investigate and report, and we don't like to do that. Why didn't you register a family boarding house? If you want to teach your guests something about farming, that doesn't concern us. We would have left you alone for the rest of your life, with a boarding house."

What should I have answered? That I came into the world a Prussian? That my ingrained concept of authority differed vastly from that of the French? The disparity between the two attitudes, the inability to leave one behind and learn the other, would cost many exiles their lives during the German occupation.

We slowly began to break up our home at Petiville. All of the kitchen and bathroom facilities we had installed had to be left behind in the old castle; these conveniences had been missing when we first moved in, with the exception of a few commodes and an outhouse in the yard. Intending to acquire the property later on, I had reserved preemptive purchasing rights. Of course this was impossible. I also lost the money I had invested in renovating the stables, grounds, and greenhouses.

Kurt Weill and his wife Lotte Lenya visited before our final departure, along with my longtime colleague Robert Vambery, in order to show me their latest musical *My Kingdom for a Cow*. They were on the way to London, where the rehearsals were to begin shortly. They urged me to give up my life in the country and to re-establish contact with the theater. I could come with them to England and direct the musical. I followed the first part of their advice, left the paradisiacal Calvados and set out for Paris.

Bunte Film-Blätter

Erscheint jeden 1. und 15. des Monats   **Illustrierte Filmzeitschrift**
Herausgeber: RICHARD BOELKE

Zuschriften sind an den Filmkunstverlag, Berlin SW 68, Ritterstraße 50, zu richten – Kleine Anzeigen die viergesp. Nonpareillezeile 1.50 M.

Jahrg. 1   **15. August 1919**   **Heft 13**

Nachdruck sämtlicher Artikel nur mit Genehmigung des Herausgebers gestattet

Ernst Josef Aufricht
Hauptdarsteller in dem Film „Baccarat" der Brandenburgischen Filmgesellschaft.

Phot. Becker und Maaß, Berlin

Ernst Josef Aufricht as the lead actor in the film *Baccarat*, 1919,
cover of the *Bunte Film-Blätter*. Photo: Becker and Maaß, Berlin.
Courtesy of Klaus Voelker, private collection.

Aufricht, left, with Georg Grosz and an unidentified child at the Aufrichts' estate in Adelsbach, Silesia (now Struga, Poland), 1924. Photographer unknown. George Grosz Archive, 1083/20/3, Academy of the Arts, Berlin.

The Theater am Schiffbauerdamm in 2010. Built in 1891–92 to a design by Heinrich Seeling, then home to Aufricht's great productions of Brecht and Weill, it is today home of the Berlin Ensemble and a historic landmark. Photo by Jörg Zägel / Wikimedia Commons / CC-BY-SA-3.0.

Brecht in his flat at the "Knie" in Berlin-Charlottenburg,
today Ernst-Reuter-Platz, 1931. Photographer unknown.
Used by permission of Ullstein Bild.

Harald Paulsen as Macheath dances with one of the Turnbridge whores in act 2, scene 5 of Aufricht's original production of Brecht and Weill's *Threepenny Opera*, Theater am Schiffbauerdamm, premiered August 1, 1928 and directed by Erich Engel. Photographer unknown. Bertolt Brecht Archive, Theater Documentation, 985-009, Academy of the Arts, Berlin.

Act 3 of Aufricht's original production of *Threepenny Opera*. The screens read: "Peachum's Song of the Inadequacy of Human Planning." In the text and title of the actual song the final word is not "Planens" (of planning), but "Strebens" (of striving), both in genitive case in the German. Photographer unknown. Bertolt Brecht Archiv, Theater Documentation, 985-011, Academy of the Arts, Berlin.

The hanging scene from Aufricht's original production of *Threepenny Opera*. Harald Paulsen as Macheath on the gallows, Kurt Gerron as Tiger Brown at left, Roma Bahn as Polly Peachum, and Erich Ponto as Peachum at right. Photographer unknown. Bertolt Brecht Archive, Theater Documentation, 985-002, Academy of the Arts, Berlin.

Credits and cast list for Aufricht's premiere production of *Threepenny Opera* from *Das kleine Magazin*. It is significant that, as related in Aufricht's text, Lotte Lenya as Jenny is missing (as she was from the original playbill). Kurt Weill, Lenya's husband, was incensed about the error. Note also that contractually the direction was by Erich Engel, as reflected here, but Brecht essentially took over from him. Courtesy of Klaus Voelker, private collection.

Hilde Körber as Berta, Peter Lorre as Fabian, and Lotte Lenya as Alma in Aufricht's production of Marieluise Fleißer's *Pioniere in Ingolstadt,* 1929, Theater am Schiffbauerdamm, directed by Jacob Geis and Brecht. Photographer unknown. Courtesy of Klaus Voelker, private collection. Published by permission of Academy of the Arts, Berlin, Elisabeth Hauptmann Archive 879.

Scene from Aufricht's original production of Brecht's *Happy End,* which premiered September 2, 1929 at the Theater am Schiffbauerdamm. Oskar Homolka, with banjo, as Bill Cracker. Photographer unknown. Bertolt Brecht Archive, Theater Documentation, 1593-009, Academy of the Arts, Berlin.

Lotte Lenya as Jenny and Harald Paulsen as Jimmy in Aufricht's production of Brecht and Weill's *Mahagonny,* Theater am Schiffbauerdamm, December 1931. Photographer unknown. Bertolt Brecht Archive, Theater Documentation, 2003-001, Academy of the Arts, Berlin.

Scene from Aufricht's production of Brecht's *The Mother*, staged
beginning January 31, 1932 in the Comedy House on the
Schiffbauerdamm. Photographer unknown. Bertolt Brecht Archive,
Theater Documentation, 2161-002, Academy of the Arts, Berlin.

Skandal um Direktor Aufricht

Der Theaterleiter aus der Haft entlassen — Dunkle Devisengeschäfte seiner Finanziers

Vor einigen Tagen ist der Berliner Theater-Direktor Ernst Joseph Aufricht auf Veranlassung der Zollfahndungsstelle verhaftet worden. Aufricht stand im Verdacht, an den Devisenvergehen des gleichfalls verhafteten Bankprokuristen Dr. Schönherr und seines Geschäftsfreundes Dr. Beye beteiligt zu sein. Der Theaterdirektor ist inzwischen aus der Haft entlassen worden. Er dementiert energisch, mit den Devisengeschäften der anderen Beschuldigten in irgendeinem Zusammenhang zu stehen. Das Verfahren gegen Dr. Schönherr und Dr. Beye nimmt seinen Fortgang.

Der Devisenskandal um Dr. Schönherr und Beye geht auf die Finanztransaktionen der „Pommerschen Bauhütte" zurück, deren Finanzberater Schönherr gewesen ist. Die Bauhütte, ein sozialdemokratisches Unternehmen, hat angeblich nach Erwerb eines französischen Patentes in Paris mehrere Bauaufträge erhalten, die sie jedoch nicht ausführen konnte, da der Devisenkommissar die Ausfuhr der zu den Bauten notwendigen deutschen Markbeträge nicht genehmigte. Nun soll die Bauhütte versucht haben, über die „Societé financière franco-allemande", deren Leiter Schönherr und Beye waren, sich trotzdem ein Guthaben in Paris zu beschaffen, indem sie französische Schulden in Berlin abdeckte. Diese Finanztransaktion wird von der Zollfahndungsstelle als s c h w e r e r V e r - s t o ß gegen die Devisenverordnung, von den Beschuldigten aber als ein n o r m a l e s G e s c h ä f t bezeichnet, das keinen Verstoß darstellen könne, weil es vor Erlaß der letzten Devisen-Verordnung perfekt gemacht worden sei.

Direktor Aufricht, der Leiter der Aufricht-Produktion, ist in den Skandal verwickelt worden, weil er geschäftlich in e n g s t e r A n l e h n u n g an Schönherr arbeitete und mit ihm zum Teil sogar die gleichen Geschäftsräume benutzte. Der zweite Verhaftete, Dr. Beye, der Kompagnon Dr. Schönherrs, gehörte eine Zeitlang der Aufrichtproduktion an und hat das Auftreten der „Nachrichter" im Renaissance-Thea-

ter finanziert. Schönherr selbst galt als Finanzier, der seinerzeit im Theater am Kurfürstendamm veranstalteten Mahagonny-Aufführung, die starke finanzielle Mißerfolge brachte. In den Devisen-Skandal soll ferner der Schriftsteller Franz Jung, der Leiter des Deko-Verlages, dessen Aufenthalt augenblicklich unbekannt ist, verwickelt sein. Der Deko-Verlag war ein von Schönherr finanziertes Unternehmen zur Ausnutzung angekaufter Patente.

Newspaper clipping from June 14, 1932, "Scandal around Producer Aufricht: The Theater Director Released from Custody—Shady Foreign Exchange Dealings by His Financier." Newspaper unknown. Franz Jung Archive, Microfilm roll 1170, image number 1, Academy of the Arts, Berlin.

Aufricht, right, with Georg Grosz, 1954. Photograph by Fritz Eschen.
Courtesy of Deutsche Fotothek, Dresden.

TEN

The old emigrant life of suitcases, threadbare and bulging with one's entire belongings, began again for me in a small Paris hotel in the Rue Galilée. One of the first to come in search of me was the film director Max Ophüls. He came with the idea of convincing me how impossible it would be to find a foothold in Paris as a theater manager, and to advise me to consider producing films instead. Perfect fluency in French would not be necessary in this line; Russian and Hungarian producers emigrated from Berlin had already found an audience. They all spoke at least four languages, fluently and full of mistakes. Aware of my dislike for the cinema, he tempted me with a strange project: making Schiller's *Love and Intrigue* into a French film. I was happy to have a project so soon, and I went about the unpleasant task of raising the necessary funds. Through a recommendation, I made contact with the son of the Swedish multimillionaire [Olof] Aschberg. He received me in his father's sprawling mansion in the Rue Casimir Périer flanked by two elegant secretaries. He was very interested. We went to dinner with Ophüls. Ophüls and I wrote a treatment and Aschberg liked it. Ophüls flew to London and hired the famous French movie star Annabella, who was filming there at the time. When he told her the story of Luise and Ferdinand, she said with tears in her eyes, "C'est trop beau!" and signed. It began as beautifully as an old-fashioned film, and ended, unfortunately, as badly as a modern one.

A telegram from the same woman who had first put me in contact with Aschberg's son now summoned the old man himself to Paris. The telegram warned of the treachery of Ophüls and Aufricht. The woman, who was in financial difficulties, assumed that we'd already received our money and were now intending to withhold her finder's fee. The elder Aschberg had already dealt with several trying episodes on his son's account, and when he heard of the latest plans for filming, the kettle boiled over. He refused the son his money, and in fact threw him out of the palatial home. The film blew up in our faces. I got a powerful scare from the bang. The film people less so; they were familiar with the sound.

One morning at dawn, on the way to Prague by express train through Switzerland and Austria—the long route in order to avoid Germany—I ran into Ophüls in the aisle. We didn't speak for the length of a cigarette, and then we told each other, openly, why we had left. Both of us, it turned out, were traveling with our families to Czechoslovakia where we hoped to raise enough money to return to Paris. His was a film project, mine a meeting with my mother and brothers, only now come out of Germany, to discuss with them how I might transfer money from our Polish stocks to France.

After half a year I was able to afford an apartment in the old neighborhood of Passy, and I returned to Paris. I would stay there until I was once again forced to leave. One could buy slightly damaged but otherwise exquisite antique furniture at the Marché aux Puces, the flea market, and I bought several pieces, and took my purchases to a wood carver for repairs. Our apartment's atelier window looked out over the Seine and the terraces of the hunting chateau of Louis XIII.

All of my detours had led nowhere; I had to return to the theater. Unfortunately I couldn't put my son Wolfgang's theory into practice, whom I had overheard discussing the future with his older brother: "First you have to be a theater manager like papa, then slowly work your way down to a proper job," was his advice.

The next year, 1937, was the year of the World's Fair in Paris. I wanted to stage *The Threepenny Opera*, by this time internationally known, under the French title, *L'Opéra de Quat' Sous*, for the international audiences that this event would bring. Once again I was on the search for a backer. I talked myself into believing that there were 126 people living in Paris who would be ready to finance my project. I found one who was willing to provide the funding for the expensive production, the elegant Edgar Heumann, theater enthusiast and emigrant from Berlin, married to a rich and kindly Dutch woman.

I leased the Théâtre de l'Etoile on the Avenue de Wagram, a house devoid of atmosphere, and the only one available. For the set design I hired the painter Eugène Berman, well known in America at the time, a Russian-born and entirely assimilated Frenchman. His studio was in the Rue des Saints-Pères on the Rive Gauche. Berman, who had never before worked for a theater company (he was later to become an eminent stage designer for the Metropolitan Opera in New York), took the offer reluctantly, and only because he needed money. He detested Brecht's and my nationality, and our idea of theater. As his assistant I hired another Russian emigrant, at one time a member of the Stanislavsky theater. An anonymous worker, he realized Berman's extraordinary designs in miniature before carrying out their full-scale construction at the Théâtre de l'Etoile.

Weill was no longer in Europe; he had finally immigrated to New York. To Brecht and Helene Weigel, in Denmark, I sent train tickets and an invitation for a four-week visit to Paris. I waited for them on the platform at Gare du Nord. As the train came in, I saw Brecht lean out of his cabin window clutching a strip of material and greeting me: "Don't worry, I brought a tie!"

The casting of L'Opéra de Quat' Sous was difficult, since I was acquainted with none of the French actors, and had to grope my way through many first impressions. René Bergeron, in the role of Peachum, whose narrow, parchment-like, spiteful face had immediately captivated me, was a mediocre actor and an unwilling worker. Long unemployed, he had accepted the role and the play without understanding either of them. He belonged to the radical right-wing group, the Croix de Feu.

I gave the role of Mrs. Peachum to France's greatest diseuse, Yvette Guilbert. It was her first experience with the theater. I often visited her at her apartment in the Rue Courcelles, where the original designs for her poster portraits by Toulouse-Lautrec hung on the wall.

Mrs. Guilbert and her husband Monsieur Schiller invited my wife and me to dinner at Prunier, a fish and seafood restaurant. We drank our apéritifs and listened as an American at the next table, bent over his menu, carefully assembled his sequence of courses. The waiter put a wine list in front of him. The American pushed it aside and ordered: "Un chocolat bien chaud!" then repeated it in a quieter tone: "Bien chaud!"—quite hot.

The waiter was astonished. He explained to the guest that his order could not be carried out. The American insisted on his hot chocolate. The maître d'hôtel was called, and the American repeated his request slowly and clearly. The maître d'hôtel made a sign to the waiter to clear the table.

"Unfortunately, we are unable to fulfill your wish. You might try another establishment."

The man stood up shaking his head and walked to the door as the waiter gathered his glasses and silverware. Guilbert nodded to the Maître d'Hôtel and said, "Well done, monsieur."

Renée St. Cyr, one of the great beauties of film and Parisian society, played Polly. For the role of Jenny I found Susy Solidor. She was an idol of the intellectuals and star of her own nightclub. Sixty portraits of her by acclaimed artists hung on the walls. The theatrical talent of Raymond Cordy, a thick-set Parisian taxi driver, was one of the luckier discoveries René Clair had made for his films. I gave him the role of Tiger Brown. The small part of Filch was played by Jean Mercure, today a well-known character actor and director. I almost had to give up the whole project because I couldn't find a suitable actor for Macheath, until Raymond Rouleau came into my office. He was at that time director of the literary experiments of the Théâtre de l'Œuvre, and his own leading man. He offered to play Macheath and to take over stage direction. I hired him as an actor. In my opinion and Brecht's, he was the best Mackie Messer ever to walk the stage.

Francesco von Mendelssohn was chosen for stage director. He had worked at the Theater am Schiffbauerdamm, spoke French fluently and without an accent, and would try as well as he could to recreate the Berlin production with French actors. Brecht and I helped him. The premiere was planned for September, and the Théâtre de l'Etoile closed all through August. We rehearsed during the day and in the evenings. The play took form and, despite our intensive work, lost it just as quickly, like mayonnaise which stiffens with the right amount of stirring, and becomes runny again the instant one stirs too long. Finally it sank in for us that our Berlin style was singularly un-French, and I gave over the direction to Rouleau. From there it went rapidly forwards. He loosed the actors from what had become a stylistic rigidity, let them develop their own lively ideas and find their own postures, allowed them more gestures. When Helene Weigel pressured Brecht to protest, he supported Rouleau. Brecht was an experienced theater pragmatist. He never stuck to principles. Theories he disseminated in the program leaflets he could disavow on the spot, when the scene demanded it.

During the rehearsals for the *Opéra de Quat' Sous*, we saw a chubby, extremely shortsighted woman sitting next to André Mauprès. Mauprès had acquired the French rights to *The Threepenny Opera* immediately after its Berlin premiere, and the woman had translated the play from German for him. Her name was Ninon Tallon. I was not on very friendly terms with either of them. Mauprès, the successful adapter of Franz Lehár's operettas, struggled obstinately against every change made to his own rather honeyed version.

Brecht's advice again was useful. "This woman could be a great help to us," he said. "She understands what we want. Why don't you talk it over with her?" He was right. I made friends with Tallon, and she supported us against her colleague. I took her to a small bar, "L'Impératrice," and introduced her to the host, Oskar Karlweis. A romance began between the two. During my time as a prisoner of war, she hid him at her vineyard near Lyon. They emigrated together to the USA and married, and it was a happy marriage.

The premiere of the *Opéra de Quat' Sous* was strongly applauded. The press found both play and production interesting and bizarre. Still, with all of their regard, they were unable to warm to it entirely. The fifty shows we performed were celebrated in the intellectual circles, but the majority of the public stayed away.

The World's Fair in Paris was an architectural wonder. It started at the Trocadéro and extended, one pavilion after the next, over a stretch of six kilometers along the Seine. One could drift by them in small boats called "vedettes." The city glowed in a euphoric beauty, before the cataclysm that would change Paris and the old Europe forever.

We expected the Viennese exile Horvath for dinner one evening. The dependable man never cancelled, and never arrived. The next morning we received a telephone call with the information that Ödön Horvath had been hit by lightning on the Champs-Elysées. We took it to be a bad joke, though an unsettling one. A gypsy had foreseen a deadly accident for him that month. He had avoided riding in elevators, had crossed avenues only in large groups of people. The newspapers confirmed his death. A bolt of lightning had struck a rotten chestnut tree on the Champs-Elysées, the tree had fallen with a groan, two witnesses leapt out of the way, and Horvath stood transfixed. Now! he must have thought.

Madame Tallon was at that time manager of the Théâtre Pigalle. It was rented as a theater for first film showings by the Bazin Bank, which distributed Russian films to Europe. Tallon spoke of the Pigalle stage as a technical wonder, and she invited me to come see it. It was indeed the finest of its kind, built as an amusement by one of the Rothschilds, who, after managing it for a year, had become bored and put it on the market.

"Why are you showing me this spectacular place? You're using it as a movie house—you won't give it to me!"

"The movies play till eleven at night. You can have it from midnight on."

I went home with this comment like a thorn in my side.

The *Threepenny Opera* performances were coming to an end, however, and I feared I would soon once again be without a theater. I telephoned Tallon from my apartment: "I agree to your terms. We'll sign a contract tomorrow for the first midnight fine arts theater in Paris!"

I offered Rouleau the position of co-manager. After a few days of consideration and calculation, we formed a plan for the partnership, and he accepted.

The *Opéra de Quat' Sous* had cost 500,000 francs. Because of my inexperience as a foreigner, I had often spent beyond what was necessary. We wanted to combine my dearly bought experience with Rouleau's—he had run an avant-garde theater in Brussels—in order to avoid wasting a single franc. We planned to come out 30,000 francs the wealthier. I set about the task of raising funds.

In the very building that we had moved into, in Passy, Avenue de Lamballe, lived the former Berlin newspaper editor Paul Lothringer. He loved Paris as much as I, and knew every corner of the city as it was then: not yet deformed by the flashy, brightly colored metal of parked cars. We accompanied each other on many walks—not for the fresh air, not to look at shop windows, not to study the architecture, not to arrive anywhere. We walked through the streets of Paris and were happy just because the houses were there. "Tu te ballades dans les rues?" Marcel Achard asked me whenever we met.

Lothringer had a rich sister. She was young and beautiful, married to an old Russian banker, Mr. de Ginsbourg, who had spirited his considerable fortune to safety in Paris during the 1917 Revolution. She was prepared to put up a part of the money I needed to fund the Théâtre de Minuit, if I could raise the rest. She gave me the name of a Hungarian banker from her bridge club.

Lothringer and I set out for one of the Grand Boulevards where the bank was located. In the car he had a sudden attack of scruples. He told me it would be unbearably painful for him to be present while I asked someone for money.

"Please, spare me, let me out of the car."

"No! I promise you I'm not going to beg or degrade myself in any way. And you'll keep your word and come. You have to deliver your sister's personal greetings so there won't be a businesslike atmosphere."

We sat in the office of Mr. Vas the banker, and Lothringer greeted him eloquently. The two chatted about their shared bridge acquaintances until, at length, Mr. Vas turned to me:

"And this is Mr. . . ."

"Aufricht!" I introduced myself again. He gave me an questioning look, and I decided to broach the issue of our visit at once. "Surely, Mr. Vas, you've lost money at the races before? At the horse or dog races?"

"At the horse races!"

"Then I have something new for you! Allow me to propose an amusement guaranteed to lose money. I'd like to open a fine arts Théâtre de Minuit." And I elaborated for him.

"Do you already have a theater?"

"The Théâtre Pigalle."

"Have you asked anyone else, or am I going to put up the entire amount myself?"

"The sister of this gentleman has also agreed to help."

He stood up: "Your project interests me. I'll discuss the matter with Madame de Ginsbourg."

She invited Mr. Vas to lunch. I was to come by unexpectedly during mocha. If the banker had agreed by that time, she would greet me with: "Quelle surprise agréable!"

I rang the doorbell and was announced by the servant. She came towards me. "Quelle surprise agréable!" My theater was financed.

Rouleau and I agreed on a piece by J. B. Priestley, *Dangerous Corner*. There were many advantages to the piece: the scenery was within our means (unfortunately the technical stage requirements were beyond them), there were only seven roles to fill, and the running time was one hundred ten minutes without an intermission. Rouleau took on the direction and one of the main roles. The rest of the cast was assembled painstakingly over several weeks out of the vast reservoir of Parisian actors. Our first requirement was that they be attuned to one another, in tone and in gesture.

We ordered the women's costumes from Worth; the men simply wore dinner jackets. Worth was the oldest of Paris's leading fashion houses, and had at one time outfitted the Empress Eugénie. They required a list of every color used in our stage design, which, once submitted, we were contractually barred from changing. Three evening dresses were ordered; the fourth, an older woman's black gown, was brought by the actress from her own wardrobe to the first dress rehearsal. The "Captain" of Worth was utterly shocked. He insisted that the dress be replaced free of charge with one from his own atelier.

In the part of the youthful lover was one of the beginners from Rouleau's theater school, a talented and beautiful young actress. We had hesitated somewhat in assigning her the role; she was a mere sixteen years old, and her movements were at times awkward as a puppy's. When she appeared at the first dress rehearsal, however, in a long, snow-white evening dress, her natural Frenchwoman's elegance showed itself and she was transformed into a perfect salon lady. Gaby Sylvia later became a star.

On the day of the first rehearsal, as I sat in my office, Rouleau came in and admitted to having made a mistake: one of the actors had to be paid at once and replaced. I reminded him of our decision not to waste a single franc. A capable actor with difficulties in finding his register was not, we had agreed, to be replaced before undergoing a period of concentrated work with us. But Rouleau insisted that he had made a mistake, and that I had best come and see for myself. I went to the rehearsal and saw for myself. The actor was paid and replaced.

In order to bring the Théâtre de Minuit to the public's attention, I turned to the owner of Paris's most ritzy club, "Gardénia," who agreed to take on the cost of the premiere, the *répétition général*, as it is called in France. On opening night the theater was decked with flowers and palm branches, and officers formed an honor guard. The performance was dazzling. According to my wife, the curtain rose and fell countless times. I let it be known I couldn't come due to illness, since I had no tails for the occasion. They had been left behind in Berlin, and I'd spent every penny I had on the production.

The press hailed the Théâtre de Minuit as an enrichment of Parisian theater, and praised *Dangerous Corner* in every detail. *The Figaro* devoted an entire page to the elegance on the stage and in the audience.

There was a bar in the basement of the Théâtre Pigalle, adjoined to the hall by a wide staircase. In the program to the premiere, Gardénia announced an open invitation to champagne before the show, in our "surrealistic theater bar." The stairs, floor, and walls of the bar were black marble, draped in gray velvet and fishnet. Over this, Rouleau's acting students had hung various props and costumes: rococo gowns, soldiers' boots, a king's crown, a tobacco pipe, a soup tureen, wigs and hats of all sizes and styles, and other artifacts dug out of storage. The haphazard arrangement made a striking impression. The guests were enthusiastic.

We later leased the bar to a man from Alsace, the owner of a small bistro in the middle of Montmartre's entertainment district, Boulevard Clichy. Over the entrance (the bar had a door to the street) he hung a neon sign with the words "La Congas." He hired a dance orchestra and opened a nightclub. The surrealistic paraphernalia was cleared away, and Rothschild's marble and mahogany elegance restored.

Like the bistro on Montmartre, the downstairs nightclub did not attract many foreigners, but was patronized mainly by entertainment district professionals. An elegant, slender, and athletic man with the face of a film beau, complete with sideburns, caught my attention with his tireless dancing. After I had introduced myself, he opened up to me and I learned that he had once been a doctor. A sordid affair had forced him to give up his profession, and he had become a pimp. He had more than ten women working for him. Any regular pimp with one or two girls was looked upon contemptuously by my friend as small fry. He would dance until the early hours, then go and collect the money. Women who didn't deliver enough cash he transferred to brothels in the province. His large brown eyes were hard as glass, his smile frozen.

Before opening the Théâtre de Minuit, I had asked my friend in London, Robert Vambery, for his advice concerning our unusual hours of operation. His answer was not encouraging: "It's hard enough to get people to come at nine; midnight will be even harder. Why not make a tabula rasa and take all of the seats out of the auditorium as well?" His opinion was soon confirmed. On the second night I sat nervously in the box office as a few stragglers came early for free tickets. In all, four tickets were sold that night.

I couldn't pay our actors' wages out of the proceeds, and was again forced to procure new funds. I'd persuaded the banker Vas that one couldn't simply drop such a successful production. He spoke with his customer, or friend, Sedlatzek, a hops dealer, who agreed to invest fifteen thousand francs in the Théâtre de Minuit. I met him before noon at a notary's office. He handed me a many-paged contract which I pretended to review carefully. The contents of the document couldn't have interested me less. I had put the actors' payment off by a day, and this was legal, but only until the evening of the next performance. After thinking up a few detailed questions for the notary about one of the clauses, I said I was ready to sign.

"And how much do you tekk for yourself?" Mr. Sedlatzek asked in his Czech accent. The sum was so little that I couldn't hold back my anger:

"I tekk nothing for myself, I tekk none of your money!"

I bowed to the notary and walked out with Lothringer, who had accompanied me. He turned to me on the stairs: "You impress me no end. But what are you going to do about the actors?"

"Let's go to lunch," I answered him.

Rouleau had an afternoon performance at the Théâtre de l'Œuvre. I drove there and found him in his dressing room.

"We have no more money! I can't pay the actors tonight."

"Servez-vous," he said, and pushed his checkbook toward me across the dressing table.

At the next morning's meeting, it was decided that the film would begin at eight o'clock, the midnight play at eleven. The theater recovered a little, and the cinema crumbled. Then our public relations manager Marc Blanquet, today a theater critic for the *France Soir*, devised a scheme yet unattempted in theater history. As both the cinema and the stage, with their unusual hours, were operating at less than satisfactory levels, Blanquet proposed that we open a combined show every evening, first the film, then, after intermission, the theater piece, for the price of one ticket. The least we could expect was the addition of the evening proceeds to those of the late night. And for its originality and generously varied program, the production seemed likely to bring in full houses. Madame Tallon and her financiers were charmed by the idea, and advanced a large sum toward promotional efforts. Our slogan ran: "Madame veut aller au Théâtre, Monsieur veut aller au Cinéma—ils vont au Théâtre Pigalle!"—The lady would like to go to a play, the gentleman would like to go to a film—they go to the Théâtre Pigalle.

The result was striking and our disappointment extreme: the theater crowd didn't want a film and the film crowd didn't want a play. Instead of doubling, our profits were cut in half.

Eventually the theater prevailed, and supplanted the cinema. Our production of *Dangerous Corner* began at normal hours and sustained itself for many months. It went on tour to Brussels, returning in 1945 to great critical acclaim in Paris under the direction of Rouleau.

I joined André Certes for our next production. He was the leader of a talented young actors' collective. We found the comedy *Apollo's Holidays*, written for a young cast by an author just as young, Jean Bertin, already the father of a large family. He provided for his children as a traveling insurance salesman. This was his first play to be staged.

Madame Tallon and I each put up a few thousand francs for costumes and props, and the Bazin Bank paid for the fully equipped house and promotion. Both the actors and Certes himself, acting and directing, rehearsed and performed for a share of the profits. The Stage Designer bought fabric for Greek costumes, only one costume for each role, and cut them according to his design. They were tailored on site in the theater, but looked nothing like home sewing; they looked distinctly Parisian.

The revolving stage, with changing scenery, was put to use. The play portrayed Apollo taking a short holiday on earth and pursuing his amorous adventures. The utterly charming performance appealed to the press, to the public, and to me. *Apollo's Holidays* ran for many months.

During rehearsals for this production, we experienced another hard political awakening. The Spanish Civil War ended, and half a million refugees, with women and children, poured over the French border. The French were not prepared for it. It was winter, and the suffering horrific. Rouleau and I collected money to buy blankets and food. He rented a truck and drove to the border. I, myself a refugee, didn't dare go with him. He came back to Paris deeply shaken. Many of the Spanish were lying without cover in the winter fields, already apathetic to the food and the first aid. In a schoolhouse, frozen limbs were amputated without anesthetic. Rouleau had brought back whatever medicine he could find at a drugstore, where he'd left his papers behind as a deposit.

After the Munich Agreement, Hitler marched into Prague. I drove to the theater in a nervous state. The stage technicians were discussing the weakness of the allied forces: France, an ally of Czechoslovakia, hadn't lifted a finger.

"We are no longer the Great Nation," one of them said, "We've given a check where our credit wasn't good." Tears were running down his face.

The performances of *Apollo's Holidays* came to an end. Madame Tallon stoutly expressed her decision in favor of a Viennese operetta, *The Imperial Loge* for our next play, in which her future husband, Oskar Karlweis, would play the lead. I withdrew from the proceedings.

The curtain fell for a long time. The war broke out. My next station was an internment camp.

CHAPTER

E L E V E N

September 1939 arrived. The Germans invaded Poland; the French and the English declared war. It was the third of September, 1939, a date that will always have its place in the history lessons.

For us emigrants and our families, who had finally begun to settle in France and to stand on new ground, that ground now began to shake. A few days after the declaration of war, there was an order for the men to appear before the police commissioner. "You understand that you are all German citizens. Are you ready to declare yourselves refugees and to fight for France?" The first part was no longer accurate, since we were one and all completely expatriated. We were between two empty chairs, and glad to be allowed to balance on the edge of the French one. We signed without exception.

"Ne perdez pas cette fiche, Monsieur," the official said when he handed me the confirmation slip, "Vous êtes maintenant presque Français."—Do not lose this piece of paper, sir, you are almost a Frenchman now.

Notices were posted the next day ordering our relocation, with a blanket and three days' food, to the stadium at Colombes. We used all our connections to find out what was in store for us. The prominent French figures we knew, themselves surprised by the outbreak of the war and uncertain about their own situations, advised us to go, that this could be nothing more than a sifting process by which the authorities hoped to identify and remove suspicious elements.

So I drove to Colombes. A legion of men holding small suitcases was lined up in silent rows. An atmosphere of terrible disappointment, as stifling as the heat and the dust, settled over these thousands standing in rows of four, to whom their beloved France had first offered asylum and on whom it now turned as its enemy.

We began to fear the worst. Rumors circulated that no one would be allowed to keep knives, scissors, or razorblades. Why such things should be taken from men who were about to be "sifted" was unclear to me. I asked one of my groupmates, Tommy. He didn't answer. Again I sensed a familiar tautness in the area of my diaphragm.

We inched forward mutely. Tommy had been handed a package by one of the postmen making the rounds. It was a delayed package out of Germany. Inside were two hundred Redbeard-Extra razorblades which he had been expecting. What would the guards make of this? Was it worth it to try to smuggle them in? We began to get nervous. How could we make the damn thing disappear under their noses? Tommy bent down as inconspicuously as possible and shoved the package into a furrow in the dirt. Normal life as we knew it had ended.

After hours of standing, they let us into the stadium. We were frisked and stripped of all sharp or pointed objects, as well as of our money and any paper with writing on it. Only "cette fiche ... presque Français" was handed back to me by the soldier: "To wipe your ass with." We were locked in, closed off from the world without an inkling of what would happen with us. We slept on the naked cement benches and between them. The September nights were cold, and at dawn strange figures, shapeless in the blankets wrapped around their heads and necks, walked briskly up and down to warm themselves. It was during these hours that the most absurd rumors were started. Across the courtyard, separated from us by a barbed wire fence, was the Austrian section of the camp. One day we heard excited voices from their side and saw them lining up in formation. Out of boredom, I started a rumor that the Empress Zita, who herself lived in Paris as an emigrant, had just arrived to liberate her countrymen. Within a few minutes my invention came back to me reported as an important new development.

When after nine days the toilets and the provisional cesspits had filled to capacity and the stench of fecal matter became unbearable for the neighbors, a decision was made to transport us in small groups to the interior of France.

Measles are very unpleasant, but nothing compared to cancer. It is hard to talk about the French camps when one has heard about the German concentration camps. If I nevertheless try to, I do it to show that the environment doesn't change the man. He remains always the same—rather shabby, a bit decent, a bit laughable, in the extreme cases deplorable, and only in the exceptions as we ourselves would like to be.

On our last night in the stadium at Colombes we were kept awake by intermittent instructions from the loudspeaker to pack our things and gather on the main concourse. There we were divided into groups of four hundred and placed under control of the military, who were marching up and down with bayonets. These were inducted members of the reserve, armed with old-fashioned rifles from the year 1914.

After hours of pointless standing around we were all at once—"*pressons, pressons!*"—packed onto buses. We rode through the almost empty dawn streets of Paris, but now as prisoners, forbidden to set foot there. From the Gare d'Austerlitz we were transported to Vierzon, an industrial city in the center of France some four hours away. We marched from there, at a fast pace and with no halts allowed, through various small villages, finally into the ruins of an old brickworks, chosen as an appropriate camp, apparently, for the high wall that surrounded it. By the next morning we had befriended the guards, farmers from Auvergne. They told us that the fast march with no halts allowed had been an emergency measure on their part; there were twenty-four of them to our more than four hundred, and they had been afraid of us.

The majority of the inmates were Jews—middle class, a few lawyers and bankers, several journalists and writers—and about a dozen working-class men. In almost all of the camps you encountered various kinds of workers, usually builders, who had been sent after World War I as part of the German reparations to heavily damaged areas of France. They had stayed in the new country, married French women and forgotten their nationality. Then one day, without warning, these expatriates were incarcerated as enemy aliens. They had walked into the same meat grinder as we had, but they reacted differently. When the armistice was signed, they said: "We've had it up to here with France, we're going over to Adolf!" and arranged their return to the German side. As a group, they kept mostly to themselves.

A few of the inmates had horribly bad foot odor—the water supply was not sufficient for washing—and it became an issue of contention for the others. At first the guards brought us to the river, but this soon ended because the water became too cold. We were put up in a large shed with a sliding wooden door and many gaping window frames. The floor was covered with red brick dust a centimeter thick. We spent the nights on a layer of straw, and slept and lived in one set of clothes. There was a well in the courtyard. On the first morning we gathered around it. Those in the front had filled their cups and were brushing their teeth. They brushed and spat over the edge of the well, then stood longer to wash out the cups that they would need later for drinking. They were told that brushing their teeth over the well was unappetizing and unhygienic, since this was our only source of drinking water. The next day they did the same, and a few more joined them. There was a confrontation that came to blows when no agreement could be reached. The guards intervened. We were forbidden to go near the well from then on. Water would be brought in buckets to a designated place and distributed in small portions. Every hour another one of us was assigned water duty.

One afternoon I went to have my cup filled. A young man stood at the pitchers, and his hands shook as he poured for me. I asked if he was sick. No, just tired.

"How long have you been standing here filling peoples' cups?" I asked.

"Seven hours," he smiled feebly. Because he hadn't complained, no one had bothered to relieve him.

In the evenings we huddled in small groups around single candles bought from first aid. We patched the walls wherever a draft came in; we made screens out of reeds from a nearby lake. From these we hung hats, bottles and pieces of clothing. Suitcases of every shape and color were spread out on the straw. The sometimes wild gestures of an excited speaker, the deranged look of his clothes and the shadows he threw in the flickering light had a romantic effect that was almost comforting. Then someone from the technically-minded group insisted on being useful and put in a light fixture. One colorless electric bulb brought all the ugliness of the place, the people and the clutter into sharp focus, and we knew where we were again.

Suddenly I became ill. My fever rose to 103, and my attacks of dysentery reached a crisis. The medical staff, unable to make a diagnosis, grew anxious at the possibility of an epidemic spreading among the prisoners. Sanitary facilities didn't exist. We had dug a pit just inside the wall and laid boards across it at intervals. During heavy rain, the effluent came up to the surface and streamed into our building. Then a new pit was dug.

The military doctor in residence gave the order that I should be transported to a military hospital, but because of my indeterminate status, as neither prisoner of war nor civilian internee, no hospital or infirmary was willing to take me as a patient. Orders finally came from a higher administrative body that a bed be made available. Instead of an ambulance, they sent a delivery truck, which was somewhat too short. Two medics pushed a board underneath me, tied my legs to it with wire, and left the back hatch open with the lower third of my body sticking out. Almost unconscious from the bumpy ride, I was unloaded in front of a military hospital in Vierzon.

They carried me through a series of passageways and finally put me down in front of an open door out of which, at that moment, a sheet-covered body was being brought on a stretcher. I asked if it was dead, and one of them nodded. They put me on the newly vacated mattress. None of it mattered to me, I could only think about how thirsty I was. I noticed an old nurse approaching my bed cautiously, peering at me. I asked her for some tea or some water. "Ni l'un ni l'autre"—not the one nor the other—she said sharply, backing away. Apparently she went to tell someone that there was a German patient in the house, because soon after that a lean French sergeant with many badges on his uniform and a stick in his hand appeared at my bedside. "You German dog, now you'll get your beating! I survived the Great War, I was badly injured by your side—and to this day I live with the pains!" I don't know what I tried to answer, in my fear and despair, I was parched beyond speaking. He stood over me silently. Then, noticing my condition for the first time, he calmed himself down and brought me water. I drank it and felt my senses return. Around me a dozen bodies lay sighing and groaning. I asked the sergeant where I was. It was the ward for vagrants, terminal cases who could claim no next of kin, awaiting their deaths.

There were boards put up at the edges of some of the beds to prevent the patients from throwing themselves to the floor in their last agonies. A man with cancer of the liver wailed so loudly that another patient dragged himself over to his bedside and struck him repeated blows in the face until he was quiet. Next to me lay an apparition of skin and bones, a black-bearded Arab who succumbed to periodic fits of coughing during which he would spit up entire sections of his lungs. After every attack he took a sip of red wine, as if he was attempting to replace the one red with the other.

An attendant came in the early mornings in order to empty bedpans, replace fallen sheets, herd those who still were able to the latrine, and bring those still able to eat breakfast a bowl of coffee and piece of bread. My thirst was unbearable. I asked the attendant for some water and received no answer. Later, a doctor came in, an older man of sedate bearing, his hands in the pockets of his white smock. The nightshift nurse was behind him. He stopped in the middle of the hall and stared blankly ahead as she made her report: "One discharge last night, otherwise nothing new. But here's the *tricheur*"—faker—"I told you about." She must have believed that I was malingering and had no excuse for being there. The doctor said indifferently: "Take his temperature." I had over 102. "What's wrong with him?" "Diarrhea." "Vegetable soup," he said, and both of them left the room. The nurse returned with a large clay pot: "Until this is finished, there's nothing else!" I was intolerably thirsty, but found myself unable to touch the soup; she had thrown in several handfuls of salt. The thirst was unbearable, and I repeated my hopeless appeal to the attendant, with the same result as earlier. Then, like a messenger from another world, the camp doctor appeared at my bedside. I did the unseemly, and clung to the sleeve of his uniform. I assured him that I had no more fever and could return to my comrades, and that I could never get better in this place.

"If there's no fever, there's no danger of you spreading the infection; I'll give the word to have you brought back right away."

A large, heavy-set soldier came to the bedside. "I have orders to bring you back to the camp. You look pretty bad. Do you have ten francs? You've got six kilometers in the rain ahead of you with that suitcase—I have to stay behind you with the bayonet to make sure we both get there—but if you have the ten francs, we can stop at a bistro first where you'll drink a liter of hot milk with coffee and few slices of bread for your strength. Otherwise you'll end up in the dirt somewhere along the way, which will be more trouble for me."

We left in the rain. He was a Parisian with a stand at the open market on Place de l'Alma. We talked about his city, and cursed the war, and he carried my suitcase. I lay once again on the scattered straw between my comrades and recovered.

There were some twelve doctors in our refugee group. Each one of them tried to prove his services indispensable to the French military doctor, with the hopes of becoming his assistant and obtaining certain privileges. The military doctor was a young man who had brought his cosmopolitan girlfriend from Nice to this desolate provincial town. The pair were lodged in a nearby castle. Every day around lunchtime, he drove into camp in his pajamas with the girl at his side, and reported for five minutes' duty. To this young man our group sent Dr. Werner Hartoch. He had intelligence, refined manners and a sense of humor, was a big drinker and eater, and established an immediate closeness with the Frenchman. The young doctor made Hartoch his assistant, and we benefitted from their association, most importantly by the unrestricted supply of alcohol.

Every morning at six o'clock, if he hadn't overslept, a young man in his early twenties would arrive for inspection. He was of medium height with broad shoulders and a pale face, a very small nose set in a flurry of red bristles, and almost no teeth. His eyes, swollen red from too much smoke and drink, were almost always blinking, and his face had a suspicious look which became grotesquely comical when he smiled. He dressed in spattered linen pants, a brown velvet jacket, and a small black hat with a pink cloakroom number on the band. The French guards never took issue with his outfit.

His name was Wolfgang Schulz, and he was the son of a ministry official of Lower Saxony. To avoid joining the Hitler Youth he had run away from home and come illegally to France, hoping to support himself as a photographer. He photographed the strangest things. I had from him an attractive photo he'd taken of a piece of Swiss cheese. He played on a small banjo, at very rapid tempos, exclusively Bach. I liked listening to him. He was mainly taken care of by his girlfriend Grethi, in whose one-room apartment the two lived. Grethi made hats, which she managed to sell with the help of connections. She was about twice as old as he, and, as the daughter of a Romanian general, belonged to an earlier wave of emigration. Because he'd had no papers, Schulz had been exiled from Paris; he'd re-registered in another district, had again been exiled, and had stayed in Paris until he was caught a third time and sent to the camp. He felt at home here, where no residence permit was demanded of him and he could be in France legally for the first time. This previously unattainable status, along with the great amount of alcohol we had in camp, prompted him to say often: "It's so wonderful here! I want to stay here!"

He got Grethi to send him a paint-box and started painting watercolors. We considered his work childish and refused to let him show it to us. After the war, living again as a free man, he named himself Wols and attained world fame as the founder of an artistic movement called Tachisme.

I came from New York to Paris in 1946 at the time of his first exhibition at Drouin, Place Vendôme. I still had the same distaste for his paintings, but because he had announced me as an American art expert, I let him talk me into playing the part. In the gallery at Drouin, an entourage of maenads with outrageous French hats on their heads were expecting me. I asked them please not to bother me, and went into the next room. After a short time Schulz-Wols came to me and said: "You have to say something, or the women won't go away."

"Leave me alone! Tell them: Shit!" I answered.

"Not original enough."

I got annoyed and told him his paintings were the ultimate dissolution of all values. His face lit up with bliss. He opened the folding doors and said to the group: "Il a dit: la destruction totale!" This met with the greatest enthusiasm.

One Sunday, which in the prisoner's camp was indistinguishable from a Monday, a group of men rushed up to me breathless with the news: "Your son is here!" I could tell from their faces that they weren't joking. At the gate stood my thirteen-year-old son Wolfgang. He wore the French Boy Scouts uniform, an organization he had joined that enabled him to move about freely despite being German. He had come from the Loire, where he had been working for farmers. He was sending his daily wages of twelve francs to my wife, who had stayed behind in our Paris apartment without any money, all accounts belonging to enemy aliens having been confiscated. I didn't show him how moved I was.

He wanted to make me a gift of something, and held out an old imitation leather case containing a mirror, a comb and a nail-file.

"Or do you want to eat some grapes?" he asked me, "You don't get a lot of fresh fruit here, do you? There's a vineyard nearby, I'll get you some grapes!"

I thanked him: "We're well looked-after here!"

I learned that he had made the roughly 200-kilometer journey by hitchhiking and on foot. I had a few francs which I wanted him to have for the return trip, but he wouldn't accept them. And suddenly he had vanished beyond the gate. The sky grew dark, and I felt dismal thinking of the boy alone at night on the country road.

After just a few weeks' encampment in Vierzon, the French began to send recruiting officers for the Foreign Legion. We had been given asylum, or rather locked in, and we had become a nuisance. They wanted to break up the camps in France as soon as possible and send us to Africa in order to be rid of us. The recruiters—officers of the feared military police—came again and again.

We lined up in the courtyard. A table had been placed in front of the entrance. The officers took their seats and prepared the papers to be signed. A colonel gave a speech. To make the offer more attractive, he declared the minimum five years' term of service in the Legion as simply lasting "the length of the war."

Even the Rothschild Committee, which since the beginning of the emigration had acted in the interest of exiled Jews, sent their recruiters. Since they didn't have anything to offer in its place, they tried to glorify the Foreign Legion, praising it as "le plus beau régiment de la France." They withdrew under a barrage of unflattering epithets.

Nevertheless, the pressure brought to bear was such that most of the group signed, and then tried to pull the others along with them. They were certain that the wives and children of those who didn't sign would pay dearly, and that they would be sent somewhere far away and forgotten by the world, never to return to France. We few who didn't sign found an unexpected support in Commander Viala.

He was an insurance official in his private life, a southern Frenchman with a small paunch and a double chin. His face was round, with dark, very human eyes, and a great power of charm when he smiled. It was his job to censor the mail. He took many men aside and said to them: "I had to read what you wrote to your wife. She has almost no money, and now you have to ask for some. Wouldn't you rather take it from me?"

Every Sunday he allowed a number of internees to meet with their wives outside of camp. When the information reached General Bloch at the Headquarters in Bourges that "the prisoners are promenading at large," a squadron of military police was sent to march at the gate. Commander Viala got on his bicycle and rode to the train station. He made sure the arriving women waited there until the squadron had retreated. After our liberation I wrote Viala a letter of gratitude. He answered that he had felt it his duty, under those circumstances, to mitigate the injustices visited on us by his country.

He too, as first in command of the camp, had to give a recruitment speech. He said:

"The Foreign Legion, for which I urge you to volunteer, is a collection of murderers, thieves, and other criminals. But the universally bad reputation of this institution will be suspended for the length of the war." Few understood what he meant. The majority, once set in motion, moved irrevocably on that path and wanted only to hear their own opinion repeated. A great many of them signed, and the camp began to empty.

One of the last transports was being assembled in the courtyard. Among the enlisted, his eyes glazed and bloodshot, stood Dr. Hartoch with a bottle of rum wrapped in newspaper, which he had almost emptied. The Marseillaise was sung to the sounds of an accordion, and we shouted "Vive la France." A man came forward and asked with emotion in his voice if he could say a few words to the comrades.

"Let us meet on the first Sunday after the war"—O eternal Schweik!—"at Café Marignan on the Champs-Elysées."

Another found the Marignan too expensive, insisting that many would not be able to pay the bill. He pushed for a different café. The pointy-bearded Henne interrupted him excitedly: "Perhaps the comrades will agree to take up a collection in advance!"

Satisfied, they marched off to the Foreign Legion.

At Christmastime Commander Viala gave a holiday banquet for the prisoners who had stayed behind. During roll-call the day before, we had seen live turkeys carried through the camp on poles. A delivery truck brought tables and benches, borrowed for a few hours, on the morning of the holiday. For the first time in ages we ate sitting down at a table. The menu began with hors d'oeuvres, then came salmon with mayonnaise, then turkey with chestnut purée, cheese, and dessert. We drank red wine or white, depending on the course, champagne for dessert and rum with our coffee, which made us drunk. I don't believe that such a meal has ever, or will ever again, be served in a prison camp.

After the meal, I sat on a stack of shingles in the winter sun and felt as sad as I've ever felt in my life.

That same day an order came from Paris to set me free. By direction of the Ministry of the Interior, the internment had been lifted for a small number of us. Some influential French friends, urged by our wives who had stayed behind, were willing to act as our guarantors. I traveled back to my house and family.

TWELVE

There was a blackout through Paris in anticipation of air raids. Lanterns burned with dark purple bulbs—"les violets," Colette called them—to help people find their way, and many walked around with gasmasks hanging from their shoulders. Motor traffic, decreased day by day due to fuel rationing, had been replaced by a flood of pedestrians. Life became frenzied under the pall of the blackout. The desire for food and amusement had never been so strong, and the usually thrifty French now filled the theaters, cinemas, and restaurants to overflowing. At the same time, a mental paralysis spread over the country. The two armies lay entrenched, facing each other. In this "Drôle de guerre," the phony war, as people called it, there was no fighting. Everyone wanted to believe it could stay this way, and knew that it couldn't.

We who had been released were mistrustful. We felt sure we would be re-imprisoned immediately if the war took a sudden nasty turn. As long as I was outside of the camp, I had to find a way to protect myself from a second internment. Was there some way to install myself somewhere in a civil occupation? I had the idea of making myself useful at the Ministry of Propaganda. According to what I could find out, there were plans to produce French propaganda for the Latin American republics.

I contacted the screenplay writer Hans Jacoby and asked him if he had any material that could be reworked into a Spanish language propaganda film. Jacoby had immigrated to Spain in 1933, and had then been forced to move to France as a result of the civil war. He understood immediately why I had turned to him. Of course he had a Spanish-French love story. Fitted with a heroic background, it would be ideal for export to South America.

The Ministry of Propaganda had established its base in the Hotel Continental, Rue de Rivoli. Madame Ninon Tallon, who was connected to all government offices through her uncle Edouard Herriot, long-time president of the Chamber of Deputies, came with me. We were received by a beautiful and elegant woman with many-carat diamonds on her fingers. It smelled exquisite in her office. One quickly saw that she was bored for lack of visitors. She was the right person to handle our request, and she was impressed with us, with the project and the story's outline. Since the film had to have a title in order to be registered, and we had not yet chosen one, she named it "La Danse Impossible"—which hit the nail on the head.

She promised every kind of help, and, naturally, no money. This I was able to procure with the assistance of Mr. Rosendorff, the owner of a private bank in Avenue de l'Opéra. Rosendorff was willing to finance our propaganda film, asking in return only that we mention his name to a certain beautiful woman at the Ministry of Propaganda. In this way each of us believed himself protected from any future trouble with the authorities. Rosendorff had a distinguished appearance, was smart, educated, kind, and reserved. He shared our affection for France. He too had had a hard time coming to terms with the idea that the French had put him in a camp when the war broke out.

The younger son of the composer Oscar Straus heard about our film project. He shared none of our interest in the Ministry of Propaganda— with his Czech passport he wasn't considered an enemy alien, and had no internment camps to worry about—but wanted to finance a commercial French version of our Spanish-language propaganda film. We met at Rosendorff's bank, and Straus introduced his backer, who owned many garages in Paris. The garagist pulled rolls of bills out of his huge leather jacket and pants pockets and laid them on the table. It was three million francs, the equivalent of about 500,000 Reichsmark. He was anxious about another inflation of the kind that had bled France dry after the First World War, and so invested all he had in the film.

Rosendorff took me and Straus into the next room and spoke to us.

"I'm sorry, I can't take this money as an investment. The man is totally naive and has no idea that he could lose his money on the film. We have to explain the risks to him."

"You have to explain the risks to my financial backer?" Straus asked.

"No," Rosendorff answered. When we went back to the man, he told him he wouldn't take his money. He urged all present to reconsider the conditions of the agreement. If the man wished, he could open an account in his name. The garagist opened an account. Straus had so fired his imagination that he wouldn't think of taking it back. Straus came the next day and produced a written proxy giving him full control over the account. He paid himself a large advance for the film production, his father an advance for composing the soundtrack, and his young, pretty, blond wife an advance for the lead role. He hired a press agent for a large sum to photograph his wife for the big film newspapers, bought a car and drove to the races (although he had no driver's license) and took to wearing the red rosette of the Legion of Honor in his buttonhole. Noticing my amazement, he explained that he'd received the rosette, red with gold filigree, from the Academy of Arts as a distinction for setting up a charity event with the help of his father. Some of the gold filigree had fallen out, he said, and if anyone mistook him for an officer of the Legion of Honor it wouldn't kill him anyway. Walter (that was the unfortunate man's first name) would later take his own life in New York when he could no longer find a way out of his financial problems.

Max Ophüls was hired as director of the French version. He had a name in France already, and he had made two films with Simone Berriau, a singer from the Opéra Comique, both of these films financed by the Pasha of Marrakesh. Mrs. Straus, who had never set foot in a film studio and barely spoke French, stayed near Ophüls, who spoke both French and German.

Born in Alsace, Ophüls had been drafted and stationed with the infantry at Bourges, two hours by train from Paris. He was, to his regret, neither a general nor a lieutenant, but a private first class. He decorated himself with the thick red Marksmanship cord, and wore his kepi cocked over his right ear, letting the black curls on his left side show, for the ladies. He agreed to commute to Paris every Sunday for an honorarium of 5,000 francs plus travel expenses. This he billed as "consultation."

Ophüls explained to Mrs. Straus in tedious detail how he envisioned her role.

"I always do the part in front of the mirror," she told him, "when I'm at home alone, and then I'm so good that I can make myself cry. But when I say the lines into the dictaphone it sounds completely different!"

I stepped into the conversation: "You need to start with acting lessons right away. I can find you a teacher!"

"Under no circumstances," Ophüls cut me off. "I want her as fresh and uninhibited in the studio as she is now."

"But it won't hurt her freshness if she learns how to speak," I insisted. She had a vulgar voice and an Austrian accent. It turned into an unpleasant confrontation. We left the couple and walked out of the building.

Jacoby raged at me on the street: "You idiot! You must think we're making a movie here!"

"Of course!" I shouted back, "What else are we making?"

"I knew you had no idea what we're doing." He calmed down. "What we're making here is a sugar-coated pill for all of us to suck on. So don't start with your acting teacher or any other ideas."

Another safeguard against the prospect of a second internment was provided by a public health officer named Rollet. For one hundred francs, Rollet would diagnose and certify anyone who came to see him as suffering from a serious illness. When the Préfecture de Police issued an order that all former internees report for *Prestation*—unarmed military service—I brought my certificate with me.

Some fifty of us were assembled in a barrack. A sergeant read from a list and called out: "Aron, Aufricht, Böhm: undress!" We undressed. A door opened to a large hall with a long table at which a military commission of two military doctors was seated. Now I noticed with horror that each of us standing there naked was holding a certificate from Rollet in his hand. I looked around for a place to get rid of mine. But I didn't have long to rack my brain: Aron, who had approached the table ahead of me, was found fit and sent out still holding his certificate. I stood in front of the two doctors.

"What's your complaint?"

"Gallstones!"

One of them pressed on my gallbladder and remained silent. The chairman at the long table spoke:

"Your profession?"

"Theater Manager."

"What are you doing at this time?"

"Making a film for the Ministry of Propaganda."

"So you're doing work—fit!"

Everyone was fit. The camps hadn't been a success, so they had found another way to take us off the streets.

On May 10th the German offensive was launched with terrific force. France awoke out of its lethargy, not to fight but to flee, and lost the battle in forty-four days. The greater part of the French Army was taken hostage. An almost joyful mood arose, for now there would be no more dead and wounded. The French seemed not to regret the occupation of their country, often repeating to themselves: "Ils sont très corrects." They meant the German military. And then came the Gestapo.

We who had so recently been liberated were interned again on the day Lüttich fell. There was no time for nuances, they still hadn't organized our draft into the unarmed service. The order applied to everyone this time, including the previously exempted men over fifty and women. My wife had the luck of having a fourteen-year-old son; the only group still exempted was women with children fifteen and under. Even in their panic, the French were not so inhuman as to incarcerate children.

I bought myself a sleeping bag this time, instead of the required blanket, packed a small suitcase, and took a taxi to Rue Scheffer to pick up Hans Jacoby. In the small apartment where his wife had once cooked marvelously for us, the two sat mute at the table, dressed and ready for the camp. I spoke after a moment, to break up the oppressive sadness in the room. "Alright, let's go!"

The two looked around the apartment they would never see again, hugged each other, and we all went quickly down the stairs. The woman went first, never looking back, and boarded a taxi for Vel d'Hiver, to the women's camp. I told our chauffeur: "Avenue de l'Opéra." When we arrived, I asked Jacoby to wait in the car a minute while I picked up Rosendorff, who was also planning to meet me. I found him in his office with his girlfriend. She was a beautiful woman, no longer young, with a classical face, dark hair and dark eyes. She turned to me with complete resignation: "Why go to the camp? In a few weeks the Germans will be in Paris, and then it's all over!" Rosendorff interrupted her and said to me: "I'm not coming with you today—I'll report tomorrow." He saw me out and, asking me at the door if I needed money, held out a roll of banknotes. Unfortunately I thanked and declined; I get nervous when I'm being offered a gift. I could have used the money later, and he wouldn't have missed it. He and his girlfriend ended their lives that day.

I got back into the taxi with Jacoby. This time we drove to the Buffalo Stadium.

THIRTEEN

After ten days in the stadium we were loaded onto buses, again at the break of day, again under a guard of rifles with fixed bayonets, and brought back to the Gare d'Austerlitz, where we boarded a train. We were forbidden to open the windows for the length of the journey. The train arrived in Limoges in the evening, from there our group was marched in quick step along a forest lane. After some time we came to a stop: a German civilian in a brown suit and beret was waiting for us with the guard detail of the camp at Braconne. When the guards had arranged us in rows of four and taken positions to the right, left, front and rear, the man addressed us in shrill German:

"You are now civil internees. You have a five-kilometer march to the camp ahead of you. Anyone who stops marching or steps out of formation will be shot without further warning!"

A number of the men shouted: "Parle français!"

He answered: "Shut your mouths, or you'll see what happens to you." Everyone was silent. To whom could one complain? We started marching. It rained, and we were quickly soaked through. We reached the courtyard of the camp after sundown. Searchlights were turned on us, and we were ordered to leave our suitcases in the quadrangle. They told us it was too late for inspection, that this would be seen to early the next morning. Someone pointed out that with the steady downpour, the contents of our suitcases would be soaked by then. We were forbidden to speak another word, and sent to the barracks. Jacoby, who was assigned to my barrack, whispered to me, "I'm going to get our suitcases!" I wanted to stop him, but he was already gone. He came back five minutes later with the baggage.

I would see him perform many other such feats after this one. He was the greatest *débrouillard* I ever knew (*"debrouillard"* is not easily translated; the French use it to describe a person who knows how to help himself in every situation).

The camp at Braconne was a strange place. It was organized and operated under the command of a German by the name of Schwob, himself an internee of the camp. Schwob was supposed to have been a reserve officer. He was about 35, middle height with a smooth, stout face and sideburns. Any misery he could put in his fellow inmates' way was justified and agreeable to him. He instituted a postal prohibition—we could neither write nor receive letters—and a smoking prohibition. Three times a day he called us to inspection and hollered at us. One man who couldn't take it anymore stepped out of formation and punched him in the face. Schwob called two French guards, who led the man away. No one revolted after that. The camp had doubled barbed wire fences and guard towers with searchlights and machine guns. The food was bad, but the latrines were freshly limed every morning.

The French military buildings stood outside the compound. We'd seen the Commanding Officer, a Lieutenant, only once, the day we were registered. He was a dry, lean old man, by profession a grade-school teacher. He ordered, in addition to our money and personal documents, that all of our watches and rings be confiscated.

For fourteen days we were cut off from the world. Then, unexpectedly, the Ecole Militaire in Paris requested two hundred men for the unarmed service. Those of us who qualified were separated from the others and placed into a unit under three sergeants. We were given back our papers and our valuables, and each received, besides, a pay book. We marched to the train station well-supplied with provisions and red wine, no longer prisoners. For those who stayed behind, who envied us, the nightmare was to last only a week longer. As the German army drew nearer, guards and prisoners alike would take to the forest.

We made ourselves comfortable in our compartments and began to eat and drink as the train pulled out of Limoges. Through the open windows came a summer wind of fields and woods, and, as the grim impressions of bayonets and barbed wire faded, we began to hope that our situation would stabilize. After many hours we stopped at a large station. Looking out our windows, we were amazed to see the people in the station make a show of turning their backs to us. One well-intentioned sergeant advised us to keep the windows closed; it had somehow been discovered that the train was carrying Germans, and there was risk of an attack. We shut the windows and tried to sleep, since by that time it was already night.

The next morning we disembarked in Albi, Département Tarn, in the south of France, and walked a short distance to the courtyard of the 99th Infantry Regiment barracks, to which we were now attached. From every window we were greeted as comrades by newly recruited French soldiers. Many came out into the courtyard to shake our hands. They were disconcerted when several of our group tried to explain to them that we weren't French, that we had escaped Germany, that we hoped our side would lose the war so that the diseased regime killing Germany and the world would fall. Our good sergeant quickly advised us to leave aside further explanations; nobody in France, especially in southern France, would understand what we meant. We ourselves felt the strangeness of our situation, and an awkward silence spread on both sides.

This camp was not our final destination. We marched from Albi, and several hours later, to our dismay, arrived at another barbed wire fence. On a wide, flat terrain stood a hundred identical concrete barracks about two meters high with small, barred windows. Inside the main gate, to the left, were kitchens and outhouses, to the right a sentry box and guards' barracks—features conforming to the Geneva Convention's specifications for prisoner-of-war camps!

The gate swung open. A captain, stocky and short-legged with a bulldog face that went well with the barbed wire, gave us the signal that he was about to speak. Our hearts dropped into our shoes. He said:

"Boys, I have to apologize. It's Sunday, lunch is over and the cooks are off. I can't offer you a hot meal. All I have is sardines, cheese and sausage. Maybe one of you can make coffee!"

Such an apathy had come over us that even this unexpected speech couldn't cheer us up. But the next morning our company was formed under a lieutenant and a sergeant, and we received our pay, along with a tobacco ration and good food from the military kitchen. We began to believe our luck had really changed. Our lieutenant announced that we were free to leave the grounds at six o'clock every evening. We took the first of these occasions to visit the post office in Albi and reestablish contact with our families. Then we walked around town. On the banks of the river Tarn, which widens at this spot, the tall, massive cathedral of Albi stood with its narrow windows and huge red brick ashlars. It had the appearance of a fortress, and indeed had been used as one. The Archbishop's palace displayed a collection of paintings by Toulouse-Lautrec, who was born in Albi. But much more important to us was the Café des Négociants. Sitting on its terrace, we forgot the difference between ourselves and the other guests.

The next day at six o'clock the guards barred our exit with lowered bayonets. The order had come from the commanding officer of the camp, an old, white-mustached nutcracker of a man. He was a harmless colonel of the reserve, furious that his model military prison had been turned into soldiers' barracks. He was determined to treat us as prisoners. He stationed guards and gave the order to let no one pass. When our lieutenant heard of this he telephoned his superiors in Albi, and the colonel had to call off his guards. This game repeated itself at intervals. The colonel, convinced of his mission, kept sending guards to block our way, forcing the lieutenant to new interventions.

One day an auspicious encounter with enemy troops gave this colonel his moment in the sun. We were ordered to vacate our barracks near the main gate immediately, and were shown into new ones at the back of the camp. German prisoners of war were approaching. The colonel had a chair brought to the gate, and sat watching the road. Near evening a car was let in. Two German pilots got out, and two guards with fixed bayonets escorted them to the first barrack. In the kitchen there was grilling and roasting in preparation for the unusual guests. After dinner we watched them strolling, under supervision, in the yard; they'd probably eaten too much. They were seen off in the car the next morning, and the colonel no longer had prisoners. He continued to be unyielding in the matter of the gate, and would not withdraw his guards.

It was on this day that Rabbi Dr. Munk was called to the gate. He was a small, fat man with a bald head and an upturned mustache. He had a friend who looked very much like him and slept next to him on the straw. Both wore dark blue suits (we had all kept our civilian clothes—the uniforms were arriving any day). The two men woke up early in the morning and brushed the straw from their suits. Rabbi Munk's wife had found her way from some part of France and was waiting, with their five children, in a hired car outside the gate. But the colonel remained unmovable: the woman and her children were not allowed to set foot inside the camp, nor could the Rabbi be let through the gate. The family, not understanding what had happened, had no choice but to turn around and drive off. The tall Mr. Schönheimer came into our barracks and announced wearily: "Mrs. Rabbi Munk and five children victoriously routed!"

We got a newspaper every day, and we followed the German Army's march towards Paris with apprehension. When I saw the photo, on June 15, of a swastika flying on the Eiffel Tower, I began walking up and down the barrack in despair. I imagined the German officers on streets of Paris: "We go now to Veba!" I muttered. "We go now to Veba . . ." I repeated louder and louder, until someone threw a brush at my head. Webèr—the accent falls on the second syllable—was a respected old two-story Paris café with a front garden in Rue Royale.

The Eiffel Tower swastika was my first full realization of what was happening to the world. But there was no time for ruminations, only the one thought of how I would save my skin. France could no longer offer us protection. The ceasefire agreement stated that all emigrants must be given up to the conquering side. We had to flee to another country, to leave Europe or fall into the hands of the hangman. Anyone who had a friend overseas renewed contact with them now and made plans to move on.

Our lieutenant could no longer stand his squabbles with the colonel. He finally received permission from his superiors in Albi to quarter us at several surrounding farmsteads.

For the French soldiers, the war was over.

One day, just as we were sitting down for a midday break in the shade of a tree, our sergeant approached and ordered us to come and unload a truck with him. No one got up, and we answered in chorus: "No!" He stood before each of us in turn and asked, "You refuse?" and each said "Yes!"

He said he would have us arrested for failure to comply, but we knew he'd had enough and just wanted to go home. After a moment's hesitation he shrugged and walked off. I felt it was time for us to get out.

We were told to report to the Bureau of Military Police in Albi for our demobilization. Not many went. France was now split in two, an occupied zone under the German Army, and an unoccupied zone in the south, where Albi was. The emigrants had come mainly out of Paris and the northeast. Having left their homes and livelihoods behind, they clamored for food and shelter. Many of them had been separated from their wives, who were being held at Gurs, a woman's detention camp in the Pyrenees. The men stayed as unarmed troops in Albi until the arrival of the German draft board, then they fled further.

Taking our younger son with her—our older son was studying in England and had joined the English Army—my wife got out of Paris the very morning the German Army entered it. She found refuge with a wine grower in a small mountain village in Département Ardèche. She sent a certificate for Jacoby and me, signed by the district council, stating that the wine grower was willing to take us into the community. This *Certificat de Domicile* was what we needed for our demobilization. A few of us in possession of this paper went to Albi and reported to the Military Police Bureau. The officer in charge, an elegant and lightly perfumed Sergeant, tore a piece of paper from a pad, entered my name on one of the lines and signed it. The scribe, a sergeant, stamped the paper and entered my name in a book.

I left the Bureau, and, on the street, read my demobilization order with curiosity. The bright summer day suddenly darkened. The certificate I held in my hands was a "Release for Prisoner E.J.A.," stamped "Prisoner of War Camp, Albi." With this paper I could return to Germany, but could not stay in France.

I went back to the camp, where I found the rest of the demobilized already discussing our situation. One of the group was Berlowitz, head of the World Student Union in Paris. He had an engaging manner, big, dark eyes, dimples and snow-white teeth, and spoke French without the slightest accent. He went to address the matter with our company commander in the small room of a farmhouse that served as the camp's administrative office. It was no longer the familiar lieutenant who had sided with us in the issue of the gate, but another one in his place, a haggard Marquis, advanced in years, who was interested only in the red wine we received with our daily rations. Berlowitz said to him: "Sir, I'm married to a French woman who is waiting for me with our child at her parents' house. Do you think I can run back into the welcoming arms of a French family with the status of a freed war criminal?" and he showed him the certificate.

The lieutenant asked him uninterestedly: "What do you want me to do?"

"Please, Sir, demobilize me and my comrades as a Soldier of the 99th Infantry Regiment in Albi!"

"Find a piece of paper, a stamp, and someone with good handwriting," the man said to Berlowitz.

On the pages of a ledger book—paper was scarce—we wrote out the new certificates, had them signed by the Lieutenant, and left Albi. Jacoby and I set out together. Buses and trains ran infrequently due to the shortage of gasoline and coal—most of the buses, anyway, had been requisitioned by the army—and after two days of traveling by any means we could find, our money was spent. We found a bistro for lunch and each devoured a hard-boiled egg and a cup of ersatz coffee. According to our map, we still had around 60 miles to go.

We walked irresolutely from one end of the town to the other. Suddenly it occurred to us to ask a man working at a garage if he had enough gas to bring us to our destination. He wanted 500 francs, which was a lot of money for us, but there was no other choice. And because I knew that my wife, if I could find my way to her, would think of a solution, we got into the car.

We drove through a hilly landscape, barren but for an occasional vine-yard, so sparsely settled that I couldn't believe we were in France. The villages consisted of five or six farmhouses each.

After two hours of travel, accompanied by the deafening song of the cicadas, we arrived in a village and pulled into a blind, overgrown alley. Far and wide we could see no one to ask, but by the map this had to be the place. I left Jacoby with our already mistrustful driver and climbed uphill through a light forest of low pines until I reached a small clearing. In the middle stood a well surrounded by three huge old farmhouses.

A young man stepped from the doorway of the middle one. I said good day to him and asked if he could give me directions. He opened the door: "Come in and drink a glass of wine!" I knew that I couldn't refuse without insulting him. We drank to each other's health, and after exchanging a few more polite words, he confirmed that I was in Sarréméjeanne.

"You're looking for a woman and a little boy?" He pointed up the mountainside, and there, standing in front of an isolated house in the middle of the vineyard, was my wife.

She brought money for the driver and bread for Jacoby and me, then we climbed the stone steps, opened the heavy wooden door and entered the house that she had rented for 16 francs a month. We would live here for almost a year. It had four small rooms, to the right and left of the narrow hallway, with concrete floors and two plank-beds in each, put there by the mayor's office. The house was intended as a lodging place for French refugees from Alsace-Lorraine. At the end of the hall one came to the kitchen, which was also the living room. The single fireplace in the house was here, and it served for heating and cooking. A sideboard, a great round wooden table, two benches and two chairs were the only furniture. Behind this room was another, smaller one with a frame-bed. Like the kitchen, it had red tile floors and an electric light. There was no water in the house, and no bathroom. We fetched our water in pitchers from a spring half a kilometer down the mountain. There was also no outhouse; we had to go in the mountains, with an umbrella when it rained. Later, seven of us would live in the house. Jacoby and his wife to the right, my son Wolfgang to the left, my wife and I on plank beds we set up in the kitchen every night. An older emigrant woman slept on the frame-bed in the back room. When she moved out, Mrs. Jacoby's sister and brother-in-law came to live with us. The brother-in-law had escaped from a camp and was very ill when they arrived. From the symptoms, it appeared he had typhus, but we couldn't get any of the local doctors to call, because the couple had no legal papers. A doctor friend wrote back recommending a strict diet of grapes, which we implemented. After several weeks the man was healthy.

Underneath the house was the wine cellar and the stable. Each of the wine-growers kept a pig for fattening in the cellar. The pigs were kept on a diet of sweet chestnuts, and by Christmas they weighed four or five hundred pounds, each with a bacon rind fifteen centimeters thick, and were ready for slaughter before the holiday. Also, each family had a small herd of goats, which gave a very fatty and goatish-smelling milk. I couldn't get used to the taste of it, although the cheese was delicious. Rabbits and laying-hens made up the rest of the livestock.

In the long-unoccupied house, scorpions had nested in the stalls and the empty cellar. The night my wife arrived there with our son, she made a fire to dry and warm their clothes, and swarms of scorpions, attracted by the heat, came up the walls. The two were horrified and, despite the rain, brought their plank-beds outside and slept in the open. Eventually these biblical creatures were scared away by the noise.

For all the primitiveness of the place, I felt restored every time I looked out through one of the small windows or took a step outdoors. The landscape was a paradise. On all sides vineyards descended into the valley. Plants and flowers of every kind bloomed in the cracks of the terraces' stone walls. At the bottom, where a wild brook flowed over a stone bed, we went with a flashlight at night and caught river crabs. Fruit trees, planted at intervals so that they didn't overshadow the vines, dotted the terraces, fig, peach, apple, apricot, walnut, and almond. The narrow paths were covered with mulberry bushes, the leaves of which were used to cultivate silk-worms and to feed the goats. Wherever there was a spring on the terraces, a small vegetable bush grew around it. After sunset we made the rounds and watered these vegetable gardens, wherever they were dry, with a ladle attached to a pole. The wine that was raised here was of modest quality, an unbottled table wine called *Pinard* in France.

The farmers were poor, but because they had no obligations to anyone, and their daily work required only a few hours, they lived as contented masters of their lives. They were proud of the fact that in the entire region there were only two wage-workers, and these were Poles. During the long summer they worked the brief hours from eight to ten o'clock in the morning and five to six o'clock in the evening. The hottest hours they spent in the shade in front of or behind their houses, where they talked with one another or sat silently and felt at ease. Only in the fall, the wine harvest season, was there any prolonged work to speak of, and even then any one of them might abruptly lay down his shears and walk off in the direction of home or the nearest shade. "He has *la flegme*," the others would say, meaning that he didn't feel like working. It was a symptom known to all. If the postman stayed away for a few days, someone would say sympathetically: "He surely has *la flegme!*"

The vineyards were barely 200 meters from their front door. When, once in a long while, a cloud appeared in the sky, the men would take an umbrella with them to work.

Each of the houses stood on a small plot among its vineyards, built over a deep cellar, with walls a meter thick, of stones from the riverbed that had been carried up the hill by these people's ancestors a thousand years earlier. The family lived in the large kitchen. In the fireplace stood an iron tripod for cooking, with a water kettle hanging from chains above it. Only the Belleville family had a stove. Their house, the first one I entered upon arriving, was at the center of the village. Three close-standing farm buildings surrounded a courtyard with a well and a stone bench. The women gathered here after lunch for the daily gossip.

A never-ending cause for talk was old Belleville himself, a man with a great white mustache and the bearing of an old soldier. He'd been a stagecoach driver. He loved to drink. After his retirement he took to his son's wine-cellar and was seldom seen above ground. Whenever he'd had too much, he caused a row and didn't let his children sleep. "Va-t-en avec ta poupée!"—get out of here with your doll—he would scream at his married son. They took the cellar keys from him as soon as he'd fallen asleep. The next morning he waited until he was alone in the kitchen, then took his revenge and peed in the hot water bottle warming on the stove. This was a big event, and the women ran excitedly to tell one another other: "Old Belleville pissed in the hot water bottle!"

The day after we arrived we set off after lunchtime to the nearby village Paysac. Jacoby and I needed to register as discharged soldiers at the mayor's office, and my wife said she would come along. Unprepared for the scorching heat of that hour, we took the narrow goatherd trail up and down hills, through vineyards and woods, and arrived in the small village drenched with sweat. My wife went to shop at the two village shops, a bakery and a general store. Aside from the few foodstuffs on ration, most items were not available at any price; often the farmers had just enough to subsist on.

I asked where I could find the mayor, and was pointed in the direction of a beautiful old house on a hill facing the village. We found him at home with his wife. He had a powerful, stocky build with a crooked nose, cunning, almost black eyes, and a good smile. He invited us onto the colonnaded terrace for a glass of wine. We discussed the sad events that had overtaken France and de Gaulle, whom we admired and respected. It was soon clear what kind of person we were dealing with, and we explained our situation openly, and the truth about our demobilization certificates. He wanted to offer us refugee assistance. We reminded him that we weren't French citizens and had no claim to such assistance, that we didn't want to create problems for him.

"But how are you going to live? You can't work for wages here! I'll register you as Alsatian refugees." He paid us the first installment. Then his wife brought out pots, bowls and a broom for us and gave my wife some helpful suggestions before we took our leave. Walking home, we felt revived by the cool dusk, and happy in the day's success. We would make this hour-and-a-half trek many times. The mayor owned a radio, a great rarity in those parts, and he would send a schoolboy to tell us whenever de Gaulle or Churchill was going to give a speech.

As we came up the last rise to our house in the dark we saw, silhouetted against the night sky, the small, still form of a woman waiting for us. Our surprise was great when we recognized Mrs. Jacoby, arrived that day from Gurs.

We became friendly with several of the six families of Sarréméjeanne. In the evenings we sat with them in front of one or another of their houses, or in their kitchens, and were served wine and roasted chestnuts. It showed their open-mindedness that they could treat us, enemy foreigners, with such kind consideration while their country was occupied and most of their husbands in prison camps. The mayor had told them we were refugees who needed protection, and that was enough for them. More than once the parish priest mentioned us in his sermon, encouraging good will towards the refugees. Then farmers whom we'd never seen before would bring us potatoes and *Marc*, a clear schnapps distilled from the skin of grapes. Of the little we had, our wives learned, with much effort and imagination, to make excellent meals on the open fire. I missed coffee, but cigarettes were plentiful. On hot days we bathed in a nearby stream at a point where it curved and formed a pool deep enough to swim in.

The end of our idyllic life in Sarréméjeanne did come, finally. The older woman who had lived with us during our first month was married to a prominent emigrant whose name was on the extradition list and who was hiding in Montauban. The woman was large and round; she had neither a waist nor a neck, nothing separating her head from her massive torso. She took no part in the daily household work, which she left to the two younger women, but spent her days outdoors in a high-laced summer dress and a large Florentine hat, her face oiled, a fringe of sun-bleached hair on her low forehead, and painted canvases. The most precious commodity in the village at that time was oil; fastidiously rationed according to the number of people per household, collected in a single flask, it was used by the drop in preparing our meals. We knew that the fat woman was secretly oiling her face with our olive oil, but no one wanted to confront her about her vain behavior. One day she filled a small bottle for herself from our supply and, to disguise the theft, poured an equal amount of water back into the flask. That evening the two young women kneeled unsuspecting in front of the fire. One heated the pan, and when the other poured in the oil mixed with water, a searing plume of oil drops shot out. By luck their eyes were spared. The two of them knocked on the fat woman's door and demanded an explanation. She began yelling that she wouldn't put up with this harassment, but my wife forced her way past her and found the bottle of stolen oil. Holding it up, she asked the woman what her source was. Now the accused began to rave, screaming: "You'll pay for this dearly! You'll pay with your child!"

The next morning I heard my son's loud crying through the window. I ran out and found him near the house, doubled up in pain. He had jumped from a wall and broken his leg. We carried him inside carefully. We had no telephone, no car, no idea what to do, and the child was whimpering. This moment of helplessness was the worst experience of my emigration. Then the door opened and the fat woman came in with her paint-box and brushes, radiant at the sight of her vindication. It was the only time my wife ever completely lost her self-control. She ran at the woman screaming: "Get her out of here, the witch! She did it with her spells! Get the witch out of here!" We held her back, and she regained control of herself and went back to the child, who clung to her wrist to suppress the pain. Someone gave us the name of a doctor in the district and found a farmer's child with a bicycle to carry the message. After an endless three hours the doctor arrived. He couldn't bring his car up the hill, and we had to saw off the legs of our dinner table and carry the boy down on it. The doctor gave him an injection and drove off with him to his practice in town, where he laid the broken leg in plaster.

A few days later the fat woman got word from her husband to meet him in Marseille: in a week they would be sailing to America.

The mayor's messenger came again, this time not with an invitation to come to hear the radio with him, but with a letter. The District Chief of Police had received orders to round up and detain all male German refugees, to be held until they could be brought before a German commission. The Pétain authorities had given their word in the ceasefire agreements to extradite all those whom they'd given asylum. The Mayor had assured the Chief of Police that there were only women and our boy in the region, that the men had all boarded ships for America. In his letter he begged us to hide ourselves well. He would explain to the community that, should anyone happen to see us, we were ghosts.

After this news, Jacoby's sister and brother-in-law felt they were no longer safe in Sarréméjeanne, and went into hiding with a family in Nîmes. They were friendly people, harmless enough, although the husband was unable to let a meal go by without saying "Dinnertime! I'm the uncle!" as we were sitting down. I waited for the phrase with apprehension every time we joined them. I didn't dare ask him to let it go, I knew I couldn't have kept a straight face.

Jacoby and I moved in with Pierre, an ancient mule who no longer worked except during the grape harvest, in his shack, in a valley that cut through the vineyards. We made our beds in the hay-loft above his stall. His passion was water. We served it to him in small amounts, as only so much could be brought at one time from the distant spring. He didn't let us sleep at night, scraping tirelessly with his front hoof for us to bring him water. From the paltry hay at the roadsides he picked out the bitter stalks with great care, pulled them out with his long yellow teeth and let them fall to the ground. His owner, old Audibert, gathered the fallen straw at feeding time and mixed it into the new hay pile. Pierre put his ears back and rolled his eyes malevolently, so that the whites showed, and old Audibert shook a fist at him and said with admiration: "He's a gourmet, the devil!"

Our nights in the loft passed restlessly, with rats scurrying back and forth over our bodies and the mule waking us at intervals, until finally we decided to spend one night in the house. It was a Saturday night, and we didn't think the French constables would ruin their Sunday morning with the difficult journey, by bicycle and on foot, into the country. At around six a.m. there was a loud knocking at the door. My wife and I were sleeping on a plank-bed in the living room. We tiptoed to the hall and took a single glance at the front door which, ending about a foot off the ground, revealed the military boots and leggings of the police. My wife called out, "Who's there?"

"District Police! Open up!"

"Just a minute, Officer, we women need to put something on!"

In the meantime, the Jacobys had crept up next to us. For a moment we stood there staring at each other. Then we pulled ourselves together and noiselessly removed the plank-bed from the living room. The women put on their clothes and shoes while Jacoby and I grabbed our things and hurried to the back room—the women were going to say that this room had been closed off by the owner. But once inside the door, we found that the key wouldn't turn, the lock was rusted. The women could delay no longer. They opened the door. Two constables entered the corridor, opened the door on the right and looked in, then the one on the left, where my son was in bed. They went into the living room. My wife asked them to sit down.

"Would you like a drink, Gentlemen?"

"No thank you, Madame!"

"A cigarette?"

"No thank you, Madame!"

Jacoby and I listened at the door. The situation looked bad. I whispered that I was going to jump from the window, try to reach the small pine forest before they could shoot, and keep running till I found a place to hide. Jacoby was sure that escape was impossible. We exchanged these words behind the door to diffuse the unbearable tension, hearing the women invent our dates of departure and addresses in America. The two officers wrote everything in their pads, then stood up—I put one leg out the window—and took their leave. We didn't dare move. We were sure it was a trap, to lure us out. It was inconceivable to us that they had sat across from this door, which they couldn't have overlooked, without opening it. Half an hour later, a neighbor came to tell us that the constables were gone.

A letter and a telegram were delivered to our hiding place by messengers. The letter was from the American Consulate in Marseille, urging me to come and arrange visas for my family as soon as possible. The telegram was addressed to Jacoby, from the film Director Curt Bernhard in Hollywood. Its content was four words: "Visa nearly nearly through." Like students of the Talmud, who spend their lives probing the meaning of a Bible passage, we sat over this telegram every day and discussed the meaning of "nearly nearly through." Our moods went from one extreme to the other depending on the latest interpretation.

Our nervousness was at its high mark. One night, as the mule scraped and the rats swarmed, Jacoby began hammering away at me that it was a matter of days, maybe hours, until the police figured out that the women had lied to them. We were a rarity and a subject of conversation in these remote parts, the parents talked about us in front of the children, the constables also had children, these children would hear about it at school and tell their fathers, the constables. I hit the floor with my fist: "I can't hear it anymore! If you keep talking I'll strangle you!"

The Jacobys didn't want to stay any longer. They packed their things, left us and went to the Spanish border to wait there for their visa. We mourned their departure. Mrs. Jacoby with her gracious, unobtrusive manner had grown close to our hearts. Her husband had spent hours with Wolfgang and with his talented hands had built adjustable platforms on which he could support his broken leg, surrealistic-looking structures of bricks, wood blocks, card decks, rags and moss, which could be raised or lowered to allow the chafed area around the plaster cast to heal. We allowed ourselves contact with the outside world only in the most serious emergencies, even when this meant performing the duties of a doctor.

My wife and I were alone now, and it was as though steam had been let out of an overheated kettle. Too many people in an abnormal situation, under constant strain, had sat too long at the same table. I took the risk and moved back into the house.

Now I had to find a way to contact the American Consulate in Marseille. I was living illegally, or as they say in France, not "en règle." Had I been asked to produce my papers, it would have meant arrest and extradition. We wrote to a Parisian acquaintance, a French soldier who was demobilized in Nîmes. He came to visit us. As I didn't have the courage to travel alone to Marseille without papers, we asked him if he would go with me. He agreed, and we set out.

In the morning half-light, with one of the locals as a guide, we struck through the countryside, keeping to back roads and circuitous paths to avoid the neighbors and gendarmes, until we reached a bus stop. We took the bus to Nîmes and stayed there overnight at the house of a tailor, where my Parisian acquaintance was also a boarder. The next day we took a train through Marseille to a small neighborhood, then a streetcar back to the city center, widely avoiding the train station and any checkpoints. We got out at the Hotel Aumage, on a side street of the Cour Belsunce, Rue du Relais, which consisted of a few rooms on the second and third stories of a narrow old house. The hotelier was a former official of the Sûreté Nationale, and his establishment was seldom disturbed by the police. We took one room together. The man didn't ask to see our papers.

That evening we met with a fellow internee from the camp at Albi. He gave me the name of an Abbé whom the Bishop had officially appointed as an aid to refugees. I wrote down the address. When we returned to the hotel, I got into a fresh bed and immediately fell asleep without worries, but exhausted after the strenuous day. I thought I must be having a nightmare when loud knocking shook the door at six in the morning.

"What is it?"

"Police!"

It was still as in a dream that I saw my companion open the door to two men in civilian dress, holding up their badges: "Your papers, please!" They inspected my companion's French passport closely, comparing his face to the photo. I showed them my expired *Paris Carte d'Identité* with photograph, and was given a sharp look of mistrust. Then they left.

"You'd better pack your suitcase," my companion told me, "they're bringing a policeman to arrest you. I'll tell your wife."

I packed and sat next to my suitcase. Was there no way out? I asked the Frenchman, and he shook his head.

"Here's my money. Give it to my wife." Perhaps I could make a run for it? I asked him: "Will they put me in handcuffs?"

"It is the custom," he answered. We waited silently for half an hour.

"I'm going to take a look around," he said at last, "they should have been back a long time ago." He left and returned soon after, and I could tell by his face that he had good news. The two officers were looking for a Spaniard of whom they had received a summary description; they didn't want to bother with me. I knew now that my first step had to be to re-establish my legality.

The one-man office of the Abbé was on the ground floor, with groups of people spilling out onto the street. When I greeted him, he asked me whether I had come to drink a *Vieux Marc* with him. He poured me a glass of wine, I drank it, and he said, "Now tell me." He was a southerner, with dark eyes and short black hair, overflowing with heartiness and good spirit. I explained to him that I hadn't come to ask for money, that I was illegal and needed papers to stay while arranging my emigration to America.

"Come with me," he said, putting on his stiff priest's hat, "we're going to the Police Prefecture. I was frightened, but he had already hurried ahead of me into the street, leaving no time for objections. For the first time in my life I was walking beside a priest, and for the first time in months I felt protected. But my fear came back to me when we entered the Prefecture.

In the waiting room Abbé Scolardi gave his name, and we were called immediately. We were told to sit. The Prefect took his place behind the desk. Scolardi showed him my letter from the American Consulate, explained my situation, and asked him to issue papers for a few months' stay in Marseille since my papers from Paris had expired. The man, who looked like an assistant grade-school teacher, had listened to him and read the Consul's letter without a sound. Suddenly he stood up and shouted at me:

"What have you done for France? The country is deep in misery, and the gentleman emigrant would like to travel to his next stop? Go, why don't you? Out! The gentlemen always want favors, favors!"

That's as far as I let him go. I had endured quite a few humiliating experiences, but the cynical slurs of this man, who knew very well that I was no tourist on a pleasure trip, were too much.

"Where do you get the nerve to speak to me like that?" I shouted back, "I'm not a tramp and I'm not a thief! You know exactly what my situation is, and you tell me I'm asking for favors!"

Scolardi tried to intervene, but it was too late. With a cutting voice the Prefect told me I had two hours to leave Marseille.

"And it's only because the Abbé brought you that I don't press this button and have you arrested and brought where you belong, with your own kind!" We were shown out. The priest bowed and walked ahead, I followed him wordlessly.

"A fine stew you got us into," he said to me on the street. "Why did you have to answer? I can't do anything for you now." I apologized, picked up my suitcase and my traveling partner at the hotel and went back to Sarréméjeanne. I didn't think of my defeat as a catastrophe, though it was one. The only measure of any action's merit was how much closer it brought me to leaving.

I had to begin to separate myself from this country, and this separation was, in its own way, as painful as it had been to leave Berlin. I was not unhappy to return to the house in Sarréméjeanne. Despite the dangers created by my illegal status, the uncomplicated, primitive life in that house was a good solution at a time when one didn't know where he belonged or how he should behave.

The winter came slowly, and we spent evenings with the neighbors, no longer in front of their houses but around their fireplaces. On colder nights the women brought flat stones the size of pancakes and put them near the fire, then walked home with them under their arms to stay warm. In the summer we lay the red wine, well-corked and tied to a stake, in the stream to cool. Now in winter it was prepared on the stove in a pot, brought almost to a boil and lit with a match. The bluish flame went out in a few seconds. This process took away some of the wine's bitterness. We used an iron pan with holes in it to roast chestnuts over olive and mulberry wood, which burned slowly and gave off intense heat. The pan was swung back and forth, then the nuts emptied into a wide, flat basket and cracked open under a sack moistened with wine vinegar.

I took walks during the day. Not on the roads, but cutting across the landscape, always careful to see people approaching before they saw me, and to hide until they had passed. One day in the woods I stopped in front of a heavy, unadorned stone cross from Roman times. I heard footsteps and ducked behind a tree. It was a young girl. She kneeled, crossed herself and prayed briefly, and when she looked up, her face had a glow that seemed to penetrate the woods all around. Living as I was in great uncertainty, this encounter made a deep impression on me.

We were invited to the house of Monsieur Sarréméjeanne in Sarréméjeanne for Christmas dinner. Of all the villagers, he had the least land but the richest yield of crops. He was far and wide the only farmer who produced household white wine. The others didn't trust his productivity, and seldom came in contact with him. From time to time we went to him to buy a pound of bacon, which we would begin to eat on the way home, so keenly did we feel the deprivation of fat in our diet.

Monsieur Sarréméjeanne was married to a large, vigorous woman who did not have the fussy way of most women of the south of France. The fourteen-year-old daughter resembled her mother: she was awkward, kind, and hard-working. None of the young men paid her any attention, though she had been tending the goats for several years. Her father comforted her: "Next year Odette gets to stir the blood!"

The pigs weren't knocked unconscious before they were slaughtered, and it took four honored guests (my son Wolfgang and I had this honor more than once) to hold them down on planks arranged across the tops of wine barrels. The scream was deafening. The carotid artery was opened and the blood collected in a bucket, to be used for preparing sausages. The wife stirred the bucket continuously with her bare arm to prevent the blood from coagulating. When Monsieur Sarréméjeanne repeated his promise to Odette that she could stir the blood at the next slaughtering, she blushed with pride.

Tall, blond Marcel, the son and heir, was open-minded and gentle. Whenever he came to visit us he brought a gift: a small sack of chestnuts, a heavy block of olivewood in his rucksack, or a flute he had carved.

Madame Sarréméjeanne prepared a Christmas meal with six courses, for which none of the ingredients were bought. For an hors d'Œuvre, she served a platter of homemade sausage and smoked ham. Next came a rabbit ragout, followed by coq au vin with pommes frites, and an omelette soufflée for dessert. After the meal there were goat cheese and fruit preserves. Carrying off such a wonderful menu on the open fire requires perfect knowledge in the choice and uses of various firewoods.

The usually taciturn wife, excited by the good food, the plentiful wine and the praise she received on all sides, grew talkative and told us that lately her husband had become a real pig. The man, whose mustache formed ringlets on both ends, smiled proudly at this sign of second youth. But he had kidney trouble that caused him great pain. He wouldn't let a doctor examine him, and was often seen wearing a deathly expression.

I had brought two packs of Celtiques Bleues cigarettes as a gift. One was opened and passed around, the other Monsieur locked carefully in a drawer. When the other relatives arrived on Christmas day, the son Marcel told me: "Father bragged the whole time about your Celtiques Bleues."

The new year came, and we received news from Marseille that the Police Prefect had been replaced. My wife, who had never thought of France as an end station and had never felt safe during our hiding, now devoted all of her energy to arranging our departure.

With the enormous demand for food and supplies to fuel the war, Germany had depleted occupied France of its resources within a few weeks. The unoccupied zone was flooded with French buyers, hired by the German government, to buy up everything that could be transported. The money came from the French, who had to pay a billion francs daily as their contribution to the war. The rate of exchange was fixed at ten marks to a thousand francs.

My outfit hung in tatters over my body. Shabby gray flannels stitched with red yarn—nothing else was available—drew too much attention to be suitable traveling clothes. My wife made the trip to Marseille alone. She was never stopped or asked to produce her Paris identity card, which was still valid. She met with Abbé Scolardi who said he was willing to bring me to the new Police Prefect. She also applied for and received money from the American Rescue Committee. The committee had a list of politically persecuted intellectuals whom they labored to save, assisting them with money and visas. At the head of the list was the agile, unstinting, and level-headed Varian Fry. He had money and helped the refugees. He hid those refugees whom Germany had ordered to be handed over, among others, the chief editor of the *Vossische Zeitung*, Georg Bernhard. Fry's work called for patient reasoning with people whose language he didn't understand, and who were often living in panic.

My wife returned with a suit for me, borrowed from friends and altered by a tailor to my measurements. We made arrangements for our journey immediately. I decided to set out a day before my wife and son.

It was not only a simple existence we had to leave behind, but also a kind of simple thinking that I had grown accustomed to: good was all on one side and bad on the other, and the sky was empty.

For some time, all roadways, trains, and streetcars into Marseille had been under police surveillance. I planned to get off at the main station and slip through the checkpoint linking arms with a farmer's daughter, employed as a maid in the city, with whom I had formed this plan on the way. She would take my ticket and give me her regular commuter's card. As we neared the checkpoint, she would begin telling me a story in the Marseille patois and leave me no time to respond; we would mingle with the crowds pressing up to the exit gate and pretend not to notice that other passengers were showing their papers.

Small and graceful, she stood with me next to the train. She grabbed my arm and began speaking excitedly about a man who had been pursuing her. As we neared the blockade I saw the guards. I became frightened and thought, maybe if I stay on the platform and catch the next train I'll be safe. I stood there for a moment, but the girl pulled me forward. If they don't stop me, I thought, and I get through the gate, then we may be done with all this mess. If they catch me, it's all over. Again I hesitated, but the girl wouldn't let me stop, she held my arm tighter, spoke louder, and I went mechanically forward. Suddenly she let go of me and laughed. We were through.

We went quickly through the streets and came to an apartment building of several stories. As was customary in those days, she occupied a *chambre de bonne* (maid's room) in the attic. In that tiny space stood a narrow bed, a night table and a stool. Her few clothes hung from a slat in the corner. "Lock the door after me, and don't open it before tomorrow morning," she said and left at once before I could thank her. I lay down on the bed. I had forgotten to buy cigarettes; there were three left in my pocket. It was seven in the evening. How would I make it through the night? Out of boredom I opened a small box next to the night table. It was full of love letters from her boyfriend. I said to myself: "You are not going to read these letters!" but the time wasn't passing, and I gave in. All of them ended: "I cover your body with my kisses!" When I had read it many times I became tired, forgot the cigarettes, and fell asleep.

FOURTEEN

First thing the next morning I went to Abbé Scolardi. As before, he offered me a glass of *Vieux Marc*. We drank, he put on his flat, round priest's hat, and we left for the Police Prefecture.

"Give me your papers and wait here," he said to me outside, "I don't want to have another scene like last time." I waited, and a few minutes later he came back with a permit for my temporary residence in Marseille. He wouldn't hear any thanks. If I ever wanted to drink a *Marc* I should pay him a visit.

I stood on the street of a big city, a legal resident. First I bought cigarettes. Then I sat down on a café terrace near the Vieux Port and ordered a cognac; the coffee still available in France was of poor quality. I listened to the city noise, saw the crowds of people and once again felt myself one of them. My wife and son were to arrive that afternoon. Maybe, I thought, we could live an almost normal life here for a few weeks or even a few months. The single, painful worry pursued us, that since the time of my wife's departure from Paris we'd heard nothing from our older son Heinz in England.

The suburbs were full of emigrants; there wasn't a bed free in Marseille. A constant stream of refugees swept through the city. I went to the Hotel Aumage, whose owner I knew from my last stay.

"You're in luck," he greeted me, "a room opened up just this morning. The woman was a refugee, she had a fight with a German fellow, he injured her. They took her to the hospital." I learned later that the man was from the Gestapo, and the woman the sister of a former Berlin film producer. She had told him about a safe in Zürich, he had demanded the combination and the key, and had hit her in the face with a chair when she refused to give him either one. They found her blind and unconscious. The bloodstains on the floor were not yet dry when we moved in.

As at the beginning of the emigration in Paris, groups of emigrants could be seen occupying the terraces of bistros and cafés. Most of them wore the same dirty suit every day. They came out of hiding places, out of camps, or, demobilized, out of the Foreign Legion. They sat where it was cheap and where they were less conspicuous. We knew the places where the police made regular raids—on gangsters, black-market dealers, passport forgers, alleged and actual spies. The wife of the man who had financed the *Opéra de Quat' Sous*, an upstanding Dutchwoman, bought a Lithuanian passport for her husband in one of these cafés in order to secure his release from a camp. Both she and the forger were arrested, and she spent several months in the holding cell of an overfilled jail among various kinds of criminals.

Yellowish and gray, his long, sharp nose on the scent of bad news, the journalist Erich Burger balanced with one half of his behind on a chair. On the other half he had a boil. He sat like this on a café terrace in the French springtime sun and symbolized the emigrants' common plight.

In accordance with the ceasefire agreement, the Marseille police arrested former Social Democratic Ministers Breitscheid and Hilferding, and turned them over to the German authorities. Neither of them survived Dachau. The area around the Gedächtniskirche in Berlin is named after Breitscheid. With this incident, the ominous extradition list resumed its foremost place among conversation topics. Every emigrant had heard from a reliable source that he was first on the list and therefore must receive immediate and preferential help. Two Viennese comedians had sung on a recording for Radio Strasbourg before the war, making fun of the Führer:

Heil Hitler, Herr von Würstel,
Heil Hitler, Herr von Kren

—was the refrain. Naturally, Hitler had a tantrum when he heard it played, and ordered that the two actors be caught at once. The writer [Leo] Lania told people, and believed it to be true, that Hitler had invaded France solely to get his hands on him.

The widow of a Berlin actor was referred to the Chief of Police to procure a temporary residence permit. In her fear of being turned away, she greeted the man with:

"Vive la France et la liberté!"

"Go on, Madame," he answered. She didn't know the rest.

"Go on, Madame," he repeated. "L'amour, Madame! Come at two in the afternoon . . ." He gave her an address. He always issued her a one-week permit, so she had to come back every Tuesday. As she was the obliging type, we often asked her to sleep an extra permit out of him, though we put it in cruder terms.

No one knew who would be arrested in the next hour. Harmless women, children, and even old ladies doing their daily shopping were apprehended by the police for prostitution and put into detention in the Hotel Bompard: a few days, a few weeks, a few months. It was said that the clerk who was responsible pocketed 12 of the 17 francs put up by the authorities for the detainees' daily room and board. The women received so little to eat, they had to devise ways of smuggling bread through the windows on twine. Men were stopped by detectives on the street, brought to the police station and asked for proof of funds for subsistence. If the officer found the amount too small, the man could be locked up for vagrancy. Strange schemes were used for making money, and honest dealing had all but ceased to exist for us. You had to pay for connections and leads. Jacoby sold the story of the *Marquis von O.* by Heinrich von Kleist as his own story to the film distributor [Adolphe] Osso, who wanted to bring some original material to America. But someone in Hollywood had read Kleist, and after both had settled there, Jacoby was forced to pay back the advance.

Jacoby heard about a relief effort where an acquaintance of his sat on the board. Apparently there was money to be had. We took the long march to an immense, light-colored brick schoolhouse crowded with homeless refugees at the edge of the city. Families with children were encamped on straw sheaves in every room and in the corridors. Some prepared meals on alcohol stoves. In the main hall people were forming a line in front of a closed door. Every applicant, we were told, would receive 200 francs.

"There's no point trying, come on," I said to Jacoby, pulling him by the sleeve, but he broke away from me, pushed to the front of the line, opened the door and went in. The people in line were in an uproar, and I ran out of the building. He came out soon after with 100 francs for me. "Stuff your face for lunch and forget the whole thing."

No one knew which visa—entrance, exit, or transit—was the best one to have at any given time, or whether France wouldn't suddenly re-enter the war on the side of the Germans. Most of all we feared that Germany would occupy the rest of the country and close off the remaining exits.

The kings among the emigrants were those in possession of a "rescue visa," or as we called it on account of easier pronunciation, the "danger visa." On President Roosevelt's order the US State Department had authorized the American Consulate in Marseille to issue special tourist visas to politically persecuted intellectuals. The German immigration quota was used up for years in advance, and this tourist-rescue visa had the advantage of a twenty-four-month validity.

To leave Europe, one had to board a ship at one of three ports: Marseille, Lisbon, or Barcelona. Securing a berth in Marseille was a lottery, since so few ships put in and at such irregular intervals, and tickets could only be bought on the black market. Spain allowed only through-travel with no stopping. Portugal wouldn't grant refugee status to emigrants, but permitted them to stay in the country a few months to wait for a ship going overseas. In order to travel to Lisbon, one needed transit visas for both Portugal and Spain. It was often a matter of months before they could be obtained, by which time it was no longer valid in the country one planned to pass through; most visas expired after three months. Then one began applying again, though by now one's residence permit for Marseille had expired and one's meager funds were used up. Crushed in this way between millstones, some became desperate and took their own lives.

One needed an exit visa from France, finally, which the authorities were afraid to issue since they couldn't be sure whom the Gestapo would ask for next. They wanted to know if you had ever written or spoken in public—meaning against National Socialism. All the applicants insisted that all they had done all their lives was buy and sell stockings, or that they were farmers and so uneducated that they'd never read a newspaper. As in many other countries, the French officials did their best to help by accepting these strange stories.

Under the same pressure were those trying to get a rescue visa from Varian Fry and the American consuls, to whom they professed to have participated in the resistance, stood on barricades, and written countless books of research or literature. When Fry was satisfied that the applicant was a politically persecuted intellectual, he cabled Washington and recommended a rescue visa.

In the cafés one often heard the question: "Are you a 'danger'?"

And the typical answer: "No, I'm only 'cabled.'"

I had it easy, I was on the first list put together by the Rescue Committee in Washington.

I had begun drinking heavily in the camps and could no longer stop. I moved about in a rosy mist, terrified of the future. By now our awful and adventuresome existence in France suited me just fine; I knew the rules here, and in New York I wouldn't. Losing everything again, my

professional experience and connections to the theater, my friends, my
home and everything we owned, was too much. There would be another
language to learn, and a living to be made in that language. I didn't want
to leave France and Europe.

"Take a look, son, that's a Kraut!" I heard a woman teaching her little
boy as I walked on the Canébière with Klaus Dohrn. Dohrn had a rosy,
round baby-face, bald with thick glasses. He was an enormous man, blonde
and fat, with a sharp political intelligence and outstanding ability as an
essayist. He belonged to the conservative Catholics. Because he preferred
pleasure to work, letting his insatiable stomach and fine tongue dictate his
decisions, he chose assignments that allowed him to meet at the restaurants of his choice.

But most of the food we could afford hardly deserved to be called food.
Occasionally we would treat ourselves to fish at Pascal. One Friday, Dohrn
and I had the *Spécialité de la Maison*, an ailaulit. The rare enjoyment of the
meal, a gentle spring sun, and a breeze from the Mediterranean had put us
in a good mood. As we stood urinating over a knee-high fence in back of
the restaurant, Dohrn said:

"You can blame all this mess on the miserable French Revolution."

I listened to him calmly and didn't feel the need to spit in his face.
Something must have changed in me, the hard-boiled leftist, and for the
first time I didn't shut my ears to the other side's argument. That a person
who held such opinions was not purely stupid or malicious was a new concept for me. A door opened, and I decided to step through it and see what
was on the other side.

On Fridays, one of the fish stores sold to customers a half-pound of
finger-thin, smoked eels. Every time we went, Dohrn wanted to bring the
eels to a lady friend of his in the neighborhood. But he never got very near
her house with the gift—he always ate it on the way.

After months of waiting in Marseille we finally had the necessary
papers and could go to the train station like normal people. And the train
station itself was once again a normal place for us, and the checkpoints no
longer scared us. We would take the train to Lisbon via Barcelona and from
there embark to America.

Suddenly I got a high fever and was confined to bed. The realization that I had to leave France was too great a shock. I truly loved
this wonderful country, with all of its weaknesses. I had been treated
badly—and worse, unjustly—but that couldn't outweigh the love and
admiration I felt.

I stayed in bed one week, until it was finally clear to me that the structure we had taken so much effort to build was about to fall apart, that my family and I were threatened with the worst. I got up from my bed. We packed the few things we owned in one suitcase and left the Hotel Aumage for Port Bou, to leave France.

FIFTEEN

O n the Spanish border we were asked to open our suitcase and the handbag containing our toiletries. The customs officer was an old, lean, ash-gray man wearing leather gloves despite the heat. He searched the handbag, and, finding nothing that interested him, turned to the suitcase, in which there were 25 packs of cigarettes I was trying to smuggle. I had assumed that our miserable-looking emigrant's baggage wouldn't be searched. The French cigarettes were very cheap since *tabac noir*, grown in France and Algiers, didn't appeal to the German occupying forces.

The suitcase was a treasure trove for the man. He felt inside and found two packs. Cigarettes were expensive in Spain, and the Spanish love black tobacco. The man went into a state of feverish excitement. He emptied the entire contents with trembling hands and turned every piece of clothing inside-out, stacking the cigarettes in a pile to the left. We were standing to his right. Our son Wolfgang stood between the handbag and the suitcase, in front of the growing mountain of cigarettes. After watching for a short time, he slowly and calmly slid a few of the packs into the already searched handbag. The man didn't notice him, he was too busy searching the lining of the suitcase. We couldn't give our son a sign to stop immediately, for this would have caught the man's attention. We watched in agonized fear. We had heard that the Border Control, aware of its indisputable power, could take away an emigrant's papers at any provocation, calling one of the guards massed around the checkpoint to take the victim to a Spanish detention camp.

The man looked up just as Wolfgang shut the handbag. He confiscated the cigarettes left on the table and marked the suitcase with chalk. We took our baggage and crossed the checkpoint into Spain with half of my cigarettes.

Barcelona with its bright lights and display windows amazed us after the wartime blackout of the French cities. We took the train as far as Madrid, arriving on a Sunday morning, and had the rest of the day, till our next train left, to see the magnificent city. We went to a bullfight, so that our son wouldn't be bored, instead of the Prado. The cold-bloodedness, talent, and elegance of the toreador impressed us.

In Lisbon we saw a Portuguese bullfight. It didn't end with the death of the bull, and the *banderilleros* with their barbed hooks weren't followed by the lancers who, in Spanish bullfights, come out on old horses for the bull to gore or slit open with its horns. The Portuguese riders sit on thorough-breds. Their method is not to infuriate the bull with lance-wounds; instead they dance about on their horses in front of the nervous and aggressive animal, and escape its attacks with brilliant stunts. After the riders, a dozen men enter the arena and approach the bull on foot. The closest man runs directly at it and, with a vault, catches its horns and twists its head down while the others help throw it to the ground. The bull is defeated. The men step quickly out of the arena, and a few old cows trot in with bells on their necks. The bull joins them and they leave the arena together. Taught a lesson by its escapades, and wounded by the barbed hooks, the bull is no longer good for fighting and is taken to slaughter.

We were told that the waiting period to sail from Lisbon would be three or four months. An American organization had reserved and paid for our cabin. The agent I spoke to was a German emigrant, who asked whether I was related to the Aufricht of the Theater am Schiffbauerdamm. I identified myself, and he said he would try to find my family a berth within the month. Again I was overcome with a terrible fear of leaving. I hoped the man would be unable to keep his word. I was crushed when he did. It had been four weeks, and we had to leave Europe.

The departure wasn't made easier by our stay in Lisbon. Situated at the southernmost point of Europe, Lisbon has all the beauty of a Mediterranean city together with the cleanliness of Holland. One could sit till dawn at any one of the countless cafés. The refugees could again be seen occupying the terraces of these cafés, exhausting one another with rumors that the entire continent would be Hitler's by morning, and that they were all as good as dead.

Rossio, in Chave d'Ouro, was a popular spot for emigrants. It was there that we often met [Erich] Ollenhauer and [Fritz] Heine, two Social Democrats. They were waiting to join their comrades in England, in order to remain as close to home as possible. They believed that there would be a need, when the war was over, for men educated in socialism. We others found this belief odd, and didn't know that the next few years would prove them right.

The emigrants' panic drew the attention of many small ship companies interested in a profit. We sailed on the *Ciudad de Sevilla*, a freight and pleasure charter with a usual route between the Iberian Peninsula and the Azores or the Canary Islands. A Spanish ship agency had had it renovated for 600 passengers by knocking out the center walls in the hold to create two great halls, one for the men and one for the women, with tight rows of bunks in each. The men's hall also had trestle tables and benches for dining. The air was sticky and hot—there was no ventilation—and the only way onto the deck was by a wooden loft-ladder. Few passengers, however, stayed in the halls; we took our mattresses and lived on deck for the length of the trip, going below only at mealtimes. Some old passengers, too weak to live outside, remained dozing and puking in the bunks, wishing to God they were off the ship. The few cabins were sold at exorbitant prices. The rest of us could barely afford our steerage tickets at $350-400 a person.

The passengers were mostly Polish Jews who had escaped to Belgium and Holland and had remained entirely unassimilated. They wore caftans, long black smocks of cotton—of silk if they were wealthy. Several were diamond merchants who carried their fortune of precious stones in pouches strapped to their bodies. In the same way, my wife had hidden our fortune of $60 in a neck pouch under her dress.

At the port of Lisbon there were folding deck chairs for 24 escudos, the equivalent of a dollar. These deck chairs were our most useful possession, by day and by night, during our three weeks at sea. I spent many hours in my chair next to [Arkadi] Maslow, the early Soviet communist and long-time companion of Ruth Fischer, former General Secretary of the German Communist Party. They had remained unmarried for ideological reasons. In 1926 they had fallen out with Stalin and were expelled from the Party. Fischer, who had many passports, managed to get into the USA. She lived in New York. Maslow only had a visa for Cuba, where our ship made a stop. He spoke volubly and engagingly, and I learned a lot from him about internal matters of the Communist Party. I also learned that in party circles I was referred to as the "Pink Puppy A." because of my theater's leftist outlook.

Maslow was a tall, fat man with an apoplectic color to his face. He ate second and third servings of the ship's food that the rest of us couldn't stomach. We lived on coffee and bread, of which there was an endless supply. Maslow moved about very little during the journey and became so fat by the second week that his deck chair broke under him. He had to squat on his mattress the rest of the way to Cuba.

Both he and Fischer began their lives abroad in extreme poverty. When Fischer managed to send him a few dollars from New York, he went first on an eating spree, and then to a brothel in Havana. There he collapsed dead. The prostitutes, who didn't want any trouble with the police, left the corpse on the street. The autopsy indicated that excessive eating, exacerbated by the tropical heat, had caused a stroke. Fischer was certain that he had been poisoned by the Soviet Secret Service.

My heart became heavier with every day that brought me closer to New York and further away from France. The unscalable wall of a new language loomed closer and closer, and I didn't like the sound of English. In truth, my English has remained inadequate to this day.

When the journey was over, we packed our few things in the suitcase, which by this time had acquired a very well-traveled look. I changed out of my swimming trunks and into the only suit I owned. My wife took our $60 out of the purse which she hid on her body and gave a few precious green bills to me and our son. Then we went on deck to see the Statue of Liberty. We sailed slowly in the oppressive heat and yellow haze past the docks. The ship stopped briefly, and officials from the Immigration and Health Departments came on board while two tugboats hitched themselves to the *Ciudad de Sevilla*; then we continued into the harbor.

Immigrants whose papers were incomplete or who seemed in any way dubious to the officials were sent to Ellis Island, at the entrance to New York Harbor, where they stayed until their case was clarified. They were allowed phone calls to friends, relatives or organizations in the city who could vouch for their identities.

My friend Dr. Herrmann Borchardt was sent to Ellis Island. He phoned the painter George Grosz, and Grosz came with his sponsor, Mr. Cohn, the matzah and noodle king. Cohn vouched for Borchardt and showed his own income tax returns by way of identification. According to Borchardt, the immigration officials knelt down when they saw Cohn's figures. They let Borchardt go at once.

CHAPTER

S I X T E E N

T he Statue of Liberty had been invisible to me in the yellow haze.
I had also been unable to admire the famous city skyline, the silhouetted skyscrapers, because we had docked not in Manhattan but at
a narrow, dirty pier in Brooklyn. The ship moved very slowly, almost
standing still. I bent over the railing and saw a stream of used condoms
float by in the brackish water. Then we halted. On the pier below us
stood the theater critic of the Berlin *Montag Morgen*, Julius Bab, his
long black beard lifting in the wind. I sat down on my suitcase. There
was no going back. Emissaries from charity organizations came on
board and offered lodging to passengers without money or a place to
stay. After long formalities with the immigration officials, we stepped
off the boat and into a taxi.

We drove through Brooklyn and over the endless, gloomy Brooklyn
Bridge, oppressive to me with its thousands of tons of iron. Berlin's
Kantstraße may not have been the height of beauty, nor certainly the sooty
streets of industrial Upper Silesia, but the houses here, put up hastily for
a quick profit, with their exposed fire escapes attached to the façades and
shapeless rooftop water tanks, were of a penetrating ugliness. The wide, flat
faces of pedestrians, without the nuance of shadow and seeming to have
no secret hidden behind them, were alien to me. All of these impressions
came to me through the sticky, foul-smelling air and were altogether too
much to take; I covered my eyes. It became clear later, through conversations with others, that the immigrants who had come directly from Berlin
had an easier time adjusting to New York than those accustomed to the
architectural harmony of Paris and to French living.

Our taxi let us off on upper Broadway in front of a small hotel. I stepped onto the street and a man pushed a printed flier into my hand. It was June 1941. Since I didn't understand a word of English—my high school studies had been in Latin, Greek, and French as a minor—I asked our friends who met us at the ship to translate. It was a flier signed and distributed by the members of the Communist Party of America, calling upon the American government to stop supporting capitalistic England in the war against Germany, which at that time was an ally of Russia. This was a part of reality I hadn't seen. The two internment camps, our year of hiding in the mountains, the months in Marseille, four weeks in Portugal and three on the ocean had all but cut us off from the political changes.

We moved into two small hotel rooms with little to unpack. We had often been without money before; now for the first time we were actually poor. I went to look for a relief organization.

Robert Vambery's father, a law professor with an international reputation, visited us at the hotel. He phoned the president of a committee, who agreed to meet with us. The taxi fare was beyond our means; we took the IRT, one of four subway lines and one of the oldest, to a side street off of Times Square. The big, filthy, steel subway cars without shock absorbers rattled so loudly on their springs that no one could speak a word.

The president greeted us warmly. She gave us the name and address of a Mrs. Polski, our benefactress from this point on. "Good luck," she said at the door, as everyone kept saying during our first days. Everyone, beginning with the taxi driver at the dock, smiled and was happy for us, for everything we would see, and for our great luck to be living in "God's own country."

Mrs. Polski, a good-looking younger woman born in the States, was of Polish descent and could speak Yiddish, which allowed us to communicate. She didn't treat us as relief seekers but as good acquaintances or distant relatives deserving the best advice.

"You need a two-bedroom apartment with furniture, a kitchen and a bathroom. Let's say ten dollars a week; food for three people . . ." she began writing in her notebook, "laundry, soap and cleaning things, razors, you smoke cigarettes, movies once a week . . ." She didn't leave out a thing. In a few minutes she had a long list.

"You'll get a check for 87 dollars from us every fourteen days."

In those days, a pound of butter cost 31 cents, a dozen eggs 30 cents, a liter of milk 10 cents. "We'll send the first check tomorrow. Do you need any money today?" We said no. "Or anything else in particular?" My wife said she would love to have an electric iron—all of her clothes were creased. Mrs. Polski left the room for a minute and came back with a check for seven dollars.

"Please try not to change your profession for the time being. You'll get the checks as long as they're necessary, and if you have extra expenses please let me know. Good luck!"

The woman couldn't have been nicer. Nevertheless it was a miserable experience for me. I sweated so heavily—this also had to do with the humid heat—that my suit was wet on the outside.

It was easy to find a furnished apartment. A third of the apartments in New York, furnished or unfurnished, had stood empty since the 1929 Depression; people had moved closer together to save money. Only after America entered the war did people start earning more money and spreading out again.

We found an apartment on 107th Street with a view of Riverside Drive and the Hudson. We were happy to see trees from the window. I remember my first English teacher asking me, "Why does every German emigrant need to see a tree from his window?" Unfortunately this apartment was $12 a week, and exceeded our budget.

Kurt Weill visited us the first day in our new apartment. He took me to see his musical, *Lady in the Dark*, which was sold out for months. It was his financial breakthrough in America. I was awed by his Buick Cabriolet, its convertible roof that could be opened and closed by a button. He invited me to see his new house in the city on the following week, when Lenya would be done moving in.

We stood near the back of the theater, under the balconies. I couldn't follow much of the action, and kept thinking about whether I should ask him for money—I knew I would have to do so at some point. Despite my dilemma I could see that the show's success was well deserved; both music and production were outstanding.

We left after an hour, and Weill drove me home. He had already said "Good Luck!" and was driving off when I finally managed to shout out: "I'm going to need a little money!"

"Of course!" he shouted back, "I'll send you a check tomorrow." The check was good for 100 dollars. I found it a bit meager, but Vambery explained to me that in America money is neither asked for nor given—in times of financial difficulty one gets a job, any kind of job, and stays with it until a way out becomes visible. Even the lowest kinds of work are not looked down on, and every dollar earned is respected. I saw pictures in the newspapers of a senator who had taken over his son's six o'clock newspaper route when the boy was sick; the father wanted to make sure that the job wouldn't be given away. The wealthy made contributions, for tax purposes, not to private enterprises but to public charity organizations established to protect those unable to work.

I still owned no clothes besides what I was wearing. At a Macy's Department Store I bought two pairs of pants and a flannel suit for $27. The same suit today would cost more than four times that amount.

At the turn of the century over 100,000 Jews had come from Eastern Europe to America every year. They had no money, spoke no English, and were intimidated by all that they saw. No one helped them. They were hard-working, though, and able to get by with little—they had always been desperately poor. They found work with their countrymen, earlier immigrants who were already established in New York. In the basements of houses in the Bronx and in Brooklyn they were given a bed and made to sew from morning to late evening, by hand or with a machine. Having a place to sleep, food, and a few dollars a week—and more than anything else rituals—seemed to them a paradise. Here they weren't persecuted, even the police left them alone, and there was no military service. The most industrious of them didn't care a bit about the world outside, but saved year after year until they had enough money to rent out their own basement and exploit newer immigrants. There was no need to learn English, since both employer and employee spoke the mother tongue, Yiddish.

These small businesses were called "sweatshops" because of all the sweat that was poured out in them, especially during the hot season. It was from such beginnings that the textile and clothing company Needle and Thread grew to what it is today. Despite larger commercial and wholesale companies, the sweatshop has not disappeared. The emigration from Eastern Europe has ended, but the old, the disabled, the Puerto Ricans, and the blacks still sit day after day sewing the same button in place.

We had a consistent weekly shortfall of twelve dollars. School hadn't begun yet for Wolfgang, and he went to look for work at a sweatshop. He was put in front of a pile of zippers that had been torn out of old clothes, and told to separate them from what was left of the fabric. The owner watched him work for several hours, then asked him for his name.

"Jack!"

"Jack, here's money for today. You can start tomorrow."

Wolfgang came home and told us: "I can give you the 12 dollars you need, I earn 13 dollars a week."

The next day he brought home a large, heavy packet full of uncleaned zippers. The contractual forty hours a week with minimum wage were enforced, but these rules were evaded. The "sweaters" had to put in extra hours at home without compensation and deliver the fruit of their labors the next morning. My wife helped Wolfgang with the work at home. The hot, humid nights didn't let us sleep.

In cramped rooms, emigres of divergent political views tried to express their irritation about the foreign country in which they found themselves. Each person tried to speak as much as possible, to attack and prove as many people wrong as possible. It sounded something like this:

"The peace of the oceans is in danger! The Americans have to enter the war!"

"They would never be that stupid. No, they'll do what's best for them and send weapons—they'll supply both sides."

"You believe that, you bum?"

"I myself have no faith in the moral clarity of the West. We Germans, knee-deep in the muck of centuries . . ." lectured a professor from the New School of Social Research, the stronghold of leftist emigrant lecturers.

"Idiot!" another couldn't keep from saying.

"Today is the birthday of Queen Luise," school teacher Dr. Borchardt remarked at his table.

"You dare to throw that at me!" shouted Eugen Fuchs and walked out. He was a highly respected scholar of Marx, and received a small pension from an American labor union.

From one corner of the room, a fat man with a small mouth lashed out: "If you bring God into it, I'm leaving the room."

Another provoked: "The poor feel better when you take the shirt off their backs!"

"If I had a piece of shit in my hand, I'd rub it in your face!" his adversary countered.

Two Hungarians discussed their wardrobe in another corner. The wholesale clothing industry, which had its center in New York, donated used and outmoded stock to goodwill societies where emigrants could clothe themselves free of charge.

"Where did you get your pants?"

"At the Self-Help."

"Not bad. But they have nicer shirts in the basement of Temple Emanuel."

"You want to eat as much as you can? Go to the Fulton Street fish market at seven in the morning, they'll give you a broom, you help them clean up. After twenty minutes of work they invite you in for a coffee, and you can have bread, as much you want. Fresh rolls and butter. Then you go to the Franciscans on 31st Street. At ten o'clock a monk comes out with a basket and gives everyone a package with two salami sandwiches and an apple. He never looks at you. For lunch you can go to the Quakers or the Salvation Army . . ."

"Are we talking about food or politics here?" someone interrupted sharply.

"Both!" several replied.

"Then we're leaving!" The Robespierre cohort departed, leaving the room to the Dantonists.

Ruth Fischer, former General Secretary of the German Communist Party, repeated the usual admonition: "Only a true Socialist movement will save us from each other." She was accompanied by two Polish Trotskyites, both of them with beards trimmed like Trotsky's. They were named Shumski and Sholzki, and I couldn't tell them apart. They often mentioned that they were in New York because it was here that they could best keep an eye on international affairs.

Eventually the various opinions crystallized into more stable factions, and the discussions became more serious and intelligent.

As today, there was left and right. President Roosevelt had stated his position as ". . . a little left of the center." The American intellectuals stood almost without exception on the extreme left, as did many emigrants. The German-language newspaper of the emigrants, *Der Aufbau*, read by all those whose English still needed practice, grew from a club newsletter to a richly supplemented weekly edition under the experienced and talented Chief Editor of Berlin's Ullstein Press, Manfred George. Contributors to *Der Aufbau* observed and judged with two left eyes, the perspective of the twenties.

I began to wonder why so many people held on to an ideology that had so weakened Europe and allowed its criminals to celebrate repeated victories. Advisors to President Roosevelt and his wife, among them exiles of various countries, bear the responsibility of a grievous error. They recommended a peace to the White House that allowed the broken Russia to rise to a second world power.

Many like us, who were able to save their lives after the collapse of France by coming to America, had difficulty finding a job. We had not yet established contact with other Americans of European background—their values were different from ours. "$50,000 Composer Arrives in New York" ran the headline of a newspaper interview: the annual income as a measure of excellence.

We held out against the country that showed us only kindness. For myself and others, this second emigration was too much; we weren't equal to the challenge.

I don't have the talent for languages that my barber in Paris had, a Yugoslavian who conversed effortlessly with a number of his customers in their native tongues. Approaching English for the first time, I found myself unable to get a firm hold of its phonetics. My profession requires a discerning ear for nuances of the written and spoken word; I manage the commercial side only insofar as it is a necessary complement to the artistic. I felt I could produce a show on Broadway despite the material difficulties, but I had grave doubts about working in English. In any case, no agent was going to trust a newcomer with promising work by an American. I began looking among the German writers. Weill brought me Hans Herrmann Borchardt.

Borchardt, who couldn't stand the heat and was trying to preserve his only suit, stayed at home in his underpants during the day. New York's apartments are overheated in the winter, and in summer the humidity is inescapable. Borchardt avoided the sun. He went swimming only if the pool had a shaded area, and covered the short distance to the diving board with a quick step. He had a peculiar dislike for trees. Upper Broadway between 96th and 110th Street, a thronging, dirty, storefront-lined strip of the thirty-mile-long boulevard, was for him the most beautiful place in the world. He was one of the best-read and politically far-sighted people I've ever met. When the war neared its end, he wrote daily letters to the Congresswoman Claire Booth Luce (married to Henry Luce, editor of *Time* and *Life*) and to various members of the Senate.

The Russian forces pressed steadily westward. General Patton had advanced almost as far as Pilsen before he was ordered back. Borchardt warned that every territory the West allowed Russia to occupy now was as good as a permanent loss. He warned about the dangers of the "unconditional surrender." Several years later, as Russian postwar politics were taking shape, Claire Booth Luce admitted that Borchardt had been right.

Borchardt had been a prisoner at Buchenwald and Dachau, and had escaped to America with a crushed hand and almost no hearing. His family, with two sons and a daughter, lived with very limited means. When we met in the evenings, he always came with seven cents he had gotten from his wife, who oversaw the family funds. He paid two cents for the *Daily News* and five cents for a cup of coffee at the Stanley Cafeteria, where customers could sit undisturbed in the gloom for two to three hours.

"Death has knocked at my door," he wrote me in Paris, in 1946 after his first stroke, "but it's not yet my turn. When you're back in New York I'll invite you to Bickford: toast with butter, baked plums and a cup of coffee!"

These were the five-cent items on the menu. The man survived four subsequent strokes in good spirits and died at sixty.

Borchardt wrote his first play, *The Germersheim Murder*, during his time as schoolmaster at the Neukölln High School in Berlin. Brecht, who knew him better than I, brought me a copy of the script. I would have liked to stage it, but the cast was too large and the set too expensive, and I could see that it had little chance of success with the public.

In America Borchardt wrote three plays that were never produced, and, because he needed the money, one screenplay of 1,700 pages. Franz Werfel recommended this valuable literary work as a novel, along with the foreword he had written for it, to Simon and Schuster of New York. The translation was published as *The Conspiracy of the Carpenters*. It had a considerable success in the press, but sold hardly any copies. Shortened to about 500 pages, it had become hard to understand.

I tried to mount a production of his play *The Halberstadt Brothers* on Broadway. It was an anti-Nazi piece about a German general who tries to save people from the Gestapo. The cost of the production was $28,000—today the figure would be well over $100,000. I found a wealthy French emigrant who could read German. The man said to me: "This play will be a success! My instincts are never wrong." He put up half of the necessary sum, and I went about raising the rest.

I was turned away from every door with disgust. It seemed that during the war Americans refused—perhaps justifiably—to make distinctions between one German uniform and another. Demoralized by my failure in this foreign city, and by our financial distress, I abandoned my efforts.

My wife took a position in the Office of War Information, established by the government for the length of the war. Wolfgang worked as a movie usher on weekends and finished high school. And we finally heard from our son Heinz, who was still in the English army. We were relieved to hear from him, but took the opportunity to start worrying anew.

Wolfgang was drafted. After passing through the hands of several doctors and hearing the last one confirm his unfitness for duty ("Mother will be happy!") he protested: "I'm not happy, I wanted to be a soldier!" The younger generation of emigrants were ambivalent about their mixed background; they had no memory of Germany, and they became American citizens three months after they were drafted.

"You can't have everything," the doctor answered.

We had no way to pay for Wolfgang's continued studies. Once out of high school, he immediately found a position in a recording studio at

Schirmer Music. Later he switched to NBC and became a producer and writer in the International Department. From that time on we had no financial worries. I took walks in Riverside Park, prepared our meals, met with friends at a forsaken cafeteria on 57th Street.

Once, at one of the more bustling cafeterias, I took out a typewritten letter and began reading it to someone at the table. The manager came out and said: "Sir, this is a restaurant, not an office!" There are no proper coffee houses or pastry shops in New York; Americans don't have time for that kind of leisure. Most of them hurry home after business hours to a bath or a shower, at six they have a drink, and then the main meal begins. With the upper class, the drinking lasts longer and the eating starts later.

I had to forego my customary walks on days of intense heat, when the humidity was at 100% and the temperature at 90 degrees and higher. I couldn't go out even at night. The evenings and nights do not cool the city; often the temperature keeps rising after dark. I saw people spending the night in the park on blankets they had brought out of their stifling apartments. Today it's too dangerous to spend the night outdoors, and most people have air conditioning in at least one room. All of the shops and restaurants are air conditioned.

My wife and I were sitting in a cafeteria at 1:00 in the morning when a group of men walked in. Each ordered a cup of coffee and a piece of cake. They were too exhausted to take off their hats, and sweat ran down their pale gray faces. They sat stiffly, as though frozen, until gradually the cool dry air thawed them, the color came back to their faces, and they took off their hats and began to drink, eat, and talk with one another.

The step from an air-conditioned room onto a New York street in summer feels a lot like being wrapped in a hot washcloth; one is instantly drenched. The irritation and exhaustion experienced on a given day is called "discomfort" by New Yorkers, and a special scale is used in weather reports to measure degrees of this discomfort.

Instead of my strolls, Wolfgang and I became members of the YMCA, the Young Men's Christian Association. The Jewish equivalent is the YMHA, the Young Men's Hebrew Association. The YMCA had several weight-training rooms, playing courts, a sauna, and a huge swimming pool. The YMHA sports facilities were stunted, although they had an impressive library and a beautiful concert hall. Since we wanted exercise, not an education, we chose the YMCA. It took great effort to put on sweatpants and a sweatshirt in the heat of the day, but we were rewarded with the swimming pool's cool water and the showers.

We tried to visit the place during its less busy hours, and found two lockers in the dressing room surrounded by empty ones. We soon had neighbors on both sides. The same thing happened in the showers. The shower rooms were empty when we arrived, but a group formed around us quickly and flung its dirty suds everywhere. This is the extent to which people go to find neighbors and a communal sense.

Yorkville, in New York, is the city's old German-American enclave. They have a "Mozartstübl" and a Café Hindenburg. At the Café Geiger, a standing violinist plays the Blue Danube, accompanied by a pianist. German restaurants and shops sell German dishes, German groceries, German baking ingredients and German wines. Over 100 clubs sing German Lieder, play skittles, and organize tours to "the old homeland."

The strongest, most insular of these communities—they existed also in Chicago, Milwaukee, and other cities—were proud of Hitler's great victories and fans of National Socialism. Their leaders were [Fritz] Kuhn and [George] Viereck. They formed SA-units and trained in brown uniforms. The United States' entrance into the war put an end to this specter; people were careful to show that they were upstanding democrats. I had an idea for how I might be useful in the war effort. There were eight radio stations that broadcast in German, through which the politically uninformed could be reached and perhaps enlightened. I saw that as my task.

I came up with the title of a radio play series, "The Schulzes in Yorkville," and commissioned the exiled dramatist Peter Martin Lampel to write some episodes for me. Members of the Schulz family, pro-Nazi and anti-Nazi, voice their conflicting opinions on democracy and dictatorship, or as they call it, the "new" and the "old" homeland. The program featured music and political commentary by prominent emigrants, among them Thomas Mann, Walter Mehring, Franz Werfel, Kurt Weill, Professor [Paul] Tillich, and Fritz von Unruh. With Manfred George's help, I acquired an office and a connection to Washington.

Our program, "We Fight Back," had been running for several months when I discovered in a listeners' poll that Germans turned off their radios whenever it was announced. Our intended audience was proud of Hitler's successes; they didn't want to listen to our defeatist opinions. It was the last time I tried to assume the role of enlightener. My employers at the Office of Strategic Service discontinued the show at the end of the year, deciding that propaganda was needed abroad and no longer at home.

For eleven months of the year we looked forward to our vacation in Maine. We boarded a Greyhound bus in the evening (or a sleeper car when we could afford it), wracked by the heat of August, and were in Maine the next morning, 400 miles away. All of our troubles were forgotten. The air is cool, dry, and spiced by forests that border the largest woodland in the world, the Canadian. The summer in Maine, and with it the flowering season, is too short to support an agricultural lifestyle. The inhabitants are foresters and fishers on the innumerable lakes, and Maine lobsters are the best in the world.

With the help of friends who owned a house in Wiscasset we found a cabin in the middle of a hilly woodland, on Damariscotta Lake. The cabin was right on the water. It was a ten-minute climb to the nearest property, a weathered gray farmhouse belonging to the widow Linscott. The farm itself, like so many in Maine, had proved unprofitable and long been out of use. She rented us the cabin for $20 a week, along with firewood and a rowboat.

Mrs. Linscott was small and bent with age, and, as it seemed, grown into the fabric of her natural environment. When she moved around outside, one had to look closely to see her. As a younger woman she had regularly covered the seven miles to the town of Damariscotta with a horse team. Now she steered the way slowly and bravely in her old car. In the loneliness of winter, cut off from the road for weeks at a time, she kept informed by listening to the radio, and if the weather permitted, went down to the road in snowshoes to pick up the newspaper. We enjoyed the conversations with her and looked forward to seeing her every year.

The Maine nights were cold, and the cabin had to be heated. There was no electric light, gas, or water, and the outhouse was some distance off in the woods. We burned petroleum lamps and cooked on kerosene burners. We used the boat to reach a general store several miles away on the lake, and, every three days, to transport the 100-pound block of ice for our icebox. These blocks were cut out of the lake in winter and kept underground, lined with sawdust. Later we bought an outboard motor and no longer had to row the long stretches. Our water source was fifteen minutes away by foot, a spring in the undergrowth. It was ice cold and had a slightly bitter taste—a wonderful drink.

Every morning, a turtle's head peered out of the clear lake water. When we swam out to it, it waited for a moment before ducking under, then emerged again further away. We saw this turtle every summer. At midday a deer often stepped out of the woods near the cabin to cross our neck of the lake. The solitude and quiet were absolute, there were no songbirds in the trees, only an occasional hummingbird buzzed by, smaller and faster than the large dragonflies.

Unfortunately there were no paths into the woods. The trees here are not planted and trimmed as they are in Europe, and they grow thick and varied out of the wild underbrush. The telegraph poles made from these trunks are as short and gnarled as when they were trees. When a forest reaches a certain age it is bought by a timber company and the usable trees are felled. A new forest grows out of the brush and dead roots. Here and there a few ancient giants are left standing to provide seeds for new growth.

We took our walks on the forest roads. Hardly a car passed without stopping to ask: "Do you need any help?" It was hard to explain to people that we didn't have a flat, but were walking for the pleasure of it.

One summer, my son got sick. High fever and shivers alternated with sharp drops in temperature. The doctor couldn't diagnose the illness, and we brought Wolfgang to a hospital near Damariscotta. It was a three-hour walk to visit him there. The news of our situation spread quickly among our neighbors, and even those we didn't know came to help. They drove us to the hospital in the morning and picked us up in the afternoon. We found cooked food in the kitchen, supplies of fresh water, ice in the icebox and new wood in the fireplace. These neighbors didn't show their faces once Wolfgang had come back from the hospital—they didn't want any thanks. Thus, in a moment of need, we had our first encounter with the uncommon generosity of Americans.

The summers in Maine did much to set our lives right.

Returning to the haze of New York, I didn't think I would live through a single night. We arrived at Central Station around midnight. I stood apathetically with my baggage ticket—it didn't matter to me how long I waited—while my wife and son dozed on a bench. I observed a small older man who was waiting for help with his luggage, and who wore the same washed-out expression as me. Finally the porter came. The huge black man lifted the old-fashioned trunk, which must have exceeded the permissible size, onto his shoulders. It must also have exceeded the weight limit. When he reached the counter where he supposed to put it down, he stopped for a moment, his eyes burning with anger, then aimed and threw the trunk at the iron edge of the counter . . . There was a crash, and the trunk burst open. The small man barely changed his expression, only looked a little sad, and the porter stood apathetically in front of him. Both were too exhausted to play-out the affair with screams, witnesses, and police. The negro received a dollar, and the small man found another porter to help him.

One afternoon, in front of the Public Library on 42nd Street, I saw a man coming toward me, a Berlin journalist whom I hadn't seen for years. I faltered for a moment; so did he, and we continued past each other with a glassy look. I thought, as I'm sure he did: why the effort of stopping and asking "how are you, where do you live and what's your telephone number?" We dragged past each other sweating and without a word.

I descended the steps to the IRT subway station. It was rush hour, and the wide passageways swarmed with commuters hurrying home with only one thought on their minds: to get under their showers. On the platform stood an impenetrable human wall. The trains came in and left one after the other, and with every arrival the crowd moved a little; for every two or three passengers getting out, hundreds got in. The cars were filled to bursting. The automatic doors with their thick rubber edges tried in vain to close. Muscular black men crammed the half-boarded passengers in and pushed the others back, the doors slid shut, and the train squeaked forward to be replaced by another one right behind it. Inside, the discomfort was so great that I spent the ride in a state of semi-consciousness and sometimes missed my station.

Time was running through my fingers. I spent a great part of my day indulging remorseful thoughts. I wanted to return to Europe, most of all to France. My memory of Germany was wiped out by the shame of what had made me leave, and by the shame and revulsion over what was happening in my birthplace.

Weill was always on the lookout for material that could be used in a musical. A cantor's son, Weill himself was an atheist, but in his conscience a Jew. I suggested the novel *Job* by Joseph Roth, but Weill felt that Job's miraculous recovery from his malady would be implausible to an American audience. A pity! He could have written the music for this great work.

My suggestion that he use *The Good Soldier Schweik*, by Jaroslav Hasek, as a model for a libretto appealed to him immediately. The New York Representatives of the Czech Government in Exile granted me the theatrical rights on the condition that Weill compose the music and Brecht write the adaptation. Brecht agreed to begin the work at once. I met with both of them in the office of Weill's lawyer, a theater specialist, and we reviewed a contract as detailed as a book, which not one of us could read or understand. We signed, and I went on the search for money.

Weill, who had experience in American "producing," estimated that I would need $85,000. I was able to raise the sum in a short time from well-to-do emigrants who had all read Hasek, and who remembered the Brecht-Weill-Aufricht *Threepenny Opera* combination.

Brecht delivered us the script in six weeks. It was a disaster. He had copied pages of dialogue out of the Schweik volumes and invented a new ending: Schweik meets Hitler on the snowy fields of Russia and the two have a conversation. It was original in concept but weak in execution. Weill declined to write the music, and I let the project fall.

Brecht had fled from Denmark through Sweden and Russia, without stopping, on his way to America. He lived with his wife, children, and very little money in Santa Monica, near Los Angeles, in a bungalow which he rented furnished for $50 a month. When he'd visited New York, he'd stayed with a friend, Ruth Berlau, on 57th Street. She had a job in the Office of War Information, and could afford to take him in. He and Feuchtwanger had written a play based on Feuchtwanger's novel, *The Visions of Simone Machard*. He gave it to me and asked me to pass it on to Borchardt when I'd read it. Borchardt and I were embarrassed by the play. It was unequivocally lousy. We went to Brecht together, having agreed that our critical response would be no more than two words: "trash can." Brecht laid it aside without a word. Feuchtwanger sold the film rights to *Simone* to Metro Goldwyn Mayer, and Brecht's money problems were taken care of. The film was never made.

I went back to my daily walks and exercise at the YMCA, prepared our meals, read a lot, and in the evenings met my friends Borchardt and Vambery. Vambery taught directing at the Brander Matthews Theater of Columbia University. From there he was called to work for the Office of War Information, where he was furious to discover that his department was making communist rather than American propaganda. Others who made this discovery were afraid of losing their jobs, and kept quiet. Vambery and his boss, an American by birth, were determined to expose the whole thing. I told him that he was only doing himself a disservice. He didn't give in. He was fired and his boss transferred to Washington. Here and elsewhere, the seeds were scattered that would later sprout the hysteria of McCarthyism.

Ruth Fischer had come into fame and money. Her political career in America began when Harvard University requested that she write a history of German Communism. After the book came out she was invited to every conservative political salon in Washington and was considered an anti-bolshevist sensation. She recounted stormy debates with Stalin, who had forced her to remain in Moscow for months and tried to corrupt her with handsome young officers. Her audience was thrilled, and liked to think that she kept a bomb hidden under her dress for all occasions. She railed exclusively against the Stalinists, not the communists, and her listeners never knew the difference.

Fischer was of above-average intelligence, within a worldview narrowed by Marxist thinking. She was witty, curious, and engaging. In her opinion, Borchardt, Dohrn, [Friedrich] Torberg, [Hans] Sahl, [Walter] Mehring, and I were political idiots. We were wined and dined in order that the great Comrade Fischer would be surrounded by people who could keep her entertained. Never were we invited together with her Trotskyite friends and followers. I can remember only once meeting with a confidant of hers; he sat alone at the furthest barstool and didn't understand how we could laugh at all of the sacred cows, and how comrade Fischer could be amused by our jibes. I watched him with curiosity. After half an hour, visibly overcome with disgust, Adolf, long-nosed, skinny, and wide-eyed, stood up and left without saying goodbye.

Fischer told us about her article in progress, "Bert Brecht, The Minstrel of the GPU," the Soviet Secret Police. She let me read it. The article was about Brecht's *The Decision*, written five years before the Moscow Trials, in which he prophesied, not denouncing but approving as necessary, their abominations. Fischer was of course justified in her position that she ought not, in blind loyalty to Brecht, expose her young students to his seductions. But my sympathies for him made it difficult to stand by while evidence was brought out that could result in his wartime deportation. I wondered how I could prevent the article's appearance. There was no talking Fischer out of it, she was too proud of her discovery.

I went to Brecht and suggested that he invite her for dinner. She didn't know her victim personally, and I hoped that she would be too curious to pass up the opportunity. A date was set, and one evening we climbed the four flights of steps to his front door. Fischer gasped for breath—she was monstrously fat and had heart trouble.

The evening began pleasantly enough (Ruth Berlau served scrambled eggs), until Fischer launched her attack: "Brecht, you with your grade-school politics began to take interest in the Party just as soon as Stalin had begun poisoning it." In normal circumstances, Brecht would have tried to out-yell her, or would simply have thrown her out. But here in America he was on the wrong horse, and she was on the right one. Brecht answered cordially, addressed her as "comrade" and tried to find the mutual proletarian bridge between them. Poor Berlau couldn't stand the tension and disappeared into the kitchen, returning with more scrambled eggs which no one noticed. By three in the morning, the hatred of the two for each other's heresies had reached such a pitch that I suggested we leave.

The article was published, and Brecht often said: "That fat pig is going to get shot. You don't settle ideological differences between comrades by bringing them to the police." Later, when she told the FBI that her brother, Gerhard Eisler, today a high functionary in East Berlin, was a communist agent, and her picture appeared in *Life*, Brecht said: "The rat must be drowned!"

Driving through the Bowery, one could turn onto a side street shortly before Chinatown and come to a large theater with over 1,200 seats in it. This was the Chinese Theater. The actors began at seven o'clock and played till midnight. Admission was 35 cents. During the five-hour performances, played without intermission, the sets were struck and rebuilt on stage. There was no curtain. The amphitheater remained lit and the audience, mostly Chinese, came and went. The four- to five-piece orchestra sat in full view on the left of the stage. We went several times; sometimes we were lucky and saw fascinating dances or heard songs to strange music. Sometimes the long incomprehensible dialogues wearied us.

Brecht came along with us once and was so interested that for a time he went every day. Through Ruth Fischer at the Office of War Information, he made the acquaintance of a Chinese man who went with him as an interpreter. Apparently he also brought his later house composer Paul Dessau to several of these performances.

In the early evening hours of Sunday a gray bell of heat and moisture descended over the city. I was walking on Amsterdam Avenue, where the funeral parlors alternated with bars and cluttered, dusty little shops. The identical four-story Brownstone houses were glazed with a sticky layer of soot. In the apartments lived large Irish families and new Puerto Rican immigrants. Part of this neighborhood has since been torn down and replanted with newer rows of identical living complexes. Millions of cockroaches and bedbugs must have died in the transformation.

If one lived near Columbia University, one way to get depressed was to walk down Amsterdam and the even poorer Columbus Avenue; another way was to stroll through the parks on the Hudson near 180th Street. Unemployed emigrants sat and stared on the benches, still in their German suits and old-fashioned hats, too tired, in the heat, to speak to each other. They couldn't figure out where they had landed. Their happiness was elsewhere, or too expensive for them to afford. Their children were assimilated, the grandchildren no longer spoke their language. But some of them did survive; I saw them later in Berlin, contented in the cafés around Olivaer Platz.

I passed into the gray squalor of Amsterdam Avenue and suddenly stopped, amazed. On a crate propped against the curb was a new bundle of the *Daily News*, on its front page in thick capitals: MUSSOLINI FIRED.

I bought a copy and hurried home with it. My wife was already in front of the radio, and we made what we could of sundry details. The Italian King had ordered Marshall Badoglio to arrest Mussolini. It was the 23rd of July, 1943, and Mussolini was deposed.

For ten years I had been having the same dream: I lose my way and somehow end up in Germany, and the Gestapo arrest me. I would wake up screaming. Now the tremendous tension stored up in me began to dissipate. It was the beginning of the end. All threats, all misery and misfortune were small now compared to the prospect of a victorious outcome to the war.

But it was still twenty months before the Reich's bestiary would be wiped out. In June of 1944 the Allies landed on the coast of Normandy. By October their troops were in Aachen, and by April of 1945 they had reached the Elbe. Hitler committed suicide and the Russians took Berlin. On May 7th the unconditional surrender was signed in Reims.

The image I had of Germany was of a mountain of waste. My thirty murdered family members, my family's expulsion, and my devastated existence all lay in this waste heap. Germany no longer existed for me. My hate was extinguished.

On the streets of New York newspaper sellers cried out the end of the war. I got onto a Number 4 bus with Wolfgang at 5th Avenue and we climbed to the upper deck. The bus drove along the Hudson. It was one of the few clear, bright days I had seen. The water of the river looked like water instead of lead, the sky was blue and transparent. We breathed out, relieved that our Heinz was no longer in danger. No more bombs, no more dead and wounded, no more tortures, and the human slaughterhouses, the vastness of which we couldn't have guessed, had ceased operations.

I should have been happy on this doubly beautiful day. The train of history was on the right rails again. But I couldn't get on, I had no ticket. I didn't want to live in America, and to start again in France without a place to live and without money seemed hopeless. And Germany was no longer on my map. I sat on the bus like a bankrupt. The day that I had so fervently awaited now forced me to make a decision.

Many emigrants got work as "re-educators" in film and theater, and returned to occupied Germany in American uniforms. I shuddered at the thought of leading such a double existence.

The Office of War Information was dissolved after the war, and the emigrants lost their jobs. My wife became joint-owner of a health studio in New Jersey. We had no material worries. I let myself be carried along by the passing time. In 1946, the advertising agency MacCann-Erickson offered my son Wolfgang a half-year in Paris to produce a radio show for Coca-Cola. He decided to take a vacation from NBC, and accepted the position.

A life-line was thrown to me. We came up with the money for my ticket. I wasn't a foreigner in Paris, and we could both live comfortably on my son's income.

CHAPTER

SEVENTEEN

For months it was impossible to find vacancies on a regular passenger ship, because so many of them had been refitted for troop transport during the war. Some had been released unmodified for passenger service, and we booked two berths. The ship had a single accommodations plan: food and service were the same for every passenger. The cabins on the two upper decks were reserved for American and British passengers, who had won the war; on the middle decks were the Scandinavians and the Swiss, whom the war had made rich. Below were the liberated French, the Italians, the Irish, and the stateless, my son and I. We still weren't US citizens, though we carried a re-entry permit.

The Italians aboard the ship had worked and saved for this trip home, where they made a prince's appearance in their villages and spent one or two hundred dollars in four weeks. Then they went back to America to begin saving for the next trip. Now the time had come again to see their relatives and to be the object of their amazement. Shortly before our arrival, they packed their cabin bedding as travel gifts.

We had sailed for 18 days on calm seas under a bright autumn sun, and were approaching Ireland. Twenty four hours before arriving, the side of the deck from which land could first be sighted was scattered with whisky bottles. A group of older Irishmen and women, who hadn't seen their home in ages, were now returning. We stopped on the high sea, a launch took them away, and we continued through the English Channel. The sun went down. We were scheduled to dock at Le Havre early the next morning. In the night, someone woke me. I got dressed. We went on deck and the man pointed off in a direction, then left me alone. The ship moved forward slowly. I saw two distant searchlights cut the dark sky. They were shining from Europe, from France. I cried a little.

The next morning we stepped on land at Le Havre. The port was unrecognizable: all of the houses had been destroyed in the air raids. We took a train through Normandy. The intense green of its fields and meadows was unchanged. But only one tower showed itself over the Cathedral of Rouen—it had lost the other one in the war. The train neared a large station, and I read on the wall: Paris. Several passengers from the ship clapped me on the shoulder; they had often heard me talk about the city.

Opposite the St. Lazare Station stood a great, ugly box: the Hotel Terminus, a transfer station for travelers. They said they could take us for a week, which I stretched into six months by tipping generously. I wanted to rent a room in one of the small hotels in our old neighborhood of Passy, but the small hotels were all full. France had hardly any tourists during and directly after the war, and the hotel managements were happy to rent long term to French guests.

We stayed at the Terminus, where they heated with oil fuel and did not have to depend on coal. This had the advantage of simultaneous room and water heating, a great rarity in postwar Paris. We were not disturbed by street noise, either; because of the gas shortage there were few taxis, and even fewer private cars.

Our first morning there we had breakfast on the terrace. The waiter served us an unidentifiable brown liquid, two saccharine tablets each and, because we still didn't have our bread ration cards, two pieces of yellow rock which he called biscuits.

"Would you like a piece of sugar?" he asked, and fished a gray cube out of his pants pocket. He asked to be paid right away, and put the banknote back into the same pocket.

We left our breakfast untouched. In my memory, the nearby Café Ruc was a good place to dine. They were serving lunch, and we ordered the only hot item on the menu. The waiter brought us each a plate with a boiled calf's brain and a potato that had a sweet taste. We ate and were still hungry. I thought about the excess in America. Perhaps I had been wrong to talk my son into this adventure.

We walked along Rue St. Lazare to the Champs-Elysées and across Place Philippe de Roule. In a few weeks one of the great actors of France would have an open-casket funeral in the church on the small square there. Famous figures of the stage and of film considered it an honor to dress and tie the shoelaces of the deceased Raimu. The people of Paris filed past his coffin for an entire day.

We stopped at the Étoile. The houses looked gray and lusterless, the pedestrians emaciated and unkempt. A few automobiles drove by. I asked my son: "How do you like Paris?"

"I can't say yet."

I helped him find Rue Pierre Charron and the MacCann-Erickson Agency, then walked back across Place de l'Alma to the bridge and looked down into the Seine. I had feared that I would find it measly, after so many walks along the two-kilometer-wide Hudson. But it wasn't measly. Notre Dame's two flat-topped towers and single, needlepoint spire rose far off in the gray light. I held my breath. I walked up the Seine to Place de la Concorde. The city's face was pale, its dress was faded and stained, but for me it glowed again as beautiful as I had ever seen it, and more beautiful than I had dreamed of it since.

In the evenings we searched the streets hungry. I had forgotten to ask my friends for a recommendation. I recognized a small restaurant in Rue Galilée and we entered. A waitress asked us curtly: "Do you want to eat here, or in the other room?"—"here" the tables had paper coverings, in the "other" room they had linen cloths and napkins. I requested the other room. The waitress became very polite and led us to a table.

The authorities had divided all of the restaurants and bars into classes, each rank with its prescribed prices. On the less expensive menu there was a little bit of the cheapest variety; in the "other" rooms, one could order an overpriced normal meal, and, for an exorbitant amount, the best French cuisine. We ate superbly. I found a bistro in Passy on the Muette run by a single family. The wife cooked, the husband stood behind the counter, and the son and daughter-in-law served. The food was so good that we came back nearly every day. Our subsistence was no longer in question.

Coca-Cola was not sold in France during the early postwar years; the winemakers were strong enough to oppose it. My son's job was to bring the name of Coca-Cola back into the awareness of restaurateurs and owners of bistros and cafés. The advertising agency in New York had produced a mock-up record in French and played it for the Coca-Cola Company directors. They accepted the model, from which my son would now create his own half-hour show. It consisted of what Americans call a "variety show": a speaker, a sketch, singers, a large orchestra with chorus—stylistically not so much in the vein of "thrills" but more dignified, as befitted the most widely drunk beverage in the Western world. The budget was such that stars like Piaf or Fernandel could be hired. Recordings were made at a studio in Passy, Rue de Marroniers, near our old apartment. One show was recorded and broadcast every week on Radio Luxemburg, which reached the better part of France including Paris, plus Belgium and of course Luxemburg. All of the French stations were state-owned and sold no advertisng time.

I went to look for my Parisian friends. André Certes embraced us and cried out joyfully: "La vie est belle!" I asked: "Pourquoi ça?" "Because we're alive and seeing one another again." My son hired him, and found in him a valuable colleague.

100 Rue Réaumur is the headquarters of several newspapers. In the canteen of *France-Soir*—the scent of Pernod was strong already on the steps—I found my friend, the theater critic Marc Blanquet. We had so many Pernods that I could hardly find my way back to the hotel. We began to meet in the canteen every day at noon, to drink a few glasses of the forbidden apéritif. When we met in the evenings it was in Rue Hirondelle, in a back room of an *épicerie*, a grocer. There the police from the prefect drank their *Pastis*, the Southern-French label of Pernod. The store owners were Corsicans. We were introduced to the place by a Corsican Count, a friend of Blanquet's.

The government had placed a long ban on this narcotic drink after the two world wars, whose victories France had bought so dearly. Nevertheless, the end of World War I saw the return of absinthe in three types: the green Pernod, the brownish *Pastis*, and the colorless *Oxygenée*. All three become cloudy when mixed with water, which must be added very slowly, in a thin stream.

Walking along Avenue Wagram one morning I was amazed to see a long line outside the Théâtre de l'Etoile. The large theater, which I had tried in vain to fill for two productions, was sold out for ten days. To get to the bottom of the phenomenon, I got in line and bought tickets. The attraction was Edith Piaf. I remembered her name from the days she had appeared in cabarets and nightclubs as "Môme Piaf," the Little Sparrow, and wasn't much talked about. That evening at the Etoile, where I was lucky to be in the audience applauding her, was one of the great experiences of my life. The burden of daily life lightens when I hear her voice on a recording.

Marcel Achard, to whom I related my enthusiasm, invited my son and me to lunch with Piaf at his apartment. She arrived late and brought her latest boyfriend, a young man from the group "Compagnons de la Chanson." "He's so vain," she explained, "he takes hours dressing. I've redone his entire wardrobe," she said and lifted one of his pant legs: "even the socks are matching brown."

She had a great time. Her laughter, which came from the gutter and reached the stars, was overpowering. She sat next to me at the table. I used my entire French vocabulary to give her compliments, which she reciprocated, telling me that she had found my production of the *Opéra de Quat'*

Sous so very interesting, and would I direct it again and let her play Polly. I was overjoyed to hear this, even though I had no desire to undertake another *Threepenny Opera* in Paris. I had suffered enough once already at the untranslatability of the language of Brecht into French.

We were drinking mocha in the music room and talking, enlivened by the various wines and champagnes we'd had with dinner, when suddenly we were distracted by a strange noise. In the middle of the room, the old poodle Coco stood on the Aubusson rug and urinated. Juliette Achard let the dog finish his business undisturbed. "He feels unnoticed—he just wants some attention!"

Back at the Hotel Terminus, the concierge handed me a note: "Your son is expecting you at the Hotel de Paris."

At first I didn't understand. I had just left Wolfgang a few minutes earlier. Suddenly I realized, it must be Heinz! He was stationed in London and not yet demobilized. I found him in the lobby, in uniform. We both sobbed. Seven years of forced separation were forgotten. The three of us sat through the night, and Heinz told us about his adventures in a special division of the English Army. He had received his training in a castle in Scotland. An English plane had dropped him over Germany wearing a German sergeant's uniform. Provided with the necessary papers, he had completed an assignment in Berlin, in constant fear of being recognized. He took pills every four hours so that he didn't have to sleep. On the third day, reeling with exhaustion, he had accidentally bumped into a civilian at the Anhalter Train Station platform, and excused himself with: "I'm sorry." He thought he was done for. He was equipped with a poison capsule and was ready to take it. There was no other way, only interrogation, torture, then a bullet in the head. But the civilian didn't react, and Heinz crossed the Swiss border that night at the planned spot.

It was wonderful to spend a few days with my two sons in Paris. Heinz needed to return to England to be demobilized. He visited us once more, this time in plainclothes, and I asked him what he would do next, now that he had been through college and the army.

"I'll have a good time!"

"Unfortunately I can't help you. I have no money to give you." To this day he manages to have a good time, because his greatest pleasure is to work and earn money.

For the coming theater season, I found a benefactor for the musical *Lady in the Dark*, by Kurt Weill and Moss Hart. Maxwell Anderson's *Joan of Lorraine*, for which I'd found a French translator, enraged Louis Jouvet: "I won't stand to have our Jeanne d'Arc drowned in American sauce!"

I tried to interest the formidable actress Edwige Feuillère in the lead female role, but she couldn't decide so quickly. Everything goes slowly in France. Those who didn't understand this at the beginning of the emigration stumbled from one fiasco to the next. In the first week back, I heard two young people at a newsstand remark about a third passing by:

"Je n'aime pas ce type-là!"

"Pourquoi pas?"

"Il est toujours pressé."

—I don't like the guy.—Why not?—He's always in a hurry!

CHAPTER

E I G H T E E N

The six months came to an end and my son's contract expired. I had
given some thought to staying in Paris to continue my projects, when
my wife wrote that my mother was coming to visit us from London. I
hadn't seen her in fourteen years. I decided to return to New York with
Wolfgang. Most of all, I didn't want to be apart from my wife any longer. It
was financially impossible for her to join me in France. Once I'd returned,
there was no way we could both go.

My son and I embarked from Le Havre in February of 1947. My mother
came to New York and fell seriously ill. She fought with death for many
weeks. There were other heavy shocks: the death of my friend Borchardt.
The death of Kurt Weill. The death of my mother-in-law, who had lived
with us since 1941. In 1950 my son was drafted into the Korean War, a
great misfortune for my wife and me. Wolfgang's consolation, "You can't
be against communism and let the others fight!" didn't make it any easier
for us.

I took walks or exercised, cooked our meals, read a lot, and met my
friend Vambery in the evenings. We walked slowly along the river in the
heat, and I dreamed out loud about the beauty of the stained glass windows
of St. Chapelle. Vambery observed: "You always talk about the beautiful
exterior—you don't know anything about what's inside!"

I couldn't get away from this thought; it wouldn't let itself be shaken
off. How could I find out about what was inside?

At the house of Klaus Dohrn I made the acquaintance of Baroness von
Guttenberg, whose son was a member of the West German Parliament.
She lived in New York and collected money for children who had lost

their parents owing to the war or expulsion. We talked about my interest in meeting with a priest. I wasn't thinking of converting, nor was I looking for an intellectual discussion. I simply wanted to come in contact with someone whose faith was absolute.

"Go to the Capuchins and ask for Father Benno. He's a saint," she told me.

I went to the monastery, a gray house indistinguishable from its neighbors on 31st Street, across from Pennsylvania Station. I was shown into a small room with a table and two chairs. A fat monk in a brown cowl, bald and white-bearded (he was 79 years old) asked me kindly how he could help.

Father Benno looked at me with deep-blue eyes. He glowed with good spirit. I thought: a man can be this happy. I told him about the conversations I'd had with various friends, and asked him whether he could do something for my ignorance, perhaps tell me something about all-merciful God. He smiled and told me to come again, he would ask the Prior for permission.

The curtain goes up on a small platform stage of a club house. I'm sitting near the front among emigrants from Berlin and Vienna. A fat, ugly man comes on stage, Kurt Robitschek, the founder and director of the Comedians' Cabaret, where I'd last seen him in Berlin in 1933 when the SA storm troopers interrupted an evening's performance. Full beer glasses flew through the air. The beer formed a tail like a comet behind the glass. Hats and coats were left behind, the theater emptied in seconds. On the street I heard that the Reichstag was burning. I drove home and said to my wife: "It's all over for the theater!" I was 34 years old at the time, and had lived the last normal day of my life.

Robitschek, who had escaped to New York via Prague and Paris, organized a group of refugee cabarettists and actors interested in putting on colorful performances in German. He addressed his audience: "Ladies and gentlemen! I'm the only theater director whose audience has been sent after him."

When Robitscheck died of lung cancer, Felix Gerstman, a Viennese emigrant, was his successor. Gerstman wanted to produce fine-arts theater and concerts that would reach an American audience. We met in his office on 42nd Street, between Sixth and Seventh Avenue, and he asked if I would help him produce a concert version of *The Threepenny Opera*. I liked the idea of taking on a project distantly connected to my former work.

Gerstman had rented the Town Hall, the best known concert hall in New York after Carnegie. I named the evening: Weill Memorial. The first part of the program consisted of songs in German, English, and French to texts by Bertolt Brecht, Maxwell Anderson, and Jacques Deval. They were sung by Grete Mosheim and Ines Matthew, the black singer with a beautiful body and beautiful voice from Weill's last musical, *Lost in the Stars*. The evening continued with songs from *The Threepenny Opera* with Lenya singing, and parts of the text read by an English speaker. It had been almost impossible to persuade Lenya to come out of the hiding she'd gone into after her husband's death. To sing Weill's music, in her grieving, was too much of a shock. On the morning of the premiere, after long and intensive rehearsals, she had called me in tears. Under no circumstances would she go through with it; I was making her and Kurt ridiculous.

The photograph of the sold-out performance shows what an exceptional success we had. The newspapers, most notably *The New York Times* and *The New York Herald Tribune*, showered praise. A small, round, gray-haired man congratulated Lenya. George Davis, American writer and journalist, with gray hair, a childlike face and dreamy eyes, impressed everyone who got close to him with his modesty, his intelligence, and unerring taste. He became Lenya's second husband. Like Weill, he died at fifty of a heart attack.

We gave many performances. Brecht was unable to attend. Summoned before the House Un-American Activities Committee, he had left the country immediately after his interrogation. A few months earlier he had come to me with the news that the Theater am Schiffbauerdamm had not been bombed; it was now in the Russian sector. He urged me to reclaim the theater, suggesting that I go to the Russian Consulate, and, he added, "Because these things are best handled capitalistically, you can use my German royalties as your working capital." I declined his comradely offer on two grounds: "I don't want to go to Germany, and I don't want to go to the Russian sector."

He traveled to Switzerland and Vienna, where he acquired Austrian citizenship, before returning to Germany and installing himself and his wife Helene Weigel at the Theater am Schiffbauerdamm in the communist sector of Berlin.

When I visited the monk a second time, he had spoken with the Prior and received permission to sit with me one afternoon a week. Since I, an agnostic, didn't know what to ask, he spoke and I listened. He began with Adam and Eve, and with anecdotes from his own life. His name was Aichinger and he came from Bavaria. His father had been a painter of churches. He had never wanted to pursue any life but that of a priest. At fifteen he had become consumptive, and the doctors forbade him to study. He begged God to let him die if he couldn't fulfill the duties of a priest. A clergyman high up in the hierarchy found a place for him in a seminary in the Wisconsin countryside and paid for the journey. He was healed, and became a Capuchin monk.

After his death I learned that Monsignore Benno Aichinger had once been *Pater General* of the Order, until poor health had forced him to leave Rome and he'd come to New York as Father Benno.

He was always delighted when I came, his face beamed kindness. But I began to be bored. One day before I came to the door of the monastery I noticed a drab, run-down cafeteria. Through the window I could see the customers jostling and pushing in their hurry. I could imagine exactly how the lukewarm food tasted, how the sour air forced itself in waves through the revolving door, especially on the days fish was served. The summer was very hot, and as I stood observing the scene, and beginning to doubt whether the walk was worth it, I noticed a change in my thinking. Not that I became a believer at that moment, but my horizon expanded, and I felt something of the uncertain and the immeasurable. The straitjacket of pure reason was loosened, and I saw more clearly that the incomprehensible cannot be comprehended.

The monk often apologized for offending my religious background when he cited departures from Jewish law in the Christian doctrine. My assurances that I was in no way religious seemed to reach him, but he had trouble imagining such a human being as I.

Heinz visited from Nice just as Wolfgang boarded a ship for the Korean War. The joy of seeing the older son alleviated the worry of parting with the younger. After Heinz had been released from the British army he had taken a position with Cook in London, and was soon transferred to the Riviera. He didn't stay long with Cook, however, and opened his own travel agency in Nice with a Frenchman, ensuring himself a good income. To my surprise he liked New York very much.

"I'm going to come back! I could make ten times as much doing the same work in America." And he did. He gave up his work in one of the most beautiful places in Europe, and now makes more than ten times as much, to his satisfaction, in bland Los Angeles. He finds our living standards in New York alarming.

I continued the visits to Father Benno's small chambers every Tuesday for a year and three months. When I asked him to christen me, although I didn't believe, he answered with a quote from Pascal: "You wouldn't look for Me if you hadn't already found Me." He wanted me to give my word that I had no objections to the dogma. I had no objections, only a request, "which is a condition for me: I've never been apart from my wife. We have to be christened together."

He said it wasn't possible; she had no instruction.

"I've told her everything you taught me," I said to him, "Let me bring her to you."

He agreed to meet with her. After their discussion, a day was set for us to come to the monastery together. At eight in the evening, with Dohrn and his girlfriend Ursula, a Swiss student and later his wife, as our witnesses, we went to the Capuchin Chapel. Father Benno was in high spirits after the christening.

"All of your sins are forgiven. If you fall over dead this minute, you'll shoot to heaven like a rocket."

I felt as though I had exchanged a comfortable old suit for a new and unfamiliar one. After several visits to mass, the Sunday suit felt no different from any other.

✳ ✳ ✳

Our cat Charlie lay rolled up on the couch. He lifted his head abruptly, stood up and made a strange noise. We heard the front door open and close, and footsteps coming up the stairs. A few seconds later our son Wolfgang stood in the room: the war in Korea was over.

Wolfgang was invited to England to meet his brother's bride, an Englishwoman. When he came back he brought us ship tickets and many dollars from Heinz, who asked us to come live in Nice. My wife sold her business in New Jersey. We bought new suitcases and clothes, left the apartment to Wolfgang and said goodbye. We knew we were lucky that, with the exception of his service time, he had always stayed with us.

We drove to the harbor on a glowing hot morning. I lay down in our cabin and didn't get up until I could breathe the fresh air of the open sea.

CHAPTER

NINETEEN

We landed in Berlin, coming from Nice. For six months we had lived an easy life on the Riviera. My son had rented an apartment for us in the quiet Quartier des Musiciens, ten minutes from the ocean. We had begun to think about staying in Nice when a letter came from Toni Mackeben in Berlin. It was an answer to the single letter we had written to Germany. Her letter was full of joy over our friendship. Both my wife and I are unable to resist human warmth, and we decided to visit Toni and stay for three days in Berlin.

We took the train to Munich. In Milan, a man took a seat in our empty compartment and spoke to us in German—a big event. For twenty years we had spoken and been spoken to in a foreign language.

Toni was waiting for us at the airport in Tempelhof. We embraced. We brought our luggage to the hotel, then drove to her apartment through the gloom of the poorly lit city. Ruins alternated with rubble heaps. Entire streetcar lines were torn up. And yet the shock wasn't there yet. I could still sleep that night.

The next morning, in daylight, we walked through once familiar streets whose houses all had vanished. At the cramped corner stores, shashlik and sausage were being sold, and the smell of cheap fat mixed with plaster dust was everywhere. We looked for Lützowplatz, which no longer existed. I saw, through the iron curtain, the ghostly landscape of the Potsdamer Platz. The horror of it overcame me. I sat up in bed at night wracked by a nervous cough. I wanted to leave, but I didn't know where to go. I had found my language again. I stayed in this half-Berlin with its visible scars, its deformed face and its sad charm and optimism, like that of the severely wounded who are happy to have gotten away with their lives.

Single houses and streets remind me of the time before my life was broken in two, before my emigration, the end of which I still haven't seen. I live in this city without admiring it or feeling sorry for it. What happened to Berlin happened to us: we couldn't defend ourselves.

In the first weeks after our return to Berlin, a man called and left his office number with my wife. I asked around about him and learned that the man was a theater critic and editor of a newspaper. I met him in the afternoon at the artist's pub, "Johnny." He made me an offer. He told me about a group of unemployed old actors supported by a modest charity fund, and suggested that I produce matinees with them, so that they could receive wages instead of welfare. I stood up and thanked the man, assuring him there were others who would be happier to accept his offer. He gave me his hand: "Take some time to think about it. I'll call you."

As I listened to him, I was reminded of an incident in 1940. We are stranded in Marseilles, waiting for our ship to America. Our money is nearly gone, and someone recommends that I go talk to the Director of the Red Cross. I am received respectfully and without delay in his office.

"There are three of you—your wife, your son and you, sir?" The Director asks after main points and details. At the end of a long interview, he opens a desk drawer and takes out a basket of coins. "Now I know your situation. Alors je vais vous décoincer!"—I'll help you out of your fix! He sifts through the coins, chooses one and hands it to me across the desk: ten francs. I stand up and thank him, assuring him there are others that could use the contribution. He follows me into the hall and puts the ten francs in my pocket, then goes back to his office and closes the door. I leave the coin in view on the top stair.

Maybe someone will find it, someone who would like to sit comfortably on a café terrace at the Vieux Port, order a drink and let the spring sun shine on him.